D1171283

HISTORICAL DICTIONARIES
OF U.S. HISTORICAL ERAS
Jon Woronoff, Series Editor

1. *From the Great War to the Great Depression*, by Neil A. Wynn, 2003.
2. *Civil War and Reconstruction*, by William L. Richter, 2004.
3. *Revolutionary America*, by Terry M. Mays, 2005.
4. *Old South*, by William L. Richter, 2006.
5. *Early American Republic*, by Richard Buel Jr., 2006.
6. *Jacksonian Era and Manifest Destiny*, by Terry Corps, 2006.
7. *Reagan–Bush Era*, by Richard S. Conley, 2007.
8. *Kennedy–Johnson Era*, by Richard Dean Burns and Joseph M. Siracusa, 2008.
9. *Nixon–Ford Era*, by Mitchell K. Hall, 2008.
10. *Roosevelt–Truman Era*, by Neil A. Wynn, 2008.
11. *Eisenhower Era*, by Burton I. Kaufman and Diane Kaufman, 2009.
12. *Progressive Era*, by Catherine Cocks, Peter Holloran, and Alan Lessoff, 2009.
13. *Gilded Age*, by T. Adams Upchurch, 2009.

Historical Dictionary
of the Gilded Age

T. Adams Upchurch

Historical Dictionaries
of U.S. Historical Eras, No. 13

The Scarecrow Press, Inc.
Lanham, Maryland • Toronto • Plymouth, UK
2009

SCARECROW PRESS, INC.

Published in the United States of America
by Scarecrow Press, Inc.
A wholly owned subsidiary of
The Rowman & Littlefield Publishing Group, Inc.
4501 Forbes Boulevard, Suite 200, Lanham, Maryland 20706
www.scarecrowpress.com

Estover Road
Plymouth PL6 7PY
United Kingdom

British Library Cataloguing in Publication Information Available

Library of Congress Cataloging-in-Publication Data

Upchurch, Thomas Adams.
  Historical dictionary of the Gilded Age / T. Adams Upchurch.
    p. cm. — (Historical dictionaries of U.S. historical eras ; no. 13)
  Includes bibliographical references.
  ISBN-13: 978-0-8108-5829-9 (cloth : alk. paper)
  ISBN-10: 0-8108-5829-0 (cloth : alk. paper)
  ISBN-13: 978-0-8108-6299-9 (ebook)
  ISBN-10: 0-8108-6299-9 (ebook)
  1. United States—History—1865–1898—Dictionaries. 2. United States—Politics
and government—1865–1900—Dictionaries. I. Title.
  E661.U66 2009
  973.8003–dc22   2008047279

∞™ The paper used in this publication meets the minimum requirements of
American National Standard for Information Sciences—Permanence of
Paper for Printed Library Materials, ANSI/NISO Z39.48–1992.
Manufactured in the United States of America.

Contents

Editor's Foreword

The Gilded Age, which lasted for several decades at the end of the 19th century, has left less of an impression than the previous period of Civil War and Reconstruction or the one that followed, known as the Progressive Era. Nevertheless, it was an important time of transition, with positive as well as negative aspects, even if the latter often appeared predominant. Of course, with a tag like "gilded," there is a tendency to look at the era's more opprobrious features such as, in the economy, the rise of so-called Robber Barons, the growing gap between rich and poor, and the wretched conditions in which many lived and worked; in politics, the election of mostly forgettable presidents, unbridled rivalry between the parties, unexciting issues such as tariffs and free silver, and rampant corruption; in society, discrimination against African Americans, Native Americans, Chinese, Eastern European immigrants, and women; and in foreign policy, the emergence of jingoism and empire building. Tentatively if not always very visibly, reformers began to address many of these problems before the end of the era. This was also the period when the United States really expanded across the continent, filling in many of the hitherto empty spaces with a rapidly growing population, tied together with markedly improved transportation and communications networks, and when mass industrialization began, transforming not only the economy but everybody's lifestyle.

As a period of transition with many countervailing good and bad features, it is not easy to get a fix on the Gilded Age, and indeed even historians are gradually revising the earlier opinions. Therefore, another look is certainly worthwhile, and an encyclopedia like this is not a bad place to begin since it contains entries on good and bad aspects of the era alike; on notable leaders of every stripe and in many fields; on political parties, trade unions, and social movements; on major events and lesser ones that give a feeling for the times; on literature and the arts;

and on changing lifestyles and popular culture. The chronology traces the trajectory from 1869 to 1899 and shows how surprisingly eventful the period was. The introduction, a particularly important section, ties things together and provides a broader perspective through which to view the entries. Admittedly, only so much can be said in this *Historical Dictionary of the Gilded Age*, and readers who want to know more will have to consult the bibliography.

Slowly but surely, this series on Historical Dictionaries of U.S. Historical Eras is filling in the blanks, and as noted above, the Gilded Age was an important but often overlooked period. Fortunately, it was possible to find an author with a broad view as well as a crucial specialization. Dr. T. Adams Upchurch is a history professor at East Georgia College where he offers a course covering this period, among others. His particular interest is racism and civil rights, a crucial issue for the Gilded Age, when it still seemed as if backsliding was just as likely as progressing on this front. He has written on this topic in several important books, including *Legislating Racism: The Billion Dollar Congress and the Birth of Jim Crow*, issues related to which are featured in entries in this volume. Dr. Upchurch has also written an award-winning article relevant to study of the Gilded Age on "Why Populism Failed in Mississippi." His expertise in this era of American history ensures that readers will find many good insights and much useful information contained in this volume.

Jon Woronoff
Series Editor

Acknowledgments

I wish to thank my friends and fellow historians who were kind enough to serve as proofreaders and fact-checkers: Dr. Connie Lester of the University of Central Florida and the *Florida Historical Quarterly*; Dr. Stanly Godbold, retired, from Mississippi State University; and Jeff Howell, doctoral candidate at Mississippi State University. Dr. Lester also deserves recognition for putting me in contact with editor Jon Woronoff of Scarecrow Press. Without the help of such able and willing professionals, this historical dictionary would not have been possible.

Reader's Note

This dictionary contains articles chosen for their comparative significance to the broad panorama of American history during the Gilded Age. Many important people, issues, and events have been excluded in the interest of brevity. Choices of what to include were subjective, so exclusion does not necessarily indicate insignificance. In some cases, collective entries proved more useful than individualized ones. For instance, the entries "Literature," "Periodicals," and "The Press" cover most of the major authors, editors, literary movements, books, and influential publications of the Gilded Age much more succinctly than several dozen individual entries could.

Except for acts of God or nature, all historical events, issues, and artifacts are shaped by people. In some cases, an individual is more important than a single item for which he or she is famous. The aphorism "the whole is greater than the sum of its parts" is applied in such cases. Thomas Edison is, for example, greater as an inventor than is any one of his separate inventions. Thus, the reader will find an article on the inventor rather than on any one of his particular inventions. In other cases, an individual is primarily remembered for a single item, such as a book he or she wrote, or an event in which he or she was involved. George Armstrong Custer is a prime example. Were it not for Custer's dramatic defeat at the Battle of the Little Bighorn, he would probably not be so remembered in history. Thus, the battle is deemed greater than the man. In some cases, both a person and an item always associated with him or her have separate entries because of their distinct significance in history. The best example is Mark Twain and his book *The Gilded Age*. People and their famous or infamous actions are, however, cross-referenced herein for the benefit of the reader, as indicated by the embedded **names** and **terms** in **bold print**.

Most people mentioned herein did not live their whole lives during the Gilded Age. Except for Stephen Crane and a few others, most were born in the antebellum period but lived to see their greatest accomplishments in the last three decades of the 19th century. The vast majority of people mentioned in this volume fall into this category. Some mentioned herein were born during the Gilded Age and/or began making a name for themselves before the turn of the century but did not achieve their greatest fame until the Progressive Era. Depending on the relative significance of their early fame, they were included in this dictionary or they were not. Examples of those excluded are George Washington Carver, Walter Reid, Charles Schwab, Scott Joplin, John Dewey, and Frederick Weyerhauser. W. E. B. Du Bois is a notable example of one who made the cut. Those who were born during the Gilded Age but had no fame at all until the 20th century have been excluded altogether from this volume.

Acronyms and Abbreviations

A & P	The Great Atlantic and Pacific Tea Company
ABA	American Bar Association
AC	alternating current
AFL	American Federation of Labor
AMA	American Missionary Association
AME	African Methodist Episcopal Church
APA	American Protective Association
ARU	American Railway Union
AT&T	American Telegraph and Telephone Company
ATC	American Tobacco Company
BIA	Bureau of Indian Affairs
DC	direct current
FBI	Federal Bureau of Investigation
GAR	Grand Army of the Republic
GE	General Electric Company
GOP	Grand Old Party (Republican Party)
ICC	Interstate Commerce Commission
IRL	Immigration Restriction League
KOL	Knights of Labor
NAWSA	National American Woman Suffrage Association
NEA	National Education Association
NFA	National Farmers' Alliance
NRA	National Rifle Association
NWS	National Weather Service
NWSA	National Woman Suffrage Association
WASP	White Anglo-Saxon Protestant
WCTU	Women's Christian Temperance Union
WFM	Western Federation of Miners
YMCA	Young Men's Christian Association

Chronology

1869   26 February: Congress passes the Fifteenth Amendment to the United States Constitution. **4 March:** Ulysses S. Grant is sworn in as the 18th president of the United States. **10 May:** The first transcontinental railroad is ceremonially completed in Utah. **15 August:** Mark Twain's *Innocents Abroad* is published. **24 September:** Black Friday hits Wall Street, causing temporary economic panic. **24 November:** The American Woman's Suffrage Association is founded. **9 December:** The first nationwide labor union, the Knights of Labor, is founded in Philadelphia, Pennsylvania. **10 December:** Wyoming becomes the first place in America where women are allowed to vote.

1870   3 January: Construction begins on the Brooklyn Bridge in New York. **10 January:** John D. Rockefeller organizes the Standard Oil Company of Ohio. **2 February:** The Fifteenth Amendment is ratified. **5 February:** Hiram R. Revels is sworn in as the first African American U.S. senator. **7 February:** The U.S. Supreme Court rules on the first "Legal Tender" case, *Hepburn v. Griswold*. **9 February:** President Grant and Congress create the National Weather Service. **25 February:** Joseph Rainey of South Carolina becomes the first black man to be seated in the U.S. House of Representatives. **15 March:** The U.S. Senate rejects President Grant's proposal to annex Santo Domingo. **31 May:** Congress passes the first anti–Ku Klux Klan law, the Enforcement Act.

1871   27 February: The U.S.–British commission to settle the *Alabama* claims convenes in Washington, D.C. **28 February:** Congress passes the Second Enforcement Act. **10 April:** P. T. Barnum opens his "Greatest Show on Earth" in New York. **20 April:** Congress passes the Third Enforcement Act. **1 May:** The U.S. Supreme Court rules on more "Legal Tender" cases, *Knox v. Lee* and *Parker v. Davis*. **8 May:** The U.S.–British commission for the *Alabama* claims signs the Treaty of Washington. **8–11 October:** The Great Chicago Fire rages in Illinois. **15 December:** The international tribunal for the *Alabama* claims convenes in Switzerland.

1872 **February:** Mark Twain's *Roughing It* is published. **4 March:** Congress creates the first national park, Yellowstone, in Wyoming. **4 September:** The Credit Mobilier scandal first comes to light in the newspapers. **14 September:** The *Alabama* claims dispute is settled via the Swiss international tribunal. **2 November:** Victoria Woodhull publishes an accusation of the Reverend Henry Ward Beecher's adultery with his church congregant Elizabeth Tilton. **5 November:** William Marcy Tweed is tried and sentenced to 12 years in jail. Susan B. Anthony is arrested in Rochester, New York, for voting. **6 November:** Grant is reelected president. **16 December:** Ned Buntline and Buffalo Bill debut "The Scout of the Plains" to a packed house in Chicago, Illinois.

1873 **6 January:** Congress begins official investigation of the Credit Mobilier scandal. **12 February:** Congress passes the Coinage Act that came to be known as the "Crime of '73." **3 March:** Congress votes itself and the other two branches of the federal government major salary increases, incensing the American public. **4 March:** President Grant is sworn in for a second term. **14 April:** The U.S. Supreme Court rules on the slaughterhouse cases. **15 April:** The U.S. Supreme Court rules on *Bradwell v. Illinois*. **18 September:** Jay Cooke's bank collapse precipitates the Panic of 1873. **23 December:** Mark Twain and Charles Dudley Warner's *The Gilded Age* is published.

1874 **13 January:** The Tompkins Square riot occurs in New York City. **26 May:** Outlaw John Wesley Hardin kills Deputy Sheriff Charles Webb in Texas, making him a public enemy of the state. **24 June:** The Battle of Adobe Walls is fought between cowboys and Indians in Texas. **21 August:** Theodore Tilton sues Henry Ward Beecher for adultery with his wife. **9–10 December:** Jesse Pomeroy is sentenced to death for first-degree murder.

1875 **7 January:** Congress passes the Resumption of Specie Payment Act. **11 January:** The trial of Henry Ward Beecher begins in Brooklyn. **15 January:** William Marcy Tweed escapes from jail. **1 March:** Congress passes the Civil Rights Act of 1875. **9 March:** The U.S. Supreme Court rules on *Minor v. Happersett*. **17 May:** The first Kentucky Derby is held. **June:** The largest locust swarm on record sweeps over the Rocky Mountain and Great Plains states, destroying crops and livelihoods. **31 October:** D. L. Moody begins his first major American revival crusade in Brooklyn, New York. **22 November:** Vice President Henry Wilson dies, leaving the office vacant for the remainder of Grant's second term. **6 December:** The first Congress controlled by Democrats since before the Civil War convenes.

1876 24 February: Members of the "Whiskey Ring" are found guilty of tax fraud. **7 March:** Alexander Graham Bell receives the first patent on the telephone. **10 May:** The U.S. Centennial Exhibition opens in Philadelphia, Pennsylvania. **23 June:** Bell demonstrates the telephone publicly for the first time at the Massachusetts Institute of Technology in Boston. **25 June:** The Battle of Little Big Horn occurs in Montana. **4 July:** The U.S. Centennial is celebrated. **1 August:** Colorado enters the Union as the 38th state. **2 August:** Wild Bill Hickok is killed in Deadwood, South Dakota. **7 November:** The Hayes–Tilden presidential election is held. **8 December:** Mark Twain's *Tom Sawyer* is published.

1877 29 January: Congress forms the Joint Electoral Commission to settle the presidential election dispute. **26 February:** Democrats and Republicans agree to the "Wormley House Bargain," which arranges the Compromise of 1877. **1 March:** The U.S. Supreme Court rules on the Granger case *Munn v. Illinois*. **3 March:** In a private ceremony, Rutherford B. Hayes is sworn in as the 19th U.S. president. **5 March:** Hayes is sworn in publicly. **10 April:** Hayes begins federal troop withdrawal from the South, officially ending Reconstruction. **21 June:** The Mollie Maguires hangings are carried out in Pennsylvania. **16 July:** The Great Railroad Strike begins in Maryland and quickly spreads to other states. **19 July:** The Great Railroad Strike leads to rioting and 25 deaths in Philadelphia, Pennsylvania. **23 July:** Texas outlaw John Wesley Hardin is captured in Florida by the Texas Rangers. **2 August:** The Great Railroad Strike comes to an end.

1878 10 January: The U.S. Senate rejects a women's suffrage amendment to the Constitution. **17 January:** The United States acquires the rights to Pago Pago in the Samoan Islands. **28 February:** Congress passes the Bland–Allison Act over President Hayes's veto. **5 April:** Massachusetts Republican congressman Benjamin F. Butler starts the "doorkeeper controversy" in the House of Representatives. **18 April:** Thomas Edison publicly demonstrates the phonograph for the first time at the National Academy of Sciences in Washington, D.C. **July:** The great yellow fever epidemic sweeps through the New Orleans, Louisiana, area killing thousands. **21 August:** The American Bar Association is founded at Saratoga Springs, New York. **28 September:** John Wesley Hardin is sentenced to prison for murder in Texas.

1879   19 February: Women receive the right to practice law before the U.S. Supreme Court. **22 February:** The first F. W. Woolworth's store opens. **22 March:** Henry George sends out the manuscript of *Progress and Poverty* for publication. **17 November:** Thomas Edison finalizes his invention of the first incandescent light.

1880   8 March: The U.S. Supreme Court rules on *Ex Parte Siebold*. **2 November:** James A. Garfield is elected president of the United States. **12 November:** Lew Wallace's *Ben-Hur: A Tale of the Christ* is published and soon becomes the best-selling novel of the Gilded Age.

1881   Jefferson Davis's *The Rise and Fall of the Confederate Government* is published. Helen Hunt Jackson's *A Century of Dishonor* is published. **4 March:** James A. Garfield is sworn in as the 20th U.S. president. **21 May:** The American Red Cross is founded. **2 July:** James A. Garfield is shot by Charles Guiteau in Washington, D.C. **4 July:** Tuskegee Institute opens in Alabama. **14 July:** Lawman Pat Garrett kills Billy the Kid in New Mexico. **11 August:** The National Civil Service Reform League is founded. **19 September:** Garfield dies. **20 September:** In a private ceremony in New York City, Chester A. Arthur is sworn in as U.S. president. **22 September:** Arthur is sworn in publicly at the nation's capitol in Washington, D.C. **26 October:** The legendary Gunfight at the O. K. Corral occurs in Tombstone, Arizona.

1882   1 January: The H. C. Frick Coke Company is organized. **2 January:** The first "trust," the Standard Oil Trust, is organized. **3 April:** Jesse James is killed in Missouri. **6 May:** The Chinese Exclusion Act is passed. **7 August:** The Hatfield and McCoy feud begins in Kentucky and West Virginia, leading to several murders over the coming days. **4 September:** The first electric lighting is switched on in New York City. **5 September:** The first Labor Day parade is staged in New York City.

1883 **16 January:** The Pendleton Civil Service Act is passed. **23 May:** President Arthur and New York Governor Grover Cleveland officially open the Brooklyn Bridge. **31 May:** Twelve people are trampled to death on the Brooklyn Bridge amid a false alarm about its collapse. **15 October:** The U.S. Supreme Court rules on the civil rights cases. **22 October:** The Metropolitan Opera House is opened in New York City. **11 November:** Nationwide time zones are instituted by railroads.

1884 **3 March:** The U.S. Supreme Court rules on *Ex Parte Yarbrough*. **9 October:** Reverend Samuel Burchard makes his infamous "rum, Romanism, and rebellion" speech, dooming James G. Blaine's presidential hopes. **11 November:** Grover Cleveland is elected president of the United States.

1885 **16 February:** Mark Twain's *Adventures of Huckleberry Finn* is published. **21 February:** The Washington Monument is ceremonially dedicated. **4 March:** Grover Cleveland is sworn in as the 21st U.S. president. **25 November:** Vice President Thomas A. Hendricks dies, leaving the office vacant for the remainder of Cleveland's first term. **December:** *Personal Memoirs of U. S. Grant* (Volume I) is published.

1886 **March:** *Personal Memoirs of U. S. Grant* (Volume II) is published. **4 May:** The Haymarket Riot occurs in Chicago, Illinois. **8 May:** The first Coca-Cola is sold in Atlanta, Georgia. **10 May:** The U.S. Supreme Court rules on *Yick Wo v. Hopkins*. **24 May:** The Brooklyn Bridge opens in New York. **31 May:** Railroads nationwide accept a standardized width for tracks. **25 October:** The Supreme Court rules on *Wabash v. Illinois*. **28 October:** The Statue of Liberty is ceremonially dedicated in New York. **4 September:** Geronimo surrenders to federal authorities in Arizona. **11 November:** The hangings of Haymarket Riot leaders are carried out. **8 December:** The American Federation of Labor is founded. **22 December:** Henry Grady, speaking to the New England Society in New York, makes his first "New South" speech to a northern audience.

1887 **4 February:** Congress passes the Interstate Commerce Act. **8 February:** Congress passes the Dawes Severalty Act. **16 February:** President Cleveland vetoes the Texas Seed Bill. **2 March:** Congress passes the Hatch Act. **27 November:** Frank Dalton is shot and killed.

1888   **1 January:** The Hatfield and McCoy feud reaches its nadir as the Hatfields kill two McCoy youths and burn down their house. **11–14 March:** The Great Blizzard strikes the eastern United States. **6 November:** Benjamin Harrison wins the U.S. presidential election despite losing the popular vote.

1889   **4 March:** Harrison is sworn is as the 22nd president of the United States. **22 April:** The first great Oklahoma Land Rush occurs. **31 May:** The tragic Johnstown Flood occurs in western Pennsylvania. **18 September:** Hull House opens in Chicago, Illinois. **2 November:** North Dakota and South Dakota become states. **8 November:** Montana becomes a state. **11 November:** Washington becomes a state. **14 November:** Nellie Bly begins her race to go around the world in less than 80 days. **21 December:** Henry Grady, in Boston, makes his final speech before dying 2 days later.

1890   **25 January:** Nellie Bly returns triumphant after traversing the earth in just 72 days. **29 January:** U.S. Speaker of the House Thomas B. Reed institutes the "Reed Rules." **18 February:** The Hatfield and McCoy feud ends with the public hanging of Ellison Mounts. **18 April:** New York's Castle Garden immigrant processing center closes its doors after 35 years and 8 million people passing through. **2 May:** Oklahoma becomes a U.S. Territory. **June:** The First Mohonk Conference on the Negro Question is held in upstate New York. **2 July:** Congress passes the Sherman Anti-Trust Act. **3 July:** Idaho becomes a state. **10 July:** Wyoming becomes a state. **14 July:** Congress passes the Sherman Silver Purchase Act. **30 September:** Congress creates Yosemite National Park. **1 November:** The new Mississippi Constitution takes effect. **15 December:** Sitting Bull is killed at the Standing Rock reservation in South Dakota. **29 December:** The Wounded Knee Massacre occurs in South Dakota.

1891   **3 March:** Congress passes the Forest Reserve Act. **14 March:** New Orleans, Louisiana, residents take vigilante justice on 14 jailed Sicilians. **5 May:** Carnegie Hall opens in New York. **6 May:** The U.S. Navy captures the Chilean rebel ship *Itata*. **15 September:** The Dalton Gang in Oklahoma stages its biggest train robbery. **16 October:** The Valparaiso Incident occurs in Chile.

1892   **1 January:** Ellis Island opens in New York. **21 January:** Secretary of State James G. Blaine sends an ultimatum to Chile demanding reparations for the Valparaiso Incident. **25 January:** President Harrison asks Congress for a declaration of war against Chile. **28 January:** Chile agrees to a settlement with the United States. **22 February:** The People's Party is created in St. Louis, Missouri. **2 March:** The Ohio Supreme Court orders the Standard Oil Trust dissolved. **4 March:** Grover Cleveland is sworn in as the 23rd president. **28 May:** John Muir founds the Sierra Club. **11 June:** Populist leader Leonidas Polk dies, leaving the People's Party with inferior leadership. **30 June:** The Homestead Strike begins in western Pennsylvania. **1 July:** The Carnegie Steel Company Ltd. is organized. **4 July:** The People's Party draws up the Omaha Platform. **6 July:** The Homestead Strike killings occur in Pennsylvania. **23 July:** The anarchist Alexander Berkman attempts to assassinate Henry Clay Frick during the Homestead Strike. **4 August:** The Lizzie Borden murders occur in Massachusetts. **7 September:** Gentleman Jim Corbett defeats John L. Sullivan in New Orleans, Louisiana, to win the world heavyweight boxing title. **5 October:** The Dalton Gang in Coffeyville, Kansas, is gunned down in its last robbery attempt. **12 October:** The "Pledge of Allegiance" is first recited in public schools. **20 November:** The Homestead Strike officially ends.

1893   17 January: American businessmen in Hawaii seize the government and appoint Sanford Dole as governor. **13 February:** President Harrison approves a plan to annex Hawaii. **4 March:** Grover Cleveland is sworn in for his second term as president of the United States. **1 May:** The Columbian Exposition opens in Chicago, Illinois. **20 June:** Lizzie Borden is acquitted of murder in one of the trials of the century. **12 July:** Frederick Jackson Turner delivers his essay "The Significance of the Frontier in American History" at the American Historical Association convention in Chicago. **16 September:** The largest of the Oklahoma Land Rushes occurs. **30 October:** The Columbian Exposition closes. **1 November:** Congress repeals the Sherman Silver Purchase Act. **18 December:** President Cleveland withdraws the treaty to annex Hawaii.

1894   1 February: Congress passes the Wilson–Gorman Tariff. **16 March:** Texas Governor Jim Hogg releases John Wesley Hardin from prison. **25 March:** Coxey's Army departs Massillon, Ohio, in a march on Washington, D.C. **1 May:** Jacob Coxey is arrested for leading "Coxey's Army" to the steps of the U.S. Capitol. **11 May:**

The Pullman Strike begins near Chicago, Illinois. **26 June:** Eugene V. Debs and the American Railway Union take charge of the Pullman Strike. **1 July:** President Cleveland has surgery on his jaw. **3–10 July:** Deadly rioting results when President Cleveland sends federal troops to end the Pullman Strike. **17 July:** Debs is sent to prison for his role in the Pullman Strike. **2 August:** The Pullman Strike officially ends. **22 December:** The Amateur Golf Association, forerunner of the United States Golf Association (USGA), is founded.

1895   12 January: The hydroelectric plant at Niagara Falls, on the New York–Canada border, begins operations. **21 January:** The U.S. Supreme Court rules on *E. C. Knight and Co. v. United States.* **20 February:** Frederick Douglass dies in Washington, D.C. **24 February:** The Cuban Revolution begins. **8 April:** The U.S. Supreme Court rules on *Pollack v. Farmers' Loan and Trust Co.* **27 May:** The U.S. Supreme Court rules on *in re Debs.* **19 August:** John Wesley Hardin is killed while playing cards in the Acme Saloon in El Paso, Texas. **17 September:** The USS *Maine* is commissioned. **18 September:** Booker T. Washington gives his "Atlanta Compromise" speech in Georgia. **17 December:** President Cleveland addresses Congress on the Venezuela Boundary Dispute.

1896   4 January: Utah becomes a state. **18 May:** The U.S. Supreme Court rules on the *Plessy v. Ferguson* case. **8 July:** William Jennings Bryan, at the Democratic National Convention in Chicago, Illinois, delivers his "Cross of Gold" speech for the first time. **16 August:** Gold is discovered in the Klondike region of the Canadian Yukon Territory. **12 October:** The first realistic "motion picture," William Dickson's *Empire State Express,* is shown in a theater. **3 November:** William McKinley is elected president of the United States.

1897   4 March: William McKinley is sworn in as the 24th U.S. president. **19 April:** In Massachusetts, the first Boston Marathon is held. **14 July:** The first ship carrying gold and prospectors from the Klondike docks in San Francisco, California. **17 July:** The second ship carrying gold and prospectors from the Klondike docks in Seattle, Washington; a *Seattle Post Intelligencer* newspaper article proclaiming the find stirs a stampede of Americans northward to the Canadian wilderness.

1898   25 January: The USS *Maine* arrives at port in Havana, Cuba. **9 February:** The *New York Journal* publishes the De Lome letter questioning President McKinley's manhood. **15 February:** The USS *Maine* explodes. **20 April:** The United States in effect declares war on Spain. **25 April:** The U.S. Supreme Court rules on *Williams v. Mississippi*. **1 May:** Commodore George Dewey destroys the Spanish fleet in the Philippines. **7 July:** The United States annexes Hawaii. **10 December:** The Treaty of Paris ending the Spanish–American War is signed.

1899 4 February: The Philippine Insurrection begins. **6 February:** The U.S. Senate ratifies the treaty ending the Spanish–American War. **23 April:** The lynching of Sam Hose occurs in Newnan, Georgia. **6 September:** Secretary of State John Hay issues the first Open Door Policy in relation to China. **3 October:** The United States settles the Venezuelan boundary dispute between England and Venezuela. **18 December:** The U.S. Supreme Court rules on *Cumming v. Richmond County Board of Education*.

Introduction

The Gilded Age was an important three-decade period in American history. It was a time of transition, when the United States began to move beyond and get over its Civil War and postwar rebuilding phase called Reconstruction. It is remembered as a time of progress in technology and industry, of regression in race relations, and of stagnation in politics and **foreign affairs**. It was a time when Wall Street grew to dominate the economic landscape, Madison Avenue began to make its mark, and the people of Main Street in small towns throughout the country built thriving businesses. It was simultaneously a time when poor southerners began farming for a mere share of the crop rather than for wages, when pioneers made lives of misery for themselves in the harsh land and climate of the Great Plains, and when hopeful prospectors set out in search of riches in the gold fields of the Rocky Mountains, from Colorado to Canada. It was a time of great optimism about the future, as inventions, **educational** expansion, the rise of the middle class, and increased leisure time for many raised the nation's collective standard of living by half. It was also a time of pessimism about many families' personal financial hardships, as they wondered how to put food on the table in an era with no government social programs to help them, no minimum wage, and widespread discrimination against **women** and minorities in the workforce. It was a time of boom and bust, and it featured two financial panics that resulted in national depressions.

With economics and society constituting the main historical focal points of the Gilded Age, it should not be surprising that the era is not generally regarded as a time of reform. Nevertheless, it played host to several important reform movements that enjoyed limited success, including women's suffrage, prohibition, immigrant assimilation, and nature preservation. Other attempts at reform—such as improving **African Americans' civil rights**, achieving more humane treatment of

American **Indians**, trust-busting, and attempting to redistribute wealth through various schemes—failed profoundly. Even so, such attempts paved the way for the 20th century's Progressive Era, which would prove more fertile ground for reform.

What follows is an enumeration and explanation of several key aspects of the Gilded Age, from its name and dates to its economics, politics, and demographics. It will provide a broad overview of the period and set the stage for the rest of this dictionary.

NAMING THE "GILDED AGE"

Eras of history are artificial creations of historians. Rarely does one era have a rigid, clear dividing line between itself and another. Usually the lines are drawn merely for purposes of packaging information in neat little boxes. These boxes are then opened by teachers and students in history classes. Sometimes the reason for the packaging seems obvious, such as calling the decades in English history that parallel the life and reign of Queen Victoria the "Victorian Age" or the centuries of American history prior to the founding of the United States the "Colonial Era." Other times the packaging is not so obvious; this is the case with calling the late 1800s in the United States the "Gilded Age." It is a catchy label, to be sure, but what does it mean? What separates it from other "ages" of American history? Why is it packaged as a separate historical entity? What are its starting and ending points? None of these questions are easy to answer, which indicates that not only is this terminology imprecise, but it may well be insufficient to describe this era, if not an altogether inaccurate description.

The Gilded Age acquired its name because a famous humorist and author living at the time, **Mark Twain**, first called it that. He was describing the United States as a nation with a beautiful, shiny exterior hiding decadent, filthy insides. Authors like Twain were celebrities in the days before the invention of electronic media. As such, they were some of the premier conversation starters and opinion shapers for the nation. If some particular event or series of events, such as a prolonged political and military conflict, had dominated the American people's attention during this time, some other author or newspaper editor would have come up with a different moniker to describe the era and thus replace the "Gilded Age" label. The "Civil War and Reconstruction," for instance, makes an easily understandable historical package, as does the "American Revolution and Early Republic." But no such defining events can be found for the era from 1870 to 1900. That, as much as for any other reason, is why the Gilded Age name has stuck.

DATING THE GILDED AGE

Some historians package the Gilded Age neatly between the end of the Civil War in 1865 and the beginning of the **Spanish–American War** in 1898. The rationale is easily understandable, for such packaging makes it one of three eras of American history that run from one war to another war (the other two being the Early Republic and the Roaring Twenties/ Great Depression). Other historians say it runs from the assassination of Abraham Lincoln in 1865 to the assassination of **William McKinley** in 1901. This assertion is equally understandable, because it confines the era between two great bookend presidents—Abraham Lincoln and **Theodore Roosevelt**—with all presidents in between being, by comparison, little more than forgettable stick figures. Still other historians say it does not really begin until the end of Reconstruction, in 1877, since Reconstruction constitutes a separate era in its own right, and it does not make sense to have overlapping eras. The problem with this line of thought is that Twain's description of this era as the Gilded Age came in 1872, right in the midst of Reconstruction. Likewise, the problem with ending the Gilded Age with either the Spanish–American War or the assassination of McKinley is that some historians give the beginning date of the "Progressive Era" as 1890, which causes another overlapping era dilemma. It can easily be argued that the Gilded Age is synonymous with the **Republican Party**'s rise to national power, which began with the Lincoln administration in 1860, and which brought the beginning of what is commonly called "big government" today. If that is the case, then deciding when the Gilded Age ended is not so easy, because Republican presidents Roosevelt and William Howard Taft were "big government" men, too, and they presided during the Progressive Era, not the Gilded Age. Coming full circle, then, eras of history are artificial creations, and one set of dates to frame the Gilded Age is just about as valid as the next.

In this book, the dates of the Gilded Age are set from 4 March 1869 through 31 December 1899. The rationale for this beginning date is that 1869 marks a symbolic turning point in the history of Reconstruction and the American people's focus on it, which effectively started the process of creating the new zeitgeist that came to characterize the Gilded Age. In that year, five important changes occurred, two of which showed immediate results, and three of which bore fruit later. First, Ulysses S. Grant was sworn into office as president of the United States, and soon the nation's attention began to move from primarily the racial and political problems of the South toward the economic and political problems of the North (and the nation) thanks to the **Black Friday** scandal. Second, the completion of the **transcontinental railroad** in that year had an enormous impact on the way Americans looked at themselves and their country—it started moving the collective consciousness of the nation away from the Civil War, Reconstruction, disunion, and impeachment, toward technological progress, economic growth, westward expansion, unity of purpose, and national pride. Third, the women's suffrage movement began a new phase at this time, as the American Woman Suffrage Association was created and the first group of women got the right to vote in a U.S. Territory (Wyoming). Fourth, the first nationwide labor union of any importance, the **Knights of Labor**, was formed in 1869. Fifth and finally, "professional" **baseball** began in this year, and with it began consumerism of organized sports as a form of entertainment for the masses. Although professional baseball, the Knights of Labor, and women's suffrage had little immediate impact, the long-term significance of any of the three could hardly be greater. One ultimately became "America's pastime," one represented the empowerment of more than half of the population, and one portended a future in which the working class—which, like women, also constituted more than half of the population—would be empowered as well.

The rationale for 1899 being the ending date of the Gilded Age is simply that most features which characterized the Gilded Age seem to have largely run their course by this time. By the close of the century, the technological advancement of **railroads**, electricity, telephones, and various other industries, as well as the dominance of corporations and trusts in business, the unbelievably wealthy tycoons they produced, and the public fascination with it all, had ceased to be a novelty. It had become the norm. In fact, the nation had already begun to experience a backlash against it.

The Populists started the backlash, but it would be left to the Progressives to finish it. By 1900, progressive thought—or reformism—had become the new prevailing zeitgeist. In other words, the notion of fixing all the problems resulting from the uneven distribution of wealth in the Gilded Age had taken precedence in the American people's minds over maintaining the status quo. In addition to this rationale, placing the end of the Gilded Age at 1900 allows for a convenient and easy-to-remember date, making a smooth transition to the Progressive Era.

DEFINING THE GILDED AGE

The study of history is largely devoted to two things: (1) chronicling the steady march of human progress and analyzing how, when, why, and by whom our species moves toward a higher standard of living and ever increasing intellectual power, and (2) chronicling whatever went wrong in the past and scrutinizing the decisions public officials made to try to correct the problems. The Gilded Age yields high volumes of both. Concerning the former, the orthodox historical interpretation holds that these post–Civil War decades were mainly characterized by economic statistics and demographic changes, such as urbanization, industrialization, unionization, technological innovation, the growth of corporations, educational expansion, the rising middle class, and increasing **immigration**. Along with economic development and apparent prosperity, however, came serious inequities, a point which brings us to the latter. The wealth was not distributed equally among classes, races, or genders, which created a notable groundswell of animosity from those at the bottom of the social hierarchy. It seemed that everyone wanted a larger slice of the pie, yet only the corporate "cooks" (sometimes "crooks") got to do the slicing. Thus, the Gilded Age had its share of socio-political issues to address and problems to solve.

The Gilded Age was, as the label implies, a time of excess and corruption, of shallowness and show. Clearly, Twain knew what he saw and how to describe it. Yet that name is not an all-encompassing description of the times. With historical hindsight, it does not capture the overall essence, or the zeitgeist, of late 19th century U.S. history. The real zeitgeist of Gilded Age America (the late 1800s) was its thrust to achieve true nationalism—that is, the quest for a national consensus on black–white race relations; the quest to reconcile the North and the South into a unified whole; the quest for a transcontinental communication and transportation network; the quest for a homogenous, nation-wide economic system that blended agriculture and industry; the quest to subdue the indigenous Native Americans once and for all; the quest to preserve and defend the post–Civil War American "nation" through a truly "national" military policy; the quest for a national consensus on morality and **religion**; and the quest to extend the American way of life overseas to subservient peoples. A better label for this era of American history, therefore, might be the "National Age," or something similar.

Although there were some "nationalists" in the United States before the Gilded Age, they were in the minority. They resided mainly in the Northeast and belonged to the either the Federalist, Whig, or Republican parties, depending upon the time period in which they lived. Meanwhile, the states' rights advocates, the **Democratic Party**, and sectionalists (regionalists) were in the majority, and hence in control of the destiny of the not-so-united United States. Before the Civil War, the region of the country with the largest concentration of states' rights Democrat sectionalists—the South—dominated American politics and the federal government to a much greater extent than did the North, despite the North's population being twice as large as the South's. There had been 15 presidents elected before Abraham Lincoln. Of them, nine were southerners. Those nine had served 49 years in office collectively, whereas the six northern presidents had served only 22 years in office. Besides that, three of the six northern presidents had held pro-southern states' rights views. Thus, the South dominated the executive branch of the federal government for all but 10 years before the Civil War. In addition to that, states' rights sectionalists tended to dominate Congress and the Supreme Court as well. When the southern states seceded from the Union in 1860–1861, however, they sacrificed all of this power in a futile attempt to become completely independent from the northern nationalists. Upon the South's defeat, the roles were immediately and dramatically reversed. From then on, nationalists began to control the destiny of the nation, but it took the first few years of Reconstruction for them to assert and prove their dominance. Those Reconstruction and Gilded Age nationalists were almost exclusively northerners and Republicans.

During the Gilded Age, the prewar notion that the Tenth Amendment to the U.S. Constitution gave some states the right to thwart the implied powers of the national government was displaced by the doctrine of national sovereignty. This does not mean that no state or section ever challenged that sovereignty during the Gilded Age. White southerners routinely tested the limits in terms of racial discrimination, and they succeeded at ensuring their race's dominance before the era had ended. This outcome was not for lack of the national government's *ability* to stop it but merely for lack of the nationalists' *willingness* to do so.

POLITICS OF THE GILDED AGE

During the last three decades of the 19th century, Americans were almost evenly divided between the two major parties, and hence almost evenly divided over conservatism and liberalism, or status quo and change. This phenomenon has been called the "politics of dead center." The 41st through 56th Congresses convened during this period. Of those 16, in the House of Representatives, 8 were controlled by Democrats, and 8 by Republicans. In the Senate, the Republicans controlled all but two (1880 and 1894). A few minor parties representing specific labor or economic interests held a few seats. The total number of congressional districts rose from 243 to 357, partly from population increase and partly from admission of new states. The latter of course accounted for all 16 of the new Senate seats, as the total number of senators jumped from 74 to 90. The only minor political party to enjoy any notable success in the Senate was the **People's Party**, but a few scattered Independents and "Readjusters" and "Silverites" also made a showing. Although the South grew increasingly "solid" for the Democrats over the period (because of disfranchisement of black voters), the rest of the country rarely voted one way or the other with consistency.

Presidential elections tell a lot about the American people. They reflect the general mood of the country in any given 4-year period. Republicans tended to win most Gilded Age presidential elections, if often by the narrowest of margins. **Grover Cleveland** was the only Democrat to break that pattern and win the White House. Although he won the popular vote all three times he ran (1884, 1888, and 1892), he won the Electoral College vote only twice, losing to **Benjamin Harrison** in 1888. The popular vote in the 1868 presidential race went 3,013,000 for the Republican Ulysses S. Grant and 2,704,000 for the

Democrat Horatio Seymour, with 317 electoral votes in play, and no serious third party in contention. In 1872, by contrast, there were six candidates in the field, although they represented only three different parties. Grant still won easily in the Electoral College. In the next three races, in 1876, 1880, and 1884, a Greenback Party or some variation of it fielded a candidate, but such parties never won a single electoral vote. In 1884, the Prohibition Party made its debut and followed with three more tries in 1888, 1892, and 1896. It failed to win a single electoral vote in any of the elections. In 1892, the only third party to enjoy any notable success during the Gilded Age, the People's Party, picked up 22 electoral votes as well as one governorship and several congressional seats. The 1896 popular vote went 7,036,000 for McKinley, 6,468,000 for **Bryan**, and 323,000 for other candidates, with 447 electoral votes in play.

Comparing the vote totals for 1868 and 1896 shows that voter participation more than doubled during the Gilded Age. It increased at a greater rate than did the overall population, which merely doubled. The increase was largely the result of the enfranchisement of some blacks and women, and the re-enfranchisement of former Confederates in the South.

ECONOMICS OF THE GILDED AGE

The focus of Gilded Age economics tends to be on industrial development, and rightly so. However, the number of farms increased during this period from a little more than two million to nearly six million nationwide. The rapid population increase and the dream of land ownership largely account for that statistic. Even so, industrial employment constituted the majority of new jobs created in the Gilded Age. Notable among the many new industries that were either created or expanded was that of steel. Although the technology to make steel had been developed earlier, it was not until the end of the 1860s that manufacturers had the mass production capabilities that would come to characterize the industry. Steel production thus grew from a mere 77,000 tons in 1870 to more than 11 million tons three decades later. To make such an increase possible, the largest steel mill in Pennsylvania, **Andrew Carnegie**'s Homestead plant, employed more than 4,000 workers. Steel largely went to build the railroads (since the tracks, the locomotives, and cars were all made of it), although the first "skyscrapers" were introduced at this time, too, thanks to the mass production of steel.

Railroad track mileage doubled in the decade of the 1880s, and the railroads employed perhaps four million by the 1890s. The railroad industry produced far more wealth for the overall U.S. economy than did any other. Yet the money was concentrated at the top, among corporate leaders and investors, while the average track layer, porter, or other laborer barely made ends meet. Not surprisingly, railroad workers became the first to stage nationwide strikes for better wages. Yet they were not the only ones. It is estimated that from 1881 to 1894, some 14,000 separate labor strikes occurred in the United States. The most notable ones were the **Great Railroad Strike of 1877**, the May Day strikes of 1886 (which led to the **Haymarket Incident**), the **Homestead Strike** of 1892, and the **Pullman Strike** of 1894. Three of these four involved either railroad workers or steel workers, while the May Day strikes involved a host of **trade unions**.

Textile mills sprang up in the South along the fall line of rivers, creating mill towns that attracted people from their isolated farms. Women and children were as likely to be employed in such establishments as men. In some areas, women accounted for 15 percent of the total workforce. Nationwide, the percentage of women working outside the home more than doubled during the Gilded Age. Approximately 1.7 million children under age 16 held full-time jobs. Such facts help account for the low pay and grinding poverty of the era; in 1890, of the 12 million families counted in the U.S. Census, 11 million earned less than $100 per month, but the majority of that number earned less than half that much. Southern sharecroppers, who often earned little monetary income, were partly responsible for depressing that figure. Despite such abysmal financial statistics, the overall quality of life increased during the Gilded Age, thanks to inventions and innovations. The United States was already a world leader in inventions prior to the Gilded Age; during the period, its output of new gadgets, industrial machinery, farm equipment, and business devices increased more than tenfold. From approximately 40,000 patents issued in all the years before the Civil War, the nation saw nearly a half-million issued by the turn of the century. Among the most notable inventions were the light bulb, the phonograph, the moving picture apparatus (all from the mind of **Thomas Edison**), the telephone, the typewriter, the adding machine, and the cash register. Such marvels were not only money-makers for inventors and investors but life-changers for homes and businesses. Consequently, by the turn of the century, the United States could boast the highest standard of living in the world.

DEMOGRAPHICS OF THE GILDED AGE

If the focus of this era was the attempt to coalesce and homogenize the disparate sections, races, political ideologies, and cultures into a true "nation," then it is important to know some demographics about the American melting pot. At the beginning of the Gilded Age, the total population of the United States stood at 38.5 million. By the end—just 30 years later—it had almost exactly doubled, to 76.2 million. Even so, the population increase averaged only about 26 percent from one decade to the next from 1870 to 1900, which was considerably less than the average of 34 percent for all the decades from 1790 to 1870. Although the locus of the population was still east of the Mississippi River, westward migration was just as much a part of the American mosaic in the Gilded Age as it had ever been. The geographic center of the population in 1870 was just a little southwest of Columbus, Ohio. By 1900, it was just a little east of Columbus, Indiana, which means it had moved about 100 miles west. In 1870, the most heavily populated state was New York at 4.4 million, followed by Pennsylvania at 3.5 million. By 1900, New York had 7.3 million, and Pennsylvania 6.3 million. They still ranked one and two. The farther west one traveled, the more sparsely populated the states became, although there were always more people living on the West Coast than in the Rocky Mountains and Great Plains states. Between the Homestead Act of 1862 and its various western state and territorial corollaries, the government disposed of some 180 million acres in the West from the 1860s to the turn of the century.

Urban population boomed during the Gilded Age. In 1870 the most populous city was New York City at well over one million. No other city came close. Baltimore, Boston, Philadelphia, and a few others were in the 200,000 range. By 1900, New York City boasted 3.4 million, and Chicago had emerged from a town that barely showed up on the map to a city claiming second place at 1.7 million. Philadelphia was the only other city to crack the one million mark. In 1870, only 25.7 percent of the American people lived in cities, with 74.3 percent living in small towns, communities, or the isolated countryside; in 1900, 39.7 percent lived in cities, with 60.3 percent living elsewhere. The number of cities with a population greater than 50,000 increased from 25 to 78.

The number of states in the union increased from 37 in 1870 to 45 in 1900. The eight states that joined the union during the Gilded Age were Colorado (1876), Montana (1889), North Dakota (1889), South Dakota (1889), Washington (1889), Wyoming (1890), Idaho (1890), and Utah (1896). Of these, six joined during the Benjamin Harrison administration (1888–1892), under the guidance of the **Billion Dollar Congress**. Colorado joined sooner because its gold and silver rushes quickly gave it more population than most other western territories. Utah joined later because its population was largely composed of Latter Day Saints (Mormons) who had to abandon the church's polygamy policy before Congress would grant statehood.

In conclusion, in a nation as large and diverse as the United States, people were bound to have a wide variety of life experiences. One person's America might look very different from another person's America. Yet, the overall tenor of the times was one of hope and expectation of better things to come. Growth, improvement, expansion—these are the terms that best describe the Gilded Age.

The Dictionary

– A –

A & P STORES. George H. Hartford and George Gilman, founders of the Great American Tea Company in 1859, renamed the nation's first great "supermarket" chain the Great Atlantic and Pacific Tea Company in 1870 to capitalize on the public excitement over the newly-finished **transcontinental railroad**. The store began as a tea and spice specialty shop in New York and grew rapidly in the 1870s–1880s through the mail-order business, heavy advertising, door-to-door sales, and expansion of its outlets and product line. By the 1880s the "A & P" had become a household name, with multiple stores in operation across the country, mainly in the Northeast. By the 1890s it had become a million-dollar-a-year enterprise. Its entry into and focus on the coffee business in the 1890s boosted both its sales and its reputation for providing high-quality and affordable products, as did its introduction of many private-label products. Its Eight O' Clock Coffee brand is still famous today. The A & P stood in the vanguard of innovative entrepreneurial ideas in the Gilded Age, paving the way for today's retail and grocery giants. *See also* WOOLWORTH'S, F. W.

A CENTURY OF DISHONOR. *See* JACKSON, HELEN HUNT.

ADAMS, HENRY (1838–1918). Born in Boston to one of the founding families of the United States, Henry Brooks Adams was the grandson of President John Quincy Adams and the great-grandson of President John Adams. As a child of American royalty, he went to **college** at Harvard University and continued his **education** abroad. During the Civil War, he tried his hand at journalism, and in 1870 he was hired to teach history at Harvard. In his 7 years as a professor,

1

he introduced into American education the graduate seminar method of teaching, which he modeled after the German system. Among his soon-to-be famous students was fellow Bostonian Henry Cabot Lodge. Adams's first great contribution to American **literature** came with his 1889–1891 publication of the nine-volume masterpiece, *The History of the United States of America (1801–1817)*, which dealt with the years of the Thomas Jefferson and James Madison administrations. In 1894, Adams was elected president of the American Historical Association. Meanwhile, he continued to write, publishing two novels before the end of the Gilded Age. He is best remembered for his semi-autobiographical *The Education of Henry Adams*, which came out in the 20th century, and is considered one of the most important works of nonfiction in American literary history.

ADDAMS, JANE. *See* HULL HOUSE.

AFRICAN AMERICANS. One reason the late 19th century was the "Gilded" Age rather than the "Golden" Age in American history was the pervasive racial discrimination of the era. Blacks held the unenviable position as the largest minority group, which made them the main target of white prejudice and stereotyping. Pseudoscientific theories that promoted racism, especially **Social Darwinism**, grew more popular every decade during the Gilded Age, which made the problem worse at the end of the era than it had been at the beginning.

The least racist part of the Gilded Age was the Reconstruction period (1865–1877). In the late 1860s and early 1870s, northern **Republican** control of the federal government gave blacks hope for a brighter future after centuries of slavery. In 1870, Mississippi became the first state to send a black man, Hiram R. Revels, to the U.S. Senate. In that same year, the 15th Amendment to the U.S. Constitution passed, which guaranteed blacks the same voting rights as whites. With this major reform, blacks voted en masse in the federal elections of 1872, directly leading to a presidential victory for **Ulysses S. Grant**. Meanwhile, many other blacks were elected to Congress from various states, and blacks temporarily held control of the legislature of South Carolina. In Mississippi, John R. Lynch served as speaker of the House in the state legislature from 1873 to 1877, and Blanche K. Bruce was sent by that legislature to serve in the U.S. Senate from 1875 to 1881. At that time, however, white southern **Democrats** began staging the "Redemption" of their government from black and Republican control, which led to the untimely demise of Reconstruction, the controversial presidential election of 1876, and the **Compromise of 1877.**

In the realm of **education** for blacks, the Freedmen's Bureau made great strides during Reconstruction. In addition, several black **colleges** were founded at this time, including **Howard** University in Washington, D.C.; Alcorn and Jackson State Universities in Mississippi; Fisk University in Tennessee; Shaw University and Bennett College in North Carolina; Hampton University in Virginia; Clark and Morehouse Colleges and Atlanta University in Georgia; Bowie State and Morgan State Universities in Maryland; Dillard University in Louisiana; and Claflin University and Benedict College in South Carolina. Some were founded at public expense, while others were made possible by philanthropy. Even after Reconstruction ended, higher education for some fortunate blacks remained the brightest spot on the horizon; several additional colleges and universities were created through the philanthropy of the Peabody and Slater Funds and through the Second Morrill Land-Grant Act of 1891. The most famous of these post-Reconstruction colleges was **Booker T. Washington**'s Tuskegee Institute. The **U.S. Supreme Court** struck a blow to black education in 1899, however, in the case *Cumming v. Richmond County Board of Education*, which allowed for state-forced segregation in public schools. As Reconstruction gave way to the Jim Crow era, blacks found themselves facing five prevalent types of racism:

Disfranchisement. The right to vote was systematically chipped away year by year in the southern states until by the turn of the century, most blacks had been disqualified altogether under new state constitutions. This was accomplished through mechanisms such as the poll tax, the literacy test, the understanding clause, and the grandfather clause, most of which were pioneered in the Mississippi Constitution of 1890.

Segregation. Each state made its own laws to keep the races separate in public places, and they did so gradually. Congress passed the Civil Rights Act of 1875 to prevent segregation from growing and spreading, but the U.S. Supreme Court struck it down as unconstitutional in the *Civil Rights Cases* ruling of 1883. Segregation did not become entrenched as an inflexible southern way of life until the U.S.

Supreme Court ruled in *Plessy v. Ferguson* in 1896 that the state-forced physical separation of the races was constitutional.

Economic Proscription. Southern whites expected blacks to stay "in their place," which often meant being locked into a **sharecropping** arrangement, working in the cotton fields, and living in a shanty in a designated black area. They generally frowned upon blacks who tried to better themselves through education or entrepreneurship.

Lynching. Vigilante justice by white mobs against blacks became increasingly common as the Gilded Age wore on. White southern society, aided by a do-nothing federal government, had come to accept not only the murder of black men accused of sexual crimes against white **women** as a necessity for preserving the social order, but in fact to romanticize and celebrate it as a manly and chivalrous action to preserve white female virtue. The Sam Hose murder in Newnan, Georgia, in 1899, became a "spectacle" lynching in which tickets were sold and whites came from Atlanta by the hundreds to watch.

*The **Convict Lease System**.* After the 13th Amendment left the door open for punishing criminals through involuntary servitude, the practice of essentially enslaving black males through the penal system and allowing the state to profit from their labor began in Georgia and spread throughout the South.

African Americans essentially had three choices for dealing with the discrimination they faced. They could protest it and fight it, they could sit and accept it, or they could try to escape it geographically. Protest and fighting generally resulted in white backlashes in which blacks died. Deadly race riots in the mid-1870s resulted from blacks trying to defend the constitutional rights they had received just a few years earlier. Even so, **Frederick Douglass** continued to encourage blacks to stand up for their rights, and he pressed for government intervention on their behalf until the end. After Douglass died, Booker T. Washington became the premier spokesman for blacks with his **Atlanta Compromise** speech in 1895. He encouraged blacks to do the opposite and thereby largely relieved government officials of their duty to correct the problem. Almost immediately after the end of Reconstruction, Pap Singleton started the **Exoduster** movement to get blacks out of the South and into the West, where he expected a brighter future for his race. Others, including some white politicians, promoted various emigration and colonization schemes to remove blacks from the United States altogether, but virtually nothing came of them.

In the end, instead of the problem subsiding over time, it had grown worse by the dawn of the new century. Advocates of civil rights reform, such as **Ida B. Wells-Barnett** and **W. E. B. Du Bois**, called for change at the time, but whites and the U.S. government generally ignored them. Some historians have judged that the last decade of the 19th century and the first decade of the 20th century were worse in some important ways for blacks than slavery had ever been. *See also* BLAIR EDUCATION BILL; BUFFALO SOLDIERS; DELANEY, MARTIN; FEDERAL ELECTIONS BILL; LANGSTON, JOHN MERCER; MOHONK CONFERENCES ON THE NEGRO QUESTION; MORGAN, JOHN TYLER; SMALLS, ROBERT; TURNER, HENRY M.

AGRICULTURAL WHEEL. *See* FARMERS' ALLIANCES.

***ALABAMA* CLAIMS DISPUTE.** This **foreign affairs** issue had its genesis in the American Civil War (1861–1865), when Great Britain indirectly aided the Confederate States of America by allowing private shipbuilders to contract with Confederate agents for the production of war ships. While the British government officially proclaimed neutrality in the Americans' war, there was no consensus among the British people as to what constituted neutrality. That, plus the fact that the Confederate ships were built without being advertised as such, kept the British government from preventing their completion or their confiscation until several had already put to sea. Once at sea, these war ships sank more than 150 U.S. vessels. The first and most destructive of these war ships was the C. S. S. *Alabama*. It thus became the namesake for all U.S. government claims against Great Britain for violations of proclaimed neutrality after the war.

With the United States bogged down in the multiple problems of Reconstruction, not much action was taken during the Andrew Johnson administration to seek reparations from Great Britain. Under the **Ulysses S. Grant** administration, however, the Americans began to push their "*Alabama* Claims" vigorously. Senator Charles Sumner argued that

Great Britain owed the United States more than $2 billion in damages, but he would allow payment to be made in land instead of money—he wanted Canada. Such outrageous demands led to a serious deterioration of Anglo–American relations but concomitantly forced the British to the bargaining table. In 1871, the two nations agreed to the Treaty of Washington, which yielded a British apology and allowed an international tribunal to judge the merits of the Americans' case for monetary damages. The tribunal of 1872 convened in Geneva, Switzerland, and took several months to arrive at a decision. Ultimately, the United States was awarded $15.5 million. More significantly, the way the two nations handled this dispute through an international arbiter set a precedent that would be followed in future crises by many other countries. Indirectly, it led to the creation of permanent international diplomatic bodies of the 20th century, including the United Nations. *See also* EVARTS, WILLIAM M.; MORTON, LEVI P.

ALGER, HORATIO (1832–1899). Born in Massachusetts, Horatio Alger Jr. hoped to follow in his father's footsteps as a Unitarian minister. He attended **college** at Harvard University, where he studied **literature** under Henry Wadsworth Longfellow, before enrolling in Harvard Divinity School, where he graduated with honors. After touring Europe, he took a job pastoring a church on Cape Cod in 1866 but was soon accused of molesting teenage boys there. Resigning his position, he moved to New York City and saw a different side of American life from that of his privileged upbringing. The hard life of poor children and teenagers who tried to eke out a living for themselves or their families with menial labor made a strong impression on him. He believed religiously that such boys who worked hard and lived virtuous lives would be rewarded in the end. In 1867, he published his first fictional portrayal of that scenario in a dime novel called *Ragged Dick*, in which a poor shoeshine boy named Richard Hunter uses honesty, integrity, hard work, and street smarts to take hold of the American dream against all odds. The book proved so commercially successful that Alger followed it in 1869 with a series called *Luck and Pluck* and another in 1871 called *Tattered Tom*, both of which followed the same rags-to-riches formula and turned out equally profitable. He eventually published more than 100 similar books. Although modern readers generally find his work too naive, simplistic, and dated to be of much literary value, he was among the top three writers of the Gilded Age both in popular appeal and name recognition.

ALTGELD, JOHN P. (1847–1902). Born in Germany, John Peter Altgeld arrived in the United States with his parents while still an infant. Growing up in Ohio, he joined the Union army during the Civil War, even though he was underage. After the war, he taught school, studied law, worked on the **railroads**, and migrated to Missouri for a time, where he served as a district attorney in Andrew County, before moving to his permanent home of Chicago in 1875. There he started a law practice and invested in real estate, which proved lucrative. Meanwhile, he began making a name for himself in the **Democratic** party, running for a seat in the U.S. House of Representatives unsuccessfully in 1884. He showed the first signs of being a Progressive reformer with the publication of an 1884 pamphlet called "Our Penal Machinery and Its Victims." Two years later, his liberal views on crime and punishment got him elected to a judicial post, which he held for 5 years. As his star rose in the Democratic party in Chicago, he won nomination for and election as governor of Illinois in 1892, appealing largely to both poor city laborers and country farmers in the midst of the Populist movement. His would prove a turbulent and controversial 4-year term.

Shortly after assuming power, Altgeld made two widely unpopular decisions. First, he pardoned the three surviving death-row inmates of the seven convicted in the **Haymarket Incident** of 1886, saying their trial had been unfair. Next, he clashed with President **Grover Cleveland** and his attorney general, Richard Olney, over how to deal with the **Pullman Strike** of 1894. When Cleveland ordered federal troops into Chicago to break up the strike, Altgeld considered it an affront to his authority as governor. He asked Cleveland to withdraw the troops while at the same time sending in the Illinois militia to quell an area of disturbance among the strikers. His militia killed several strikers, which then put him at odds with both labor and the **railroad** capitalists simultaneously. Chicago newspapers, **Republicans**, and Populists, as well as some members of his own party, condemned him as an **anarchist**, a communist, socialist, un-American foreigner, and the like. Altgeld blamed Cleveland for it all and spent the campaign season of 1896 trying to ensure that the incumbent president did not get renominated. It worked, and he threw his support behind losing candidate **William Jennings Bryan** and the unsuccessful **free silver** platform. Meanwhile, he lost his own bid for reelection and thereafter faded into obscurity, although he briefly reemerged in a losing bid to become mayor of Chicago in 1899. Perhaps his most important legacy as governor was his push to expand **college** and university facilities across the state.

AMERICAN ANTI-IMPERIALIST LEAGUE. Founded in 1898 at the onset of U.S. military occupation of the Philippines in the **Spanish–American War**, the American Anti-Imperialist League was devoted to preventing the United States from becoming a colonial power. It failed in this initial effort when the **William McKinley** administration and the U.S. Senate approved the Treaty of Paris of 1898 with Spain, which gave the United States official ownership of the Philippines for a mere $20 million. Thereafter, the league campaigned to get the United States out of the colonial business as quickly as possible, arguing that the Filipinos wanted and deserved independence. Composed of both **Democrats** and **Republicans**, the league boasted some of the most influential people in American politics and society as members. Notables included former President **Grover Cleveland**, author **Mark Twain**, steel magnate **Andrew Carnegie**, educator John Dewey, social reformer Jane Addams, editor E. L. Godkin, and labor leader **Samuel Gompers**, among many others. Former Treasury Secretary George Boutwell served as its first president.

In 1899, once the Filipino insurrection against American occupation began, the league felt vindicated and hoped government leaders would change course accordingly. This hope soon failed. By the presidential election of 1900, Democratic candidate **William Jennings Bryan** had come out clearly on the anti-imperialist side. Even so, many of the Republican members of the league could not bring themselves to vote for him. The league survived this minor schism, but it never actually achieved its objective of an immediate American withdrawal from colonial activities. It did succeed in raising public awareness of an important issue at the end of the Gilded Age, however, and it laid the foundation for future anti-war organizations. *See also* TELLER AMENDMENT.

AMERICAN BAR ASSOCIATION (ABA). Established in 1878 in Saratoga Springs, New York, the ABA was an important Gilded Age creation. Prior to its founding, the United States had no national bar association or other nationwide organization offering a set of standards for the practice of law. Each state regulated the practice, some through their own bar associations, but there was no uniformity across the country. Consequently, what passed for ethical legal conduct in the deep South or the "wild West" might be quite unacceptable in the Northeast. Likewise, what seemed proper in regions with large Catholic or various ethnic populations might seem improper everywhere else. Finally, what seemed good to **Democrats** might be deemed extremely improper by **Republicans**, or vice versa. The ABA's founders sought to rectify the problem by offering a forum for lawyers and judges from around the country to discuss legal issues and to codify a national system that would be acceptable in all parts of the United States, by all **religious** and ethnic groups, and by all political parties.

The infamous financial scandals of the **Ulysses S. Grant** administration brought the need to the fore, with the Whiskey Ring case of 1875–1876 as the final straw. The Whiskey Ring operated mostly around the St. Louis area, which served as the center of American alcohol brewing. Not surprisingly, therefore, the catalysts of the ABA's founding were St. Louis lawyers who were also Missouri congressmen or Grant's cabinet members with a good grasp of local law and customs, national law, and East Coast ethics. James Broadhead, Henry Hitchcock, and Benjamin Bristow were three such founders, each of whom served a 1-year term as president of the ABA. Other notable founders and presidents included Yale law professor and foreign diplomat Edward J. Phelps; Kentucky governor, senator, and University of Cincinnati law professor John W. Stevenson; former Confederate general Alexander Lawton of Georgia; Iowa senator George G. Wright; Connecticut governor Simeon E. Baldwin; **Tammany Hall** Democrat Clarkson N. Potter of New York City; and Boston civil rights advocate and president of the National Association for the Advancement of Colored People Moorfield Storey. *See also* CORRUPTION.

AMERICAN FEDERATION OF LABOR (AFL). *See* GOMPERS, SAMUEL.

AMERICAN PROTECTIVE ASSOCIATION (APA). Founded in Clinton, Iowa, by Henry Bowers in 1887, the APA, as the American

Protective Association was commonly called, was an ephemeral anti-Catholic organization that sought without much success to affect public policy on the national level. With its socio-political roots in Freemasonry and the Know-Nothing movement of the 1850s, the APA likewise engaged in secret, ritualistic activities. It campaigned against Catholic candidates, sought legislation to restrict Catholic **immigration**, opposed the hiring of Catholic teachers in public schools, and railed against any organization that had a Catholic founder or leader, such as the **Knights of Labor** (led by Terence Powderley). Its membership is difficult to ascertain, but APA leaders claimed up to 2.5 million at its peak in the mid-1890s, although 1 million may be closer to the truth. Composed mainly of Protestants who had emigrated from Ireland, Germany, and other nations where tension ran high between Catholics and Protestants, the APA seemed to be a throwback to an old European socio-**religious** structure. It made gains in local politics in the Midwest, Great Plains states, New England, and California, but it barely dented the South or big eastern seaboard cities with large Catholic populations, such as New York City, Boston, and Baltimore.

The APA worked mainly under the auspices of the **Republican** party, although most national GOP political leaders wanted nothing to do with such a defamatory and discriminatory group. While perhaps 20 Republican congressmen expressed agreement with the APA on some points, virtually none openly supported the group. Several influential non-Catholic public figures, meanwhile, blasted it in their speeches and writings, including **Theodore Roosevelt**, **George Frisbie Hoar**, **John P. Altgeld**, and **Washington Gladden**. Republican President **William McKinley** largely sealed the fate of the APA, however, by appointing Catholics to conspicuous federal posts and by shifting the national focus away from domestic concerns to **foreign affairs** via the **Spanish–American War**. The APA thus died out quietly around the turn of the 20th century.

AMERICAN RAILWAY UNION. *See* DEBS, EUGENE V..

AMERICAN RED CROSS. The International Red Cross, a humanitarian organization founded in Switzerland in 1864, produced dozens of national chapters, including one in the United States in 1881. Organized in Washington, D.C., by Clara Barton, the American Association of the Red Cross, as it was technically called, spawned its first local chapter in Dansville, New York, in the year of its inception. In 1882, Barton, the first president of the organization, persuaded Congress to accept the directives of the first Geneva Convention for the treatment of those wounded in war. For the next 14 years, Barton and the American Red Cross worked to relieve the suffering of victims of various domestic disasters, such as the **Johnstown Flood** of 1889. In 1896, Barton led the group's first expedition onto foreign soil, intervening in a now-forgotten war in Asia Minor. During and after the **Spanish–American War**, the group labored in Cuba. From its small beginning in the Gilded Age, it evolved into one of the world's most important humanitarian organizations during the 20th century.

AMERICAN TOBACCO COMPANY. *See* DUKE, BUCK.

AMERICAN WOMAN SUFFRAGE ASSOCIATION (AWSA). *See* ANTHONY, SUSAN B.; STANTON, ELIZABETH CADY; WOMEN.

ANARCHISM. Anarchism, a political philosophy or worldview that became prominent (albeit not mainstream) during the Gilded Age, originated in Europe. At its core lay an idea that dates back to the ancient Greek Stoics—that government is by nature oppressive and should thus be abolished. Through an evolutionary process, that idea came to be convoluted with Karl Marx's notion that capitalism is equally oppressive and ought to be abolished. Since every industrialized nation in the world had some type of capitalism as its economic system at the time, manifestations of Marxism and anarchism appeared in each, in one form or another. Syndicalism, **trade unionism**, socialism, revolutionary socialism, collectivism, utopianism, and communism were all variations of this common ideology. The precise mixture of anti-government and anti-capitalism that any particular person or group espoused created variations that ran the gamut from mildly reformist versions of anarchism to radical and terrorist versions.

Anarchism first came to the American working class's attention in the early 1880s when German **immigrant** Johann Best arrived and began organizing labor in the Chicago area. In 1883, he led in drafting the "Pittsburgh Manifesto," analogous to Marx's famous 1848 "Communist Manifesto" but targeted only at major American corporations. Most Americans took little notice of such reformist teachings until the May Day labor strikes and rallies of 1886 that produced the **Haymarket Incident** in Chicago, which resulted in several deaths and subsequent executions. Thereafter, anarchism was, rightly or wrongly, equated with violence, revolution, and anti-Americanism in popular perception.

One of Best's disciples, Emma Goldman, ultimately became the most renowned anarchist writer, speaker, and recruiter in American history. A smart, feisty, young Lithuanian immigrant, Goldman plotted with fellow anarchist Alexander Berkman to murder **Henry Clay Frick**, manager of **Carnegie** Steel Company, in the midst of the **Homestead Strike** of 1892. Berkman went to prison for his assault on Frick, while his accomplice Goldman walked free for lack of evidence against her. The incident turned all but a few workers and labor organizers against anarchism in the United States. The nail in the proverbial coffin of American anarchism came at the end of the Gilded Age as Leon Czolgosz, a young follower so zealous and strange that even Goldman would not keep company with him, took center stage. His assassination of President **William McKinley** led to immigration reform and the outlawing of anarchism in the United States.

ANTHONY, SUSAN B. (1820–1906). Born to a Quaker father and Baptist mother in Massachusetts, Susan Brownell Anthony never married but instead devoted her life to the crusade for **women**'s rights. With longtime friend **Elizabeth Cady Stanton**, she founded the National Woman Suffrage Association (NWSA), which petitioned for the right to vote based on the 14th and 15th Amendments to the U.S. Constitution. Unsuccessful, Anthony voted anyway in the presidential election of 1872, for which she was arrested and fined $100. Four years later, at the **U.S. Centennial** Exposition in Philadelphia, she read her "Woman's Declaration of Rights" to a mostly shocked and unreceptive audience. In 1880, she, Stanton, and Matilda Joslyn Gage began compiling their four-volume *History of Woman Suffrage*, the last volume of which was published in 1902 and was mostly Anthony's work. In 1890, she was instrumental in getting the rival American Woman Suffrage Association to merge with the

NWSA to form the National American Woman Suffrage Association (NAWSA), the organization that would eventually be responsible for the ratification of the 19th Amendment. Elected the second president of the NAWSA, she served from 1892 to 1900.

ARMOUR, PHILIP (1832–1901). Raised on a farm in upstate New York, Philip Danforth Armour moved to California as an adult to seek his fortune in the 1849 gold rush. Making a handsome profit in supplying miners with the necessities of their trade, he invested in a grocery business in Milwaukee before launching into the slaughtering and meat packing industry at the time of the Civil War. The Union army demanded meat year-round, and Armour made the beginnings of his fortune by supplying it. This led to his developing several innovations, including the first modern animal disassembly line, the tin-canning of meat, the icing down of meat for sale days after butchering, and the use of every part of the hog and cow with nothing wasted. In 1875, he centralized his business, "Armour and Company," in Chicago, Illinois, adjacent to **Union Stock Yards**, although he had branches in New York City and Kansas City. In 1883, to compete with rival **Gustavus Swift**, Armour began using new refrigerated boxcars to ship his meat. Soon he owned several thousand cars of his own, which allowed him to cut shipping costs. By the time he died, he and his son Jonathan Ogden Armour had turned the company into one of the largest trusts in the United States. Like most Gilded Age tycoons, he was simultaneously a ruthless capitalist/exploiter of labor and a generous philanthropist. Perhaps his most important legacy was helping organize the agricultural commodities futures market in Chicago.

ARTHUR, CHESTER A. (1830–1886). Born in Vermont, Chester Alan Arthur first achieved notoriety as Collector of the Port of New York, a position he earned in 1871 because of his loyal support of President **Ulysses S. Grant** and New York's **Republican** party boss **Roscoe Conkling**. In 1880 he won the vice presidency of the United States on the ticket with President **James A. Garfield**. Succeeding to the presidency upon the death of Garfield in September 1881, he faced a nation of critics who assumed him unqualified and unworthy of the job, skepticism coming because he had been put on the ticket to appease Conkling and the **Stalwart** faction rather than because of any impressive political pedigree he had. Arthur surprised his many naysayers, however, by becoming an honest and effective leader in the White House. During his tenure, two major laws were enacted, the **Pendleton Civil Service Act** (with his approval) and the **Chinese Exclusion Bill** (over his veto). Arthur alienated many members of his own party by vigorously prosecuting cases of graft and **corruption**, as well as by taking the opposing side in several battles with Congress. In the end, his integrity proved his undoing. **James Blaine**'s faction of the party, the Half-Breeds, defeated Arthur's renomination in 1884. He left office in 1885, retired to New York City, and died the following year.

AT&T. *See* BELL, ALEXANDER GRAHAM.

ATHLETICS. *See* SPORTS AND RECREATION.

ATLANTA COMPROMISE. The "Atlanta Compromise" ranks as perhaps the most important speech of the Gilded Age. This name, given to **Booker T. Washington**'s address at the Atlanta Cotton States and International Exposition on 18 September 1895, was made famous by rival **W. E. B. Du Bois**, who disapproved of it. In this brief speech, Washington offered words of racial reconciliation for black and white southerners before a mostly white audience that included the governor of Georgia, the editor of the *Atlanta Constitution*, and many other influential people. Soon the transcript was printed in newspapers throughout the nation, and a copy was sent personally by Washington to President **Grover Cleveland**. Whites received the address enthusiastically.

Realizing that the situation of **African Americans** in the South, and indeed the nation, had deteriorated in the 1890s, Washington sought to approach the problem with an appeasement policy he labeled "accommodationism." He pointed out that since one-third of the South's population was black, it behooved both races to figure out a way to get along with each other better than they had so far. To his fellow blacks, who were often enticed by either emigration and colonization schemes or grand delusions of political power, he said, "Cast down your bucket where you are," meaning to stay in the South and humbly learn a trade. In so doing, they would make themselves valuable as a labor force in the so-called New South. To white employers, who just as often looked forward to an influx of white **immigrants** to supply the South's labor needs, he said likewise, "Cast down your bucket where you are," meaning they should hire their black neighbors instead. He made a strong case for blacks, as a whole, having been loyal to their white employers whether in slavery or freedom. He assured whites that black workers would "stand by you with a devotion that no foreigner can approach."

The most memorable line in the speech was: "In all things that are purely social, we can be as separate as the fingers, yet one as the hand in all things essential to mutual progress." This statement would prove accurate over the coming years (although not exactly in the way Washington hoped) as whites imposed greater and greater degrees of segregation and inequality upon blacks in society while simultaneously exploiting their labor for mutual, albeit racially disparate, economic benefit. The compromise contained within these words was clear to whites: Washington, the head of the most successful black school in the South, Tuskegee Institute, was willing for his people to accept an inferior position in society in exchange for living in peace with whites and widening economic opportunities in the New South. For this, the white media elevated Washington to the status of *the* spokesman for blacks going into the 20th century, but many black intellectuals increasingly came to see the accommodation strategy as surrendering to injustice without putting up a fight. *See also* GRADY, HENRY W.

– B –

BABCOCK, ORVILLE. *See* CORRUPTION; GRANT, ULYSSES S.

BARBED WIRE FENCING. Rarely has such a simple development had such a monumental impact on life in the United States. Prior to its invention and widespread use, no fencing material existed that was cheap, abundant, and strong enough to allow for cordoning off hundreds of acres of farmland to keep out roaming livestock. This was especially a problem on the western prairie, where the so-called "law of the open range" operated, in which cattle herds grazed freely or were driven by **cowboys**, with no concern for property rights. The need for crop protection was thus a major factor leading to the invention of barbed wire.

Joseph Glidden, a farmer from DeKalb, Illinois, is generally credited with inventing barbed wire. In 1874, he earned a patent on the version that eventually became the standard of the industry, although he had to wage a protracted legal battle to ensure his patent rights. Others had experimented with primitive versions of barbed wire, which was essentially a "thorn fence," but none proved commercially viable. Along with two other men from DeKalb—Isaac Ellwood and Jacob Haish—Glidden developed the still commonly used two-strand wire rope with a single "barb" twisted perpendicularly between the two and protruding outward. It was designed to stop a cow in its tracks, and it worked. Soon, Glidden and Haish parted ways, becoming rivals in the barbed wire business, but Ellwood partnered with Glidden. In 1876, Glidden sold his interests to the Massachusetts-based Washburn and Moen Manufacturing Company, which employed Ellwood for a while. Soon, he formed his own company, but the patent rights went to the Washburn company. Thanks to the marketing prowess of John Wayne Gates, who sold Texas ranchers on the idea of barbed wire, the Washburn company became the largest and most lucrative in the industry. In 1898, Gates gained a controlling interest in the company and combined it with some competitors into a monopoly called the American Steel and Wire Company, which subsequently sold out to the megacorporation U.S. Steel.

BARNUM, P. T. (1810–1891). Born in Connecticut, Phineas Taylor Barnum became a successful and famous show businessman long before the Gilded Age. In his early career, he worked in newspapers, advertising, and traveling entertainment, and owned a museum in New York City. His most notable successes in those years were his display of the 2-foot-tall dwarf "General Tom Thumb" and his tour of vocalist Jinny Lind, "the Swedish Nightingale." In the 1860s and '70s he tried his hand at politics, winning office in the Connecticut legislature and as mayor of the town of Bridgeport. In 1871, however, show business beckoned again, and he started a circus he called "The Greatest Show on Earth." Thanks to the ubiquity of the

railroads, he was able to perform across the United States over the coming years. Soon he combined with several other circus owners, including J. A. Bailey, whose shows had played in other parts of the world, and formed what eventually became known as the Barnum & Bailey Circus. The main attraction was "Jumbo" the elephant, which brought in more than $1 million in revenue before the animal died in 1885. Even then, Barnum sold tickets just for the privilege of viewing Jumbo's huge, stretched hide. Whether he actually made the statement so often attributed to him, "There's a sucker born every minute," he certainly applied the principle. Competition in the traveling entertainment industry was fierce in the 1880s–1890s, and, after Barnum's death, one of the competitors—the Ringling Brothers—bought out the Barnum & Bailey Circus, and turned it into the icon of all American circuses in the 20th century.

BARTON, CLARA. *See* AMERICAN RED CROSS.

BASEBALL. The most important team **sport** of the Gilded Age, baseball had already been America's "pastime" for a decade, according to one New York newspaper. Actually, it had been merely a New York area recreational phenomenon before 1869, when the first fully professional team of paid players took the field. That team, the Cincinnati Red Stockings, proved nearly unbeatable. At that time, however, most businessmen involved in the planning side of the game considered paying the players to be scandalous, and they tried to keep the game pure, fielding only amateur players. Yet the wave of the future lay in enticing the best players with money. In 1871, therefore, the National Association of Professional Base Ball Players was formed. Its organizational and financial difficulties soon forced it to fold, but in 1875, millionaire William A. Hulbert created the National League to replace it. It proved commercially viable, despite its attempt to cater to a high-society audience with Victorian age values, by charging a 50-cent admission price, refusing to stage games on Sundays, and not serving alcoholic beverages in concessions. In 1882, Albert Goodwill Spalding gained control of the league, and took it to a new level through shrewd marketing, strong management, and codification of the game's rules. Under Spalding, the league survived a challenge from the American Association, formed in 1883 by

Christopher Van der Ahe, who wanted to increase revenue by catering to the uneducated working-class immigrants, charging a lower admission price, holding Sunday games, and serving alcohol. Spalding's National League weathered another storm in 1890 when the players rebelled against the owners and struck out on their own, forming the Players League, hoping to make more money. This attempt at **trade unionization** lasted only one season. In 1891, the National League resumed operations, practically undaunted, for the rest of the Gilded Age. Not until the 20th century would it take on many of the modern characteristics of the sport that current baseball fans know and love.

BATTLE OF ADOBE WALLS. *See* INDIANS, AMERICAN.

BATTLE OF LITTLE BIG HORN. The most famous episode of the larger Black Hills War, in which the U.S. Army sought to subdue the free-roaming **Indian** tribes of the northern Great Plains, this battle occurred in southern Montana on 26 June 1876. It pitted U.S. Lieutenant Colonel George Armstrong Custer and the 7th Cavalry against an alliance of Sioux, Arapahoe, and Cheyenne, led by Crazy Horse. It came only 9 days after the Battle of the Rosebud, in which General George Crook and a small cavalry detachment had engaged Crazy Horse's forces indecisively only a few miles to the north. As the Indian alliance of perhaps 10,000 people (including probably 3,000 warriors) camped in the valley of the Little Big Horn, Custer's forces split into three columns and launched a surprise attack. The Indians reacted quickly, however, and seized the advantage. As a column led by Major Marcus Reno fell on one side, Custer's column fell on the other. Legend has it that Custer was the last white soldier left standing as his men died all around him. He supposedly made a heroic "last stand," but the Indians showed no mercy and took no prisoners. Some 268 people on the side of the U.S. Army died in the battle, making this the greatest military victory for the Native Americans in the history of the western Indian wars. *See also* BUFFALO BILL; SITTING BULL.

BATTLE OF THE STANDARDS. *See* FREE SILVER.

BEECHER, HENRY WARD (1813–1887). Born in Connecticut to the famous Beecher family of New England, Henry Ward Beecher grew up around outspoken, puritanical Congregationalists who were noted for their denunciation of American slavery during antebellum times. Following in his father's footsteps, he became an abolitionist and Congregationalist preacher himself. After the Civil War, he championed **women**'s rights and Christianity's embrace of secular science, among other liberal causes. By the early 1870s, he had been pastoring the 2,000-seat Plymouth Church in Brooklyn, New York, for a quarter-century, and had begun filling it beyond capacity with his exuberant and inspirational sermons, which touched on virtually every social and political issue of the day. At the same time, he published the best-selling book *Life of Jesus Christ* (1871), sealing his reputation as, in the words of *Harpers' Weekly*, the most brilliant religious figure that the United States had ever produced.

At the height of his fame, however, a scandal of monumental proportions threatened to destroy Beecher's career and his good name. A longtime close friend and member of Plymouth Church named Theodore Tilton accused him of committing adultery with his wife Elizabeth Tilton. Elizabeth had supposedly confessed to her husband, who then confronted Beecher privately while spreading the rumor of the affair to people who publicized it. Elizabeth then changed her story (she would ultimately change it five times in all), but by then the damage had already been done. In 1872, radical women's rights advocate **Victoria Woodhull** published a scathing indictment of the pious preacher via her weekly paper, basically calling him a world-class hypocrite, thus putting the Beecher–Tilton affair squarely in the public eye. In 1873, Beecher and Tilton agreed to a public truce in the *Brooklyn Eagle* newspaper, to put an end to discussing the case in the press. The Plymouth Church's governing council, however, decided that Tilton had already brought too much ignominy to the congregation and its pastor and voted to rescind his membership. That, plus continued agitation from other sources, led Tilton to renew his accusations in 1874. He sued Beecher and demanded $100,000 in damages. The trial began on 11 January 1875, lasted 6 months, and resulted in no clear and irrefutable evidence for the alleged adultery. Famed attorney and politician **William M. Evarts**, among others, represented Beecher.

Although Beecher walked away free, he could have easily allowed the incident to scar him for life, but he did not. Instead, he resumed preaching, lecturing, and writing books, trying to put the ordeal behind him. In 1885, he published his last important work, *Evolution and **Religion***, which secured his place in history as one of the foremost intellectuals/theologians of the Gilded Age. *See also* LITERATURE.

BEEF BONANZA. *See* ARMOUR, PHILIP D.; COWBOYS; SWIFT, GUSTAVUS; UNION STOCKYARDS.

BELL, ALEXANDER GRAHAM (1847–1922). Born and reared in Scotland, "Aleck" Bell moved with his family to Canada in 1870. His father was a speech teacher who did pioneering work with the deaf, basically inventing sign language. Young Aleck followed in his path, studying sound and communication all his life. He, too, worked with the deaf and in 1872 became a professor of speech at Boston University in Massachusetts. While there, he began experimenting with ways to communicate electronically. Bell and his chief competitor, Elisha Gray of the Western Electric company's research team, each worked feverishly and independently to build a working model of a "talking telegraph." They both succeeded and, ironically, their lawyers arrived at the patent office on the same day, 14 February 1876, to file their patents. After a short dispute, the patent office issued the patent to Bell, rather than Gray, on 7 March, due to a paperwork technicality. Interestingly, at the time, the telephone had not yet actually produced a clear, audible communication. Three days later, however, in Bell's laboratory, it did. More importantly, a few months later, at the great **Centennial** Exposition in Philadelphia, Pennsylvania, he demonstrated it before what amounted to the eyes of the world.

Various other competitors soon mounted challenges, claiming they had invented something like the telephone, or part of it, before Bell. After a series of long, drawn-out battles that finally wound up in the **U.S. Supreme Court**, Bell won the exclusive right to claim ownership of the telephone in 1893. Bell had proceeded from the start on the assumption that he would win. He and his financial backers thus formed the Bell Telephone Company in 1877, which expanded to become the American Telegraph and Telephone (AT&T) corporation in 1885. In 1878, Bell's company opened the world's first commercial telephone exchange/switchboard in New Haven, Connecticut. Within 3 years, it had similar exchanges in most major American cities.

Bell did not confine his research to the telephone. Like his equally famous counterpart **Thomas Edison**, he had a broad range of interests. He invented the metal detector, founded the journal *Science*, helped charter the National Geographic Society, and experimented with artificial flight, among other things, all during the Gilded Age. He spent his last years working primarily in the controversial field of eugenics.

BELLAMY, EDWARD. *See LOOKING BACKWARD.*

BERKMAN, ALEXANDER. *See* ANARCHISM; FRICK, HENRY CLAY; HOMESTEAD STRIKE.

BILLION DOLLAR CONGRESS. This 51st Congress, a **Republican**-majority body, was elected in November 1888 in conjunction with President **Benjamin Harrison**, seated in December 1889, and voted out in November 1890 in the largest turnover in American history to that time. It earned its nickname because it became the first Congress to pass a $1 billion budget for a single year. Led in the House of Representatives by Speaker **Thomas B. Reed**, it was noted for passing the revolutionary "Reed Rules," which placed time limits on debate. Its debates in the Senate, however, had no time limits, and, consequently, one of the longest and most bitter filibusters of all time occurred over the **Federal Elections Bill**. The House and Senate agreed in passing several important laws, including the **McKinley Tariff**, the **Sherman** Anti-Trust Act, and the Sherman Silver Purchase Act. This Congress ultimately became the most legislatively active one by far to that time, proposing more than 17,000 bills and resolutions, and passing more than 1,000 of them before adjourning in April 1891. *See also* BLAIR EDUCATION BILL; EVARTS, WILLIAM M.; MORGAN, JOHN TYLER; MORTON, LEVI P.

BILLY THE KID (1859–1881). Using several aliases, this infamous western outlaw mainly went by William H. Bonney, although he was probably born Henry McCarty in New York City. Many aspects of his short life are shrouded in legend, but what his biographers generally hold to be true is that his father died when the Kid was a small child, his mother remarried, and the family moved to New Mexico. Then his mother died, leaving him orphaned at the age of 14. Apparently a decent, honest young man for the next year, he supported himself with the help of sympathetic neighbors before running afoul of the law. Jailed on a charge of teenage mischief, he escaped and fled farther west, eventually joining a cattle-rustling ring, which got into a shootout that resulted in several deaths. New Mexico Territorial Governor Lew Wallace, a former Union Civil War general and soon-to-be author of what would become the best-selling book of the Gilded Age, *Ben-Hur*, offered him amnesty in exchange for his testimony against the adult leaders of the ring. The Kid accepted the offer and testified against his *compadres*, but was kept in custody contrary to his agreement with Wallace. Escaping again, former acquaintance and newly elected sheriff Pat Garrett caught him and put him on trial for murder. Found guilty, he was sentenced to hang. The Kid refused to go quietly to the gallows, however. This time he killed two guards in order to escape custody. Garrett, now on a personal vendetta, tracked him down and shot him in cold blood on 14 July 1881 at Fort Sumter, New Mexico. Ironically, the Kid was not widely known nationally until Garrett published an account of his life and death, which sensationalized the facts for self-serving purposes. The legend of Billy the Kid grew to claim that he had been a heartless, crazed killer of some 21 men. Evidence suggests, however, that he actually killed only four by himself and that he was an accomplice in the murder of five others.

BIMETALLISM. *See* FREE SILVER.

BILTMORE ESTATE. Located in the Blue Ridge range of the Appalachian mountains on the outskirts of Asheville, North Carolina, the Biltmore Estate represents the epitome of gaudy Gilded Age opulence. Built at the behest of George W. Vanderbilt, the grandson of multi-millionaire **Cornelius Vanderbilt** and son of William Henry Vanderbilt, it became the largest private estate in the United States, and it remains so today. Although conceived in the 1870s and '80s, the Biltmore mansion's actual construction did not begin until 1889, and the home was not opened to guests until 1895. **Richard Morris Hunt** was the chief architect of the

175,000-square-foot, 250-room mansion, which covers 4 acres. Imitating some well-known European castles, the mansion housed a library with 23,000 volumes, an art collection that rivaled many galleries and museums, exquisite furnishings and tapestries, and state-of-the-art technology. The landscape architect was **Frederick Law Olmsted**, who imported exotic flora from the ends of the earth, took advantage of indigenous varieties of trees, shrubs, and flowers to fill the hills and valleys, and surrounded the mansion with gardens. Originally, the whole estate totaled 125,000 acres, but much of it was forested and uncultivated. Most of the land eventually was sold, and the grounds were whittled down to the current 8,000 acres, much of which is manicured, cultivated, or otherwise maintained, and almost all of which, thanks to Olmsted's impeccable design, serves to accentuate the attraction of the mansion. The estate required more than 400 servants, farm hands, mechanics, and supervisors of various types, to tend the home, the grounds, and the fully self-sufficient Biltmore farm daily. While the estate shows the best taste in Gilded Age design and decoration, it also exhibits the worst aspects of stereotypical "Robber Baron" wealth acquisition in the sense that, other than selected guests, no one outside the Vanderbilt family got to enjoy its unparalleled magnificence until many decades later when it was reformed as a tourist attraction.

BLACK FRIDAY GOLD SCANDAL. The first in a series of money scandals of the **Ulysses S. Grant** administration involved New York financiers **Jay Gould** and Jim Fisk and their attempt to corner the gold trading market. This scheme and the notorious **Credit Mobilier Scandal** are what gave this era of American history the opprobrious sobriquet the "Gilded" Age. The genesis of the scandal lay in the U.S. government's issuing of Greenbacks (paper money) to help fund the Union cause in the Civil War by allowing for deficit spending. The Greenbacks were supposed to be redeemable in gold at face value after the war, but their actual value fluctuated as investors' confidence in them ebbed and flowed. Redemption of Greenbacks became a central issue of Reconstruction and of the presidential campaign of 1868. In Grant's 1869 inaugural address, he promised to make them redeemable in gold at a discounted rate that most holders would gladly accept. His secretary of treasury and economic advisor, George Boutwell, would be in charge of carrying out the policy.

Gould and Fisk, both of whom were already rich men, saw a "golden" opportunity to make even more money by manipulating the gold market. Their plan was complicated, and it depended upon patience, several people's cooperation, and events unfolding just the right way. To simplify, they would try to get the Grant administration to halt its redemption policy temporarily. At the same time, they would buy gold on the open market in large quantities at the going rate. As they and the U.S. treasury hoarded gold, the supply in the market would decrease, demand would increase, and the value of gold would skyrocket. They would then sell their gold at a great profit, and the government could resume its redemption policy, and no one would get hurt, and no one needed to know. To make this plan work, however, Gould and Fisk had to gain access to the busy, popular, and financially naive president. They enticed Grant's brother-in-law Abel Corbin, who was married to sister Virginia Grant Corbin, into their scheme. Corbin arranged several social gatherings in which Grant, Gould, and Fisk were all present, so they could discuss economic issues and discourage the new president from continuing his redemption policy. Corbin also convinced Grant to appoint another of Gould's and Fisk's alleged henchmen, Daniel Butterfield, as assistant secretary of treasury. Butterfield would have inside information about any decisions Grant and Boutwell made and would supposedly be able to notify Gould and Fisk in advance. Thus, four rogues, according to the standard historical interpretation, stood to make a killing in the gold market.

As this scheme advanced, and as the price of gold began its precipitous rise in the market, Grant and Boutwell became suspicious. Through communication between his sister Virginia and his wife Julia, as well as Corbin, Butterfield, and Boutwell, Grant caught on and actually did the opposite of what Gould and Fisk expected. He abruptly ordered the treasury to sell a huge cache of gold to deflate the market value and ruin the scoundrels. This caused a panic on Wall Street on 24 September 1869—"Black Friday"—as shocked investors in gold (including Fisk and Corbin but excluding Gould) began selling their holdings, absorbing enormous losses, and sending the overall national economy into a tailspin. Gould got word to sell just before the collapse and thus escaped any significant losses.

Technically, what Gould and Fisk did, although highly unethical, was not altogether and necessarily illegal. The subsequent investigation was brief and inconclusive for several reasons: the **Republican** majority in Congress had no interest in destroying a president of their own party; most Americans had no interest in defaming a man who had been the greatest Civil War hero for the Union army; no such scandal had ever been used by opponents to ruin a presidential administration before, and no one yet knew that this one would not be an anomaly for Grant; **Democrats** were complicit in the scandal to some extent, too, because of Gould's and Fisk's ties to **Tammany Hall**, so many of them did not want to probe too deeply into this financial morass; and the nation had just moved on from the impeachment of Andrew Johnson a year earlier, and most Americans did not want to go through something like that again. The main opposition that arose to the Grant administration in the wake of this scandal came from a group of reformers who soon called themselves the **Liberal Republicans**. For all these reasons, Butterfield ended up taking the fall, although he vehemently denied his part in the plot. Corbin suffered financial ruin, and returned to private life and obscurity. Fisk had worse problems to deal with than losing money or reputation in this particular scheme, and was later murdered for some of his other unscrupulous dealings. Gould went on to a long life and more riches. *See also* CORRUPTION.

BLACKS. *See* AFRICAN AMERICANS.

BLAINE, JAMES G. (1830–1893). Born in rural southwestern Pennsylvania, James Gillespie Blaine moved to Maine in 1854, got involved in state politics, worked his way through the ranks of the **Republican** party, and ultimately became speaker of the House of Representatives in Congress from 1869–1875. From 1876–1881, he served in the United States Senate and made two unsuccessful attempts to secure the Republican nomination for president. Appointed secretary of state by President **James Garfield**, he resigned soon after Garfield's death rather than remain in **Chester Arthur**'s cabinet. Called the "Plumed Knight of Maine," Blaine was implicated in the infamous **Credit Mobilier Scandal** of 1872 and other lesser scandals, but managed to finagle his way out of legal punishment through sophistry and clever defenses, including selective public reading of the "Mulligan Letters." In 1884 he finally got his wish and became the GOP's presidential nominee, but because of his past scandals, a large number of Republicans did not support his candidacy. These defectors, called the **Mugwumps**, voted with the **Democrats** instead. An even greater factor contributing to Blaine's defeat, however, was the Reverend Samuel Burchard's ill-timed and poorly worded "rum, Romanism, and rebellion" description of the Democratic party just before the election. This comment drove Catholic Irish-Americans away from Blaine and cost him the election.

After a 4-year hiatus, Blaine emerged once again in 1888 to support the candidacy of **Benjamin Harrison**, who rewarded him with the office of secretary of state, which he held for 3 years. In that post he became an early proponent of American imperialism, and his policies helped push the United States toward the **annexation of Hawaii**, among other imperialist objectives. He died in Washington, D.C., never having realized his life's ambition—to be elected president. Yet he stamped his identity on the politics of the Gilded Age to as great an extent as any individual of the day. *See also* CORRUPTION.

BLAIR EDUCATION BILL. In 1881, Henry Blair, a New Hampshire **Republican**, introduced this bill in the U.S. Senate for a federally funded and supervised public **education** system in America. Designed primarily to help **African Americans** catch up with whites in economic, political, and social skills as quickly as possible, the bill would have helped poor whites in undereducated regions of the country, particularly Appalachia, as well. In the Republican-controlled Senate, the bill passed easily after much debate in 1884 by a vote of 33 to 11, but the **Democrat**-controlled House of Representatives would not allow it to be voted upon. Two years later it passed by a wider margin in the Senate only to meet the same fate in the House. In 1888, it passed yet again in the Senate, but by a much narrower margin, before being tabled in the House for the third time. In 1890, the situation seemed perfect for passing the bill, as the GOP controlled both houses of Congress and the presidency for the first time since it had been introduced, and the U.S. government enjoyed a large treasury surplus that could have been spent on such a national program. Strangely, however, the Republican majority in the Senate was not able even to bring it up for a vote this time, mainly because the **Billion Dollar Congress** had such an unusually large number of pressing issues waiting in the dockets.

Although support for the bill among the general public came overwhelmingly from blacks and northern white progressives, as well as from Republicans in Congress, there was no strict party line on the measure, and many otherwise conservative southern Democrats supported it. The primary objection to it was based on the fact that founding fathers such as James Madison and Alexander Hamilton, among others, had written explicitly a century earlier that the Constitution did not give Congress the power to create or control a public school system. Supporters maintained that times had changed, and the Constitution was sufficiently flexible to allow it now. In the end, the Blair Bill simply faded into obscurity. Not until the Progressives became entrenched in the federal government some 30 years later did such a public education program get started.

BLAND-ALLISON ACT. *See* FREE SILVER.

BLY, NELLIE (1867–1922). Born Elizabeth Jane Cochran in northwestern Pennsylvania, her pen name comes from a song by Stephen Foster. She made her reputation as a muckraker more than a decade before muckraking became common in journalism. As an investigative reporter, she first wrote of the pitiful conditions of poor **women** and children in factories in the Pittsburgh area by going undercover to work alongside them. In 1887, while working for the *New York World*, she feigned mental illness in order to be admitted to Blackwell's Island insane asylum in New York City, whereupon she exposed the horrid treatment of patients. Her report, published as the book *Ten Days in a Mad-House*, brought her instant international fame. Seizing the moment, she next turned to one of the most ambitious and celebrated undertakings of the Gilded Age: proving it was possible to travel "around the world in 80 days," as French novelist Jules Verne had written. Departing on 14 November 1889, she arrived back in New York City on 25 January 1890, beating the mark by more than a week, successfully traversing the globe in less than 73 days. Soon after, she married a millionaire industrialist, inherited his fortune and business responsibilities, retired from journalism, and spent most of the remainder of her life in New York and Europe working for various reform movements. *See also* LITERATURE; PRESS, THE.

BORDEN MURDERS CASE. On 4 August 1892, two murders in Fall River, Massachusetts, brought the most sensational criminal investigation and trial of the Gilded Age. Less than 4 years after the infamous Jack the Ripper murders in England, the American news media was primed for a similar case on this side of the Atlantic. The murders of Andrew J. Borden, a prominent and wealthy citizen of Fall River, and his wife Abby, allegedly by hatchet-wielding youngest daughter Lizzie, were a news editor's dream, sparking a frenzy of coverage and speculation that lasted for nearly a year and ended only after a verdict was reached in this trial of the century. This became the first famous "axe-murder" case in American history.

On the morning of 4 August, only two people were home at 92 Second Street in Fall River when the Bordens were murdered—the 32-year-old unmarried Lizzie and the family maid, Bridget Sullivan. They found the slain victims and notified police. Andrew had been chopped in the head 11 times, Abby 18. As the investigation commenced, all the evidence was circumstantial. Because of primitive forensic methodology and technology, the police and prosecutors botched the investigation. No murder weapon could be positively identified, although a broken hatchet in the family barn was thought to be it. No suspect could be found other than Lizzie. Prosecutors targeted her mainly for three reasons: she had recently tried to buy cyanide at a local pharmacy, and the family had indeed caught food poisoning the day before the axe murders; she had burned a dress that police suspected but could not prove had blood on it; and she gave inconsistent testimony about what happened that fateful day.

The trial lasted 15 days, from 5–20 June 1893. In the end, the jury took less than 2 hours to return the verdict: not guilty. There was clearly reasonable doubt that Lizzie did it. One factor that played into the jury's decision was that a similar axe murder had been perpetrated in town not long before this case. Perhaps the axe murderer was the same person and still at large. Later events in Lizzie's life (she was caught shoplifting and was alleged to have had a lesbian affair with a married woman) impugned her reputation, although they did not prove her to be a killer. She remained in Fall River for the rest of her life, a curiosity to some residents, a pariah to others.

BROOKLYN BRIDGE. Among the most important and impressive engineering feats of the Gilded Age, this bridge has spanned the East River from Manhattan to Brooklyn, New York, since 1883. Its genesis came from a New Jersey wire manufacturer and accomplished bridge builder named John Roebling. He began drawing up plans in 1855, but the New York City Council did not approve them until 1869. His plans called for using his own company's wire cable to make the world's first steel suspension bridge. To allow for future growth in **railroad** traffic, he designed it to be about six times stronger than necessary. He persuaded a group of prominent businessmen and politicians to begin securing the funding in advance. Projected to cost about $7 million, it ended up costing more than twice that much. When John Roebling died in a freak accident before construction began, his son Washington Roebling took over and carried out his father's design.

In 1870, Roebling's crew sank caissons on the river bottom and began building the foundations for the main towers that would support the bridge. Tragedy struck again, however, as Roebling developed the bends during one of his submersed supervisory inspections. Unable to continue his hands-on supervision, he delegated authority to his wife Emily, who became his representative. Within 3 years, the twin 276-foot gothic limestone towers were complete. By 1876, the main cable was stretched and anchored to each side. Two years later, the vertical cables holding up the bridge were in place, and in early 1883 the final touches were added. The end result was a bridge that stood 135 feet above the river at midspan, extended more than 6,000 feet across from tip to tip, contained some 14,000 miles of steel wire, and sported the third tallest towers in the world. On 23 May 1883, President **Chester Arthur** and soon-to-be President **Grover Cleveland** ceremonially opened the bridge. The bridge had claimed the lives of 20 construction workers over 12 years. Within a week, however, it claimed a dozen more—all pedestrians who were trampled under foot by a panicking mob that thought the bridge was collapsing.

BRYAN, WILLIAM JENNINGS (1860–1925). Born in southern Illinois, Bryan attended Illinois College before going to law school in Chicago. He practiced law in his home state before moving to

Nebraska in 1887. Entering politics there as a **Democrat**, he won a seat in the U.S. House of Representatives in 1890 and kept it for two terms. He lost a bid for the U.S. Senate in 1894 but thereafter made such an impressive speech at the Democratic National Convention in 1896 that the 36-year-old Bryan received the nomination for president. His "cross of gold" speech, which argued for **free silver**, and which he subsequently delivered repetitiously on his whistle-stop campaign, ranks among the classic political orations in American history. At the same time as Bryan began bearing the standard for the Democrats, the **Populists** likewise chose him as their presidential nominee, putting him in the unlikely and awkward position of serving two parties at once. Even with the combined votes of both parties, he still fell short of defeating **William McKinley** in the election. He got a rematch 4 years later, but his candidacy garnered even fewer votes the second time. In between the two elections, Bryan became a leader of the **American Anti-Imperialist League**. Once again, he found himself in the minority, though, as the McKinley administration pushed ahead with imperialist ambitions, with the consent of most of the people. After the Gilded Age gave way to the 20th century, Bryan continued to enjoy a long career in the public eye. Sadly, he seemed destined always to be on the less popular side of most issues, as was the case when he resigned the office of U.S. Secretary of State in the Woodrow Wilson administration in protest of Wilson's decision to enter World War I in 1917 and when he represented the State of Tennessee in the Scopes Trial of 1925.

BUFFALO BILL (1846–1917). Born William Frederick Cody in east central Iowa near the modern-day Quad cities on the Mississippi River, he moved with his Free Soil family to Kansas in 1854, where his father became a casualty in the infamous "Bleeding Kansas" dispute over slavery. Brought up on the frontier of the "wild West," young William claimed to have experienced many historic adventures, including prospecting for gold, riding for the Pony Express, working for the U.S. army as a scout, and fighting with the Union army in the Civil War, among others—all before his 18th birthday. While some of his claims cannot be proven, he certainly lived the hard life of a frontiersman. After the war, he went to work for the Kansas Pacific **Railroad** as a bison hunter. Killing the large, free roaming animals supplied meat for the railroad workers and helped reduce the nuisance of stampedes. So adept was Cody as a hunter, equestrian, and marksman, that he won a contest in 1868 for killing the largest number of buffalo in a single day, earning him the nickname "Buffalo Bill." Fame found him in 1869, when dime novelist **Ned Buntline** introduced Buffalo Bill as a heroic character in one of his books. Only 23 years old at the time, Buffalo Bill had his greatest exploits yet to come, and Buntline and other writers cultivated the legend as Cody's real life played out.

From 1868–1872, Buffalo Bill worked as a scout for the U.S. army in the Plains **Indian** wars. In 1872, he won a Congressional Medal of Honor for gallant service in that arena, purportedly putting his life on the line to save his fellows from an Indian attack. In the same year, he entered show business as a character in a play that mimicked his real life. He toured off and on for the next 10 years, while occasionally reverting to the real thing. In 1876, after the U.S. army's defeat at the **Battle of Little Big Horn**, Buffalo Bill supposedly got revenge on behalf of George Custer and his men by scalping Yellow Hand, a Cheyenne Indian allegedly complicit in the massacre. Whether true or not, Buffalo Bill began reenacting "Custer's Last Stand" and his own act of revenge thereafter, to the delight of his white audiences.

Cody's most lasting legacy, of course, is his "Buffalo Bill's Wild West" show, which he produced and starred in from 1883 until his retirement some 30 years later. This show greatly expanded his original production, adding a cast of stars that included **Annie Oakley**, **Calamity Jane**, and **Sitting Bull**. It was an outdoor, open-air rather than an indoor stage performance, fielding a cast too large for a theater. The show not only toured the eastern United States but also played in Europe for a full decade as well, impressing the likes of the Pope and the Queen of England, among many others. The high point in the show's 30-year run came in Chicago, when the organizers of the **Columbian Exposition of 1893** rejected Buffalo Bill's Wild West extravaganza as a featured attraction. Buffalo Bill simply set up his show next door to the Expo and competed with it for tourist dollars. One estimate holds that the great frontiersman drew 6 million people away from the Expo and raked in a fortune.

By the turn of the 20th century, Buffalo Bill was possibly the most famous and easily recognizable person in the world with his trademark western attire and goatee. He did more to create the stereotype of "**cowboys** and Indians" and the wild West of the late 1800s that has been immortalized ever since in movies, television shows, and novels, than any other individual.

BUFFALO SOLDIERS. Created by Congress in 1866 and stationed at Fort Leavenworth, Kansas, the all-black U.S. 10th Cavalry Regiment got the nickname "Buffalo Soldiers" from the American **Indians** they frequently engaged in battle on the western frontier. The name was soon applied to all black troops in the West, including the 9th Cavalry and four infantry units. Historians are not certain about the origin of the name, but evidence suggests that the Indians were describing these **African American** troops as having the color and hair texture of buffalo. They are primarily remembered for their service in the Indian Wars from 1867–1890, in which they fought the Comanche, the Apache, and the Cheyenne, among others in some 177 skirmishes and battles. Congress issued 18 Medals of Honor to Buffalo Soldiers for their exploits in the Indian Wars. Some of these troops also served as scouts, translators, surveyors, cartographers, road builders, defenders of homesteaders, protectors of the **railroads**, escorts of the U.S. mail, and national park rangers. They fought valiantly in the **Spanish–American War** of 1898 as well, especially at the Battle of San Juan Hill along with **Theodore Roosevelt** and the Rough Riders. Despite their valor, they suffered the same kind of discrimination that routinely plagued black civilians during the early Jim Crow period. Although they were not the only black soldiers in the U.S. army, they were the only ones to take on a legendary status during the Gilded Age.

BUNTLINE, NED (1823–1886). Born Edward Zen Carroll Judson in upstate New York, his family moved to Pennsylvania when he was 10 years old. He took his pen name "Buntline" (a type of rope on a sail boat) after running away to sea from the docks in Philadelphia as a teenager. From a stowaway cabin boy to a naval midshipman, he traveled widely, and his life thereafter became one of constant adventure and turmoil, which, combined with a vivid imagination and clear writing style, provided much fodder for his future prose. From New York City to Boston, from Florida to California, and most points in between, he found stories to write about, mostly fictionalized portrayals of real events and people. During the Civil War, he noticed that reading dime novels was a favorite pastime of the soldiers, and he decided to cash in on it by giving them more current and more masculine reading material.

In 1868, Buntline went to San Francisco to be among the first to ride the new **transcontinental railroad** back east and write about it. On the trip, while passing through Nebraska, he sought to interview **Wild Bill Hickok** but instead became acquainted with William F. Cody, whom he dubbed "**Buffalo Bill**" in a series he quickly began writing and publishing in New York. The public's appetite for reading about the "wild West" was voracious at the time, and Buntline scored big. He then convinced Buffalo Bill to star in a play he wrote and produced called "The Scouts of the Plains," which was first performed in Chicago in 1872. Again successful, Buntline took the show on the road for several months before the two parted company. In 1875, he contracted with the Colt Manufacturing Company of Connecticut to make a pistol called the "Buntline Special," in order to give it to lawmen in the West, such as Wyatt Earp of Dodge City, Kansas, to woo them for interviews. It worked, and he managed to publish hundreds of novels, short stories, and plays about such people, turning some into legends. Indeed, many of the enduring myths of the "wild West" of the late 1800s came from his pen. *See also* LITERATURE.

BUTLER, BENJAMIN F. (1818–1893). Born in New Hampshire, Benjamin Franklin Butler attended **college** in Maine before being admitted to the bar in Massachusetts. He achieved fame as a controversial Union general in the Civil War and, although a **Democrat** before the war, became a Radical **Republican** at the beginning of Reconstruction. Serving in the House of Representatives, he led the prosecution against President Andrew Johnson in the 1868 impeachment proceedings. Thereafter, he became a staunch supporter of President **Ulysses S. Grant** and proponent of legislation to benefit **African Americans**, most notably a law to eradicate the Ku Klux Klan. After Reconstruction ended, he tied his future to various third-party movements and/or the Democratic party. He won the gubernatorial election of 1882 in Massachusetts as a Democrat, but 2 years later lost a presidential bid on the Greenback-Labor/Anti-Monopoly party ticket. He spent the last years of his life practicing law, from which he earned a small fortune. Despite his notable distinctions in the Gilded Age, he is primarily remembered in history by the moniker that southerners gave him in the Civil War—the "beast."

– C –

CABLE, GEORGE WASHINGTON (1844–1925). Born and reared in a slaveholding family in New Orleans, he grew to become the foremost novelist of the deep South during the Gilded Age. Despite his southern heritage and his service in the Confederate Army in the Civil War, he developed a more progressive view of race relations than most of his peers. Wounded in battle, he returned home and became a bookkeeper. He wrote for the *New Orleans Picayune* newspaper from 1870–1879, but left after publishing his first book, *Old Creole Days*, which was a collection of short stories that first appeared separately in *Scribner's Monthly*, and which proved quite profitable. He followed with two more successful novels about the racial complexities of southern society, *The Grandissimes* (1880) and *Madame Delphine* (1881). In 1885, he published two important critiques of southern race relations, "The Silent South" and "The Freedmen's Case in Equity" (1885), for which he was ostracized in New Orleans. He then moved to New England, where he remained for the rest of his life, and where he continued his criticism of southern racism, publishing *The Negro Question* in 1890. His racial views notwithstanding, Cable never ceased to love his homeland, and wrote and spoke fondly of other aspects of southern life. His other lasting contribution to American **literature** is that his work inspired the southern novelist *extraordinaire* William Faulkner.

CALAMITY JANE (1852–1903). Born Martha Jane Cannary, she moved from Missouri to Montana with her family at the age of 13. After both parents died within the next 2 years, she did odd jobs and raised her 5 siblings until she turned 18. Fiercely independent, unusually resourceful, and already well traveled in the West, she found work as an army scout. She soon abandoned all pretenses of femininity and began dressing like a man, as well as cursing and swearing, drinking, chewing tobacco, practicing marksmanship, and trick riding. Moving constantly from one western state or territory to the next, she soon was keeping company with famous characters **Wild Bill Hickok**, **Buffalo Bill** Cody, Colonel George Armstrong Custer, and generals Nelson Miles and George Crook. She had a famous romantic attachment to Hickok, and she was there in Deadwood, South Dakota, when he was killed in 1876. She allegedly acquired her nickname "Calamity" Jane by riding into a hail of gunfire to save the life of an army officer. Although she also saved a stagecoach full of travelers from an **Indian** attack and saved the lives of several people with smallpox by nursing them back to health, her legend largely derived from the fact that she became a character in a "wild West" dime novel series called *Deadwood Dick* by Edward Wheeler. Toward the end of her life, she contributed to her own celebrity by publishing a short autobiography in which she exaggerated her exploits and, in some cases, either lied or showed a very faulty memory. Even so, she really was the wildest woman of the "wild West" in the Gilded Age, and the "heroine of the Great Plains." At her death, she requested to be buried beside Hickok in Deadwood, where she remains.

CANDLER, ASA. *See* COCA-COLA.

CARNEGIE, ANDREW (1835–1919). Born in Scotland, Carnegie immigrated with his family to the United States in 1848, settling in Pittsburgh. Poor but intelligent and ambitious, young Andrew worked his way up from textile mill labor to telegraphy to railroad administration, all by the age of 20. Investing in **railroad** sleeping cars, oil wells, and steel bridges, he began accumulating wealth in the 1860s. By 1870, at the age of 35, he was rich enough to retire to a life of leisure. The allure of the commercial possibilities of the steel industry beckoned him, however, and by 1875 he had founded his first steel-making company, the Edgar Thompson Works, in southwestern Pennsylvania. In the 1880s, he began acquiring stock in **Henry Frick**'s coke mill and soon came to own the controlling interest in it. He also bought out one of his main rivals, the **Homestead** Steel Works and began the slow consolidation of his steel empire, which would ultimately make him the richest man in the world.

After achieving the beginnings of his fortune, Carnegie began writing articles for **periodicals** in England and the United States, and in 1886 he entered the ranks of notable published authors with *Triumphant Democracy*. His most enduring contribution to American history, however, came in 1889 with an article entitled "Wealth" (later renamed "The Gospel of Wealth"), which proffered what might be called the conscientious capitalist viewpoint. He argued in essence that accumulation of wealth by the most able business leaders was natural and therefore good, but giving back to society thereafter through philanthropy was the highest calling of the wealthy. His economic philosophy basically represented a fusion of the prevalent ideology of the day, **Social Darwinism**, and what would soon come to be known as the **Social Gospel**. He practiced what he preached by endowing more than 1,000 public libraries in the United States, as well as funding numerous other projects.

Meanwhile, in 1892, Carnegie showed that his generosity did not extend to laborers in his steel mills. When they went on strike at the Homestead plant, he and Frick put down the strike with a strong and merciless hand. In 1898, he made another controversial decision. His anti-imperialism sentiments at the time of the **Spanish–American War** led him to offer to buy (literally) the independence of the Philippines. A year later he went back to what he knew best—corporate consolidation. He created a virtual monopoly in the steel industry with his Carnegie Steel Corporation, which he sold to **J. P. Morgan** in 1901 for roughly half-a-billion dollars, making him the richest man in the world at the close of the Gilded Age. *See also* AMERICAN ANTI-IMPERIALIST LEAGUE; LITERATURE; TRADE UNIONS; WASHINGTON, BOOKER T.

CASTLE GARDEN. This joint creation of New York City and the state of New York was the nation's first official **immigrant** processing center. Originally called Fort Clinton and built in anticipation of the War of 1812, it was converted to an immigration facility in 1855. Since New York already received approximately two-thirds of all immigrants arriving on American shores at the time, the city and state considered a special new welcome and inspection station necessary. It operated for 35 years, closing on 18 April 1890. During that time, it processed some 8 million people, including such famous ones as **Joseph Pulitzer**,

Nikola Tesla, Emma Goldman, and Harry Houdini. On 10 December 1896, the renovated facility reopened as the New York City Aquarium. Today it is called Castle Clinton and serves as the main departure point for tourists visiting its more famous successor, **Ellis Island**.

CENTENNIAL, THE U.S. On 4 July 1876, the United States celebrated its 100th birthday. Although people all across the country observed the day (with the exception of diehard ex-Confederates in the South), the festivities centered around the city of Philadelphia, which had served as the nation's capital in 1776. Here, a century later, it hosted an international exposition (world's fair)—the first of its kind in American history. Both the city, and the whole state of Pennsylvania, began preparing for the event in 1870. Two years later Congress joined in the preparations by creating an official Centennial Commission to coordinate the project. In 1873, Philadelphia set aside 450 acres for the expo, and organizers began soliciting exhibits from both Americans and Europeans. The fair's theme was industry and technology, and all participants were expected to demonstrate their most impressive creations accordingly. The centerpiece was the giant Corliss Engine, which President **Ulysses S. Grant** turned on to get the fair started on 10 May. That day alone brought nearly 200,000 spectators to the fair. Although attendance dropped precipitously thereafter, on 28 September, nearly 250,000 people showed up. Undoubtedly the most important invention displayed at the fair was **Alexander Graham Bell**'s telephone. The most enduring legacy of the Centennial was that its success spawned imitators, leading to a host of other similar expositions around the nation during the Gilded Age. *See also* COLUMBIAN EXPOSITION OF 1893.

CHAUTAUQUAS. Begun in 1874 in western New York at a former Methodist camp meeting spot called Lake Chautauqua, these socio-religious and **educational** retreats became the most popular vacation getaways in America during the Gilded Age. Methodist minister John H. Vincent and business partner Lewis Miller opened the original retreat as a Sunday school teacher-training seminar. Although only a few people were expected to show up, some 500 came within the first 2 weeks. The phenomenal growth of the retreat thereafter mirrored that of the biggest corporations of the day. Within a decade, the original vision of stimulating, inspiring, and uplifting Christian lay leaders through Bible study had been expanded to offer a wide variety of educational opportunities and entertainment venues that catered to large families as well as individual adults. Likewise by that time, imitators had sprung up all over the country, servicing perhaps 100,000 vacationers. One of the most famous was the Lake **Mohonk** Mountain House built by Quakers. Whatever these imitators' official names may have been, they were popularly and generically termed "Chautauquas." They spawned various social clubs and journals and gave rise to celebrities making "circuit" tours. Ultimately, Chautauquas became a combination of traveling circus and mobile university. The success of the movement can be attributed to the lack of other educational opportunities and entertainment venues available to the rural middle class, as well as the family friendly atmosphere and relatively inexpensive price tag of the Chautauquas. The movement lasted well beyond the Gilded Age, finally dissipating in the 1920s. *See also* RELIGION.

CHICAGO FIRE OF 1871, THE GREAT. Chicago, Illinois, at the beginning of the 1870s had a population of about 300,000. On the southwestern bank of Lake Michigan, the city stretched some 10 miles in length and measured approximately 3 miles wide. In the heart of the city sat the business district, from which residential areas fanned out on all sides. Most of the city's buildings and accouterments were made of wood. On the night of 8 October, the Great Chicago Fire of 1871 broke out. The cause of the initial blaze remains unknown to this day, but guesses have ranged from a cow kicking over a lantern in a barn full of hay to meteor showers raining down on the city that night. Whatever the cause, the fire quickly turned into a conflagration as high winds spread it. Compounding the problem, the region suffered from a drought that year, making the wooden city literally a tinderbox. The fire burned for almost 3 days, covered nearly 4 square miles, killed perhaps as many as 300 people, destroyed more than 17,000 buildings, and cost more than $200 million in damages. It left a fifth of the city in smoldering rubble, but that fifth happened to be some of the most valuable real estate in town, making the devastation seem out of proportion to the size of the area affected. Nearly a third of the denizens of Chicago were left homeless as a result. Afterward, the fire proved to be something of a blessing in disguise, as builders reconstructed the city out of more durable materials. Chicago thus played host to some of the first modern steel-frame skyscrapers in the world, and the population tripled over the next two decades.

CHINESE EXCLUSION ACT. Chinese **immigrants** had first begun arriving in the United States soon after the California gold rush of 1849. The Central Pacific Railroad corporation of **Leland Stanford** recruited these "coolies," as they were known, as cheap labor for building West Coast **railroads**. Indeed, their efficient, cost-effective labor made completion of the first **transcontinental railroad** possible by 1869. By the late 1870s, some 250,000 Chinese had settled in the United States, mostly in the San Francisco area. Although not enough to constitute a national threat to Anglo-American superiority, this quarter million certainly posed a threat to the white working class in California, since the Chinese would work cheaper and perform even the most dangerous construction jobs. Complicating matters, the Chinese tended to cluster together and did not assimilate easily into the dominant culture, and many had come to America as slave laborers or indentured servants. Some white Californians thus despised them as non-white, non-Christian, non-English speaking foreigners, and began calling for restriction of their immigration and limitations on their civil rights once here. Dennis Kearney, an Irish immigrant who helped establish the Workingman's Party in California, led these nativists and socialists in opposing Chinese immigration. China, a nation filled with peasants, held many push factors that threatened to send many thousands—perhaps even millions—of emigrants to America. The fear, therefore, that struck lawmakers on Capitol Hill in the early 1880s was about the future, rather than present conditions in the West. This sinophobia (fear of Chinese) led them to pass the Chinese Exclusion Act in 1882. It barred all Chinese immigration for 10 years. In 1892, Congress revisited the issue and extended the exclusion indefinitely.

CHISHOLM TRAIL. *See* COWBOYS.

CHURCH OF CHRIST, SCIENTIST. Founded in Boston in 1879, this church is known primarily for teaching a form of mind over matter for the healing of sicknesses in the human body. Its founder, Mary Baker

Eddy, was born Mary Baker in New Hampshire. Growing up a traditional New England Congregationalist, she was frequently ill. In 1866, while on what she believed was her deathbed, she suddenly recovered after reading and believing a Bible passage regarding healing. Thereafter, she began formulating a theology around healing, which culminated in the publication of *Science and Health with Key to the Scriptures* in 1875. In this manifesto, she claimed to have found the key to unlocking the hidden truths of the Bible, which would restore humankind to its right relationship with the Creator. Essentially, the key was her revelatory knowledge that the material world is an illusion, sickness is not real, and once people embrace this knowledge, they are set free from sickness and all other Satanic lies and curses. In 1877, she married a man named Eddy, and 2 years later founded her church, with 15 charter members. In 1881, she opened the Massachusetts Metaphysical College, which both practiced and taught the science of healing. Two years later, she began publishing the *Christian Science Journal*. In 1892, she erected the architecturally impressive edifice in Boston called the "Mother Church" of Christian Science. Three years later, the newly reorganized church codified its doctrines and government in its *Manual of the Mother Church*. Although the church grew beyond the confines of Boston in these Gilded Age years, it was widely regarded as a heretical cult by other mainstream denominations. Not until the 20th century did it begin to gain a measure of respect from outsiders through the publication of the *Christian Science Monitor*. *See also* RELIGION; WOMEN.

CIVIL RIGHTS CASES. The **U.S. Supreme Court** ruled on this collection of legal suits in 1883. The cases stemmed from the Civil Rights Act of 1875, which began as a bill written by Charles Sumner, the **Republican** senator from Massachusetts, in 1872. This federal law forbade discrimination based on race in public accommodations, among other things. Its intent was basically to nip in the bud the burgeoning practice of segregation in the South. The conservative court, however, headed by Chief Justice Morrison R. Waite, declared it unconstitutional on the grounds that Congress had no authority to regulate private businesses or individuals' behavior toward minorities. Only the various state governments could constitutionally pass laws pertaining to such matters. Moreover, Justice

Joseph P. Bradley, who wrote the 8 to 1 majority opinion, asserted that the expansion of federal power for the expressed purpose of promoting civil rights for minorities would make southern blacks "the special favorite of the laws" by granting them rights that not even whites possessed.

Bradley's rationale was that private enterprises could deny service or admission even to whites if the owner or manager found something objectionable about their presence, something that hurt business. **John Marshall Harlan**, as usual in cases involving race, provided the one dissenting vote. He looked at the spirit rather than the letter of the law, and considered the special protection of blacks necessary since they had been singled out for slavery before. This ruling, coupled with the earlier *Slaughterhouse Cases* ruling in 1873 and *U.S. v. Cruikshank* in 1876, emasculated the original intent of the 14th Amendment to the point of making it essentially meaningless for the next 80 years. Meanwhile, it opened the door wide for segregation to become the new cultural paradigm of the South after 1883, and was soon reinforced by the court in *Plessy v. Ferguson* in 1896 and *Cumming v. Richmond County Board of Education* in 1899. It thus served as a major blow to **African Americans** for the rest of the Gilded Age.

CLEVELAND, GROVER (1837–1907). Born in New Jersey, Stephen Grover Cleveland spent most of his life in western New York, in the Buffalo area. In the 1870s, when Buffalo had a reputation as the most crime-and-vice-ridden city in America, Cleveland made his first claim to fame as a "hanging sheriff." In 1881, he won the office of mayor, and the following year was elected governor of New York. The reputation he built, which propelled him to the White House in 1884 was that of an honest, conservative, no-nonsense leader. The campaign of 1884 between Cleveland and **James G. Blaine** marked a low point in American politics for mudslinging during the Gilded Age. The **Republicans** exposed a scandal in which they claimed Cleveland, a **Democrat** and a bachelor, had fathered an illegitimate child. Newspapers poked fun at the situation with cartoons showing a baby crying, "Ma, Ma, where's my Pa?" Cleveland proved his mettle by admitting to paying child support to a woman with whom he had been intimate. Upon winning one of the closest presidential elections in American history, Democrats delighted in adding a twist to the jibe, "Ma, Ma, where's my Pa? Gone to the White House, Ha, Ha, Ha!" Cleveland thus became the first Democrat since before the Civil War to win the presidency.

Cleveland's first term in office was largely successful, albeit uneventful by historical standards. One of the most important issues of the day was securing pensions for Union Civil War veterans. Cleveland, the only president of the Gilded Age who had not served in the Union Army, expressed little sympathy for veterans and none at all for those who filed fraudulent claims for pensions. He vetoed a major pension bill accordingly. He took an equally hard-line approach to helping suffering farmers in Texas, refusing to support a plan for their economic aid. The fact that the United States was running the largest surplus in its history at the time made Cleveland seem unnaturally cruel in the opinion of the **Grand Army of the Republic** and the National **Farmers' Alliance**, both of which worked for his defeat in 1888. In his defense, Cleveland did not want to run a surplus; he favored lowering the **tariff** to reduce both the surplus and the tax burden on the people.

Laws passed in Cleveland's first term include the **Dawes Severalty Act** and the **Interstate Commerce** Act, both of which he signed. He also presided over the dedication of the **Statue of Liberty** in 1886. In that same year he became the second president to get married while in office, and the first to do so in the White House.

Despite winning the popular vote, Cleveland lost the election of 1888 to **Benjamin Harrison**. He returned to defeat Harrison soundly, however, 4 years later, making him the only president in American history to serve nonconsecutive terms. Unlike the first, his second term was disastrous. He discovered he had cancer in his jaw in 1893 and underwent a debilitating operation and recovery process. The **Panic of 1893** devastated the economy, the **Pullman Strike** of 1894 made it even worse, and Cleveland's harsh response to the march on Washington by **Coxey's Army** in 1894 once again made him appear to be an unusually callous man. He left office after 1896 and retired to Princeton, New Jersey, where he spent the rest of his life. *See also* ALTGELD, JOHN P.; HENDRICKS, THOMAS A.; STEVENSON, ADLAI.

COCA-COLA. Perhaps the best-known product in the world today, Coca-Cola had its origins in the Gilded Age. In Atlanta, Georgia, wounded Confederate Civil War veteran-turned-pharmacist John S. Pemberton formulated the original recipe for this soft drink under a different name around 1869–1870. He intended it to be a "patent medicine"—popular pain relievers and cure-all remedies created by local druggists and pseudo-pharmacists in the years before the professionalization and standardization of the pharmaceutical industry—partly to help himself and fellow veterans cope with pain and morphine addiction, and partly because he was an entrepreneur looking for a good product to sell. The beverage's main ingredients were coca leaves and kola nuts, mixed with sweetener and carbonated water. Pemberton modified the formula several times before arriving at his final version. On 8 May 1886, Pemberton sold the first glass of it under the name "Coca-Cola" for 5 cents from a soda fountain in an Atlanta drug store. Business partner Frank M. Robinson coined the name, scripted the now-famous logo, and made it a trademark. Pemberton began advertising in the local newspaper almost immediately, and Coca-Cola quickly developed fans, probably more from the fact that prohibitionists were turning Atlanta into a dry city than from the originality of the product. (Several similar products were already on the market at the time, including root beer, ginger ale, and other "cola" drinks).

Asa Candler, an Atlanta businessman immediately bought some legal rights to the product, but not exclusive rights. After a 2-year legal battle with Pemberton's son, Candler emerged as the owner of the company. Through shrewd marketing, Candler turned the product into a regional, then national, and international success. Although Coca-Cola did contain small amounts of cocaine, which comes from the coca plant used in the product, the version of it that Candler sold never contained a harmful amount, and he removed it entirely within a few years. Coca-Cola was first sold in bottles by the Biedenharn company in Vicksburg, Mississippi, in 1894, but not until the turn of the 20th century did bottled "Coke" displace soda fountain Coke as the main source of sales.

CODY, WILLIAM F. *See* BUFFALO BILL.

COINAGE ACT. *See* FREE SILVER.

COLFAX, SCHUYLER, JR. (1823–1885). Born in New York City, Schuyler (pronounced "Skyler") Colfax moved as a teen with his family to St. Joseph county in northern Indiana, just south of the Michigan line near South Bend. He became a newspaperman, a Whig, and a friend of *New York Tribune* editor **Horace Greeley**. In the mid-1850s, he became an organizer of the **Republican Party** in the Hoosier State. As such, he won a seat in the U.S. House of Representatives in 1854, where he routinely enjoyed favorable **press**, thanks to his congeniality toward fellow newspapermen. In 1862, he was elected speaker of the House, a post he held until being elected vice president of the United States for the **Ulysses S. Grant** administration in 1868. As vice president, he fell out of favor with his former friends in the press, supposedly because he developed an aloof, aristocratic demeanor. Not thriving in his new position, he talked of stepping down after one term. Indeed, he had already notified party officials that he did not want a second term as vice president when, on the eve of the election of 1872, he was implicated in the infamous **Credit Mobilier Scandal**, which sealed his fate. In the subsequent congressional investigation, he denied any impropriety, but evidence suggested otherwise, and his credibility as a witness and a public servant was irreparably damaged. Congress could have brought impeachment charges against him, and rightly so, but since his term was about to expire anyway, he escaped that ignominious distinction. He went on to have a lucrative career on the lecture circuit, however, primarily by speaking about the life of Abraham Lincoln and his relationship with the slain president. Oddly, by the time of his death in 1885, he had become such a forgotten figure that, when he fell dead of a heart attack at a **railroad** depot in Mankato, Minnesota, his body had to be identified by the personal effects he was carrying.

COLLEGES AND UNIVERSITIES. The Gilded Age saw an explosion in the growth of institutions of higher **education**. More than 340 new colleges opened for business during this time, which represents about one-fourth of all 4-year colleges in America today. Several factors led to this dramatic increase. First, the rising middle class of the rapidly urbanizing and industrializing nation created greater need in the workforce, and simultaneously more demand among consumers, for specialized, professional degrees. Second, the two

Morrill Land Grant Acts of 1862 and 1890 gave state governments financial incentives to establish public colleges. Third, several Gilded Age multimillionaire philanthropists used significant portions of their fortunes to start new colleges or enlarge existing ones. Fourth, the need for world-class universities that could compete with the best that Europe had to offer spurred the development of professional research schools and departments in existing institutions as well as new ones. Fifth, more specialized colleges for **African Americans** and **women** were needed because of the blatant, rampant racism and sexism of the day. In addition to these catalyzing factors, there were the natural increases that went with population growth. State governments and church denominations largely supplied those new institutions.

Ohio State, Oklahoma State, Virginia Tech, Washington State, Texas A & M, Mississippi State, Colorado State, Purdue, Clemson, and the universities of Arizona, Nebraska, Nevada, and Rhode Island were among the more prominent universities to be built during the Gilded Age through the 1862 Morrill Act. Many others were enlarged through the first Morrill Act, as well. The 1890 Morrill Act focused primarily on black colleges including Prairie View, Fort Valley State, Florida A & M, Alcorn State, Jackson State, and North Carolina A & T. Some of these colleges predated the Morrill Act, having origins as Freedmen's Bureau schools in the late 1860s. **Booker T. Washington**'s Tuskegee Institute in Alabama was unique among all Gilded Age colleges in that it was neither a Freedmen's Bureau school nor a Morrill Act school, but was built for blacks mainly with white northern philanthropists' money. Some of the prominent women's colleges included Wellesley, Smith, and Mississippi University for Women.

Some of the more prominent philanthropic universities included **Vanderbilt**, **Stanford**, the University of Chicago (built with **John D. Rockefeller**'s money), Cornell (which also received land grant funding), and Johns Hopkins in Baltimore, Maryland. The latter is especially important because, before it opened in 1876, there was no modern Ph.D.-granting university in the United States. The oldest, most respected private universities in the United States, Harvard and Yale, had to reinvigorate their faculties, reform their curricula, and revitalize their facilities to keep up with the prestigious new philanthropic research universities. Under the able guidance of Charles W. Eliot, Harvard managed to keep pace with Johns Hopkins. The other

Ivy League schools tried to follow suit, but not until the 20th century would some of them achieve parity.

COLUMBIAN EXPOSITION OF 1893. This Chicago, Illinois, extravaganza stood as one of the high points of the Gilded Age and perhaps the grandest event of its kind ever. The name derives from the United States government's desire to commemorate the 400th anniversary in October 1892 of Christopher Columbus's landing in the Americas. Unfortunately, the expo actually did not open until May 1893, due to construction delays. And once it opened, ironically, it focused very little attention on its namesake. Most of the expo was instead concerned with technology of the present and future, not with Columbus or the past. The significance of the expo occurring in 1893 rather than 1892 was that it offered a great, if only temporary, relief from the economic depression that hit the nation at that time, the **Panic of 1893**. It also had another unintended benefit; it showed off American industrial and technological strength to visitors from all over the world at a time when the United States was just beginning to flex its muscles in world affairs.

The plans for staging an event to honor Columbus began in Congress in 1889. Several cities competed for the right to host it, but Congress awarded the honor to Chicago in 1890. The city had to raise $10 million up front to finance the massive project, and then sell about 25 million admission tickets at 50 cents apiece to break even. The list of directors and planners for the event reads like a who's who of the Gilded Age. It included **railroad** car tycoon George **Pullman**, financial advisor Charles Schwab, architects Daniel Burnham and **Richard M. Hunt**, landscape designer **Frederick Law Olmsted**, and Harvard educator Charles Eliot Norton, among others. Supervising the project was former U.S. Senator George Davis. After much disagreement, the planners decided to build the fair upon 633 acres of marshy land on the shore of Lake Michigan called Jackson Park. Olmsted designed a series of canals, lakes, and reflecting pools to make a garden out of a swamp. The architects meanwhile designed 14 large buildings, each with its own unique character but all with a common classical European motif, and all covered in white stucco on the exterior. By all accounts, the large white, classical buildings situated in the beautifully landscaped garden gave the great "White City," as observers immediately dubbed it, the aura of heaven on earth.

President **Grover Cleveland** opened the festivities on 1 May by flipping a golden lever that turned on the 127 electric dynamos and 43 steam engines that powered the fair. Over the next 6 months, admissions topped 27 million, more than enough to make a profit. Once inside, the paying customers were treated to both amusements on a "Midway" and educational exhibits inside the buildings—a total of 65,000 separate attractions. Few were disappointed; most were elated beyond their wildest dreams. One would have needed to travel the world extensively to have seen something grander than this expo, and few Americans of that age had been anywhere exotic. The White City made such an impression upon author Frank L. Baum that he based his Emerald City in *The Wizard of Oz* (1900) on it. Future theme park visionaries would later copy the Midway idea for **Coney Island** and the overall buildings and grounds design for Disneyland and Disneyworld. Other lasting legacies of the expo include new food products that have since become staples of the collective American diet, such as soda pops (most Americans had never tasted them before), Juicy Fruit chewing gum, Pabst Blue Ribbon beer, Quaker Oats, Aunt Jemima pancake syrup, and Shredded Wheat cereal. Likewise, the "Pledge of Allegiance" made its debut at the Columbian expo, and Scott Joplin debuted his new ragtime music. *See also* HEINZ, H. J.; HERSHEY, MILTON S.

COMPROMISE OF 1877. The presidential election of 1876 between **Republican Rutherford B. Hayes** and **Democrat Samuel J. Tilden** was the most controversial and hotly contested election in American history. Although Tilden carried a 250,000 popular vote majority and held a 184 to 165 lead in Electoral College votes, 20 electoral votes were still in dispute. Because of long-festering problems of Reconstruction in the South, Democrats and Republicans both claimed victory in three states, each party casting separate electoral votes and calling the other's invalid. Tilden needed only one of these electoral votes to carry the election; Hayes needed all 20. In addition to the seven in South Carolina, four in Florida, and eight in Louisiana, one electoral vote in Oregon was also up for grabs. The latter was settled quickly in favor of Hayes, but the former 19 remained in dispute from November 1876 to late February 1877. During that time, both parties jockeyed for position in the three southern states and in both the Senate and the House of Representatives, as the Electoral College turned the problem over to Congress.

Tradition had always allowed the House of Representatives to count electoral votes, but in this case, the Democrats controlled the House, so the Republicans who controlled the Senate demanded the right to count the votes. Unable to agree, party leaders formed a special bicameral and bipartisan Electoral Commission comprising five senators, five representatives, and five U.S. Supreme Court justices. Although the commission was intended to be as balanced as possible, it ultimately had to choose one side over the other, and it went with Hayes, to the delight of Republicans and the chagrin of Democrats. House Democrats reacted with a month-long filibuster to prevent implementation of the decision. During that month, behind the scenes Democrats and Republicans bargained and reached a compromise at what came to be known as the Wormley House conference. The agreement stipulated that Democrats would acquiesce to a Hayes presidency in exchange for Hayes appointing a southern Democrat to his cabinet, building a southern **transcontinental railroad**, securing federal internal improvements in the South, and most importantly, removing all federal troops from the South and promising to end Reconstruction. Hayes actually carried out the first and the last of these points, but not the two in the middle. Most important to the big picture of American history was the stipulation to end Reconstruction. It had profound implications for **African Americans** over the coming decades, essentially setting up the Jim Crow era.

COMSTOCK, ANTHONY (1844–1915). Born in rural Connecticut to a strict Christian family, he moved to New York City after the Civil War, where he had his moral sensibilities challenged at every turn by big city sleaziness. He saw cursing, gambling, prostitution, and sexually explicit **literature** as immoral vices, and he believed it his calling in life to suppress such things. Working through the local Young Men's Christian Association, he helped form the New York Society for the Suppression of Vice in 1872. A year later, he succeeded in getting Congress to pass a law prohibiting the U.S. Postal Service from distributing what he deemed obscene and indecent material, and won appointment as a special Postal Inspector. In so doing, he became, for better or worse, the moral conscience of

America, a man with power to determine what constituted acceptable and unacceptable literature for public consumption. The prevailing outward religiosity of the Gilded Age, which paralleled the Victorianism of the British Empire, largely resulted from this moral censorship that critics dubbed "Comstockery." Both Comstock and Comstockery lasted well beyond the Gilded Age, affecting the first generation of the 20th century as well. Not until after World War I did Comstock's influence on American society and politics begin to wane. *See also* RELIGION.

CONEY ISLAND. America's first large, permanent amusement park, Coney Island is located on the southern edge of Long Island, New York, in the borough of Brooklyn. It is not actually an island, but a peninsula. Although it began as a local playground many years before, it expanded into a national, and even international, collection of theme parks during the late Gilded Age. The rise of the middle class, which had both money to spend and leisure time to spend it, made Coney Island possible. For much of the time prior to 1894 it was under the control of **Tammany Hall** and **corrupt** political bosses who profited by taking bribes from gambling and prostitution houses in exchange for not enforcing local vice laws. In 1895 the first enclosed theme park, Sea Lion Park, opened there, which featured the world's first roller coaster with a loop. Two years later the unique Steeplechase Park opened as a competitor, sporting its impressive artificial horse-racing ride. By the turn of the century, Coney Island was set to become the world's greatest amusement park, which it remained until the post–World War II years. *See also* SPORTS AND RECREATION.

CONKLING, ROSCOE (1829–1888). Born in Albany, Conkling practiced law in western New York, ultimately making Utica his home in the 1850s. There, when the **Republican Party** formed, he became one of the original members. In the 1860s he won a seat in the U.S. House of Representatives and strongly supported President Lincoln. During Reconstruction, he stood among the "Radical" Republicans. Elected to the U.S. Senate in 1867, he soon developed a reputation as the most powerful political boss in New York and one of the leading men in his party nationally. He supported President **Ulysses S. Grant**

through his administration's many scandals and, as such, became the leader of the **Stalwart** faction in and after 1872. He led the drive to nominate Grant for a third term as well, but failed. His disagreement with the reform-minded Half-Breeds within the party, and his intense dislike for fellow Republican **James G. Blaine**, created one of the most serious and interesting dramas in American politics in the Gilded Age—one that eventually led to his downfall. Supporting the moderate **James A. Garfield** for president only marginally and begrudgingly in 1880, and only after his friend **Chester A. Arthur** was put on the ticket as vice president, he felt betrayed thereafter when Garfield made important federal appointments in New York without consulting him. Out of spite, he tried to block those appointments in the Senate, but he failed. In protest, he resigned his seat, thinking wrongly that the New York state legislature would stand with him against Garfield and Blaine and send him right back to Washington.

With the severe disappointment of that rejection, Conkling retired from politics in 1881 and set up an extremely lucrative law practice in New York City, where he remained for the rest of his life. When an assassin shot Garfield in 1881 making Arthur president, suspicion immediately arose that Conkling had ordered the killing. Indeed, the assassin was a Stalwart, but there was no evidence that Conkling had any involvement in the murder. In the end, his contributions to the American polity have been notable, although mixed. For one, he helped write the convoluted 14th Amendment, and as one of the authors, he later argued credibly and successfully in court for the inclusion of corporations as "persons" as defined therein, which brought him much money as a corporate attorney. For another, he helped create the bipartisan committee that determined the outcome of the disputed presidential election of 1876 with the **Compromise of 1877**. *See also* MORTON, LEVI P.; WHEELER, WILLIAM A.

CONVICT LEASE SYSTEM. In 1868, southern state governments began leasing prisoners to private companies for a fee. The first contract was between the state of Georgia and a local **railroad**-building firm for **African American** prisoners. The idea was fourfold: to punish criminals with hard labor, to let the prisoners pay for their own incarceration through their labor, to provide railroad companies and other businesses with labor at a cheaper rate than they could otherwise get, and to instill fear in the black population and discourage criminal behavior. Although some white prisoners were also farmed out through the convict lease system, blacks were the main victims. Because the 13th Amendment allowed for involuntary servitude on the basis of a prisoner having been duly convicted of a crime, and because a few whites were also forced into hard labor, the system was not overtly unconstitutional. Over time, however, it quickly became apparent that this was a convenient, legal way to keep blacks "in their place" by forcing them back into an arrangement approximating slavery, and to make a profit for the state in the process. In some states, such as Georgia, the system not only paid the cost of the incarceration for those inmates forced into hard labor, but also yielded hundreds of thousands of dollars of net profit. Consequently, it encouraged the arrest, conviction, and harsh sentencing of more and more black males, resulting in an exponential increase in the black prison population in southern states. It also resulted in the deaths of many of these prisoners, since they were considered expendable. Reformers soon took notice. By the 1890s, a movement was begun to abolish the convict lease system, but it would be left to the Progressives in the early 20th century to accomplish that goal.

CORRUPTION. Typically defined as the abuse of political power for personal gain, corruption comes in several different forms, all of which were present in abundance in the Gilded Age. Corruption was in fact what "gilded" the Gilded Age. **Mark Twain** coined this name for this era of American history mainly because of the corruption that ran rampant through the federal government in the Reconstruction period, and particularly the first 2 years of the **Ulysses S. Grant** administration. He was also commenting on state and local corruption, as well as the American people's seeming acceptance of it as an unavoidable byproduct of democracy. The infamous **Credit Mobilier Scandal** involving the construction of the first **transcontinental railroad** actually began before Grant took office, but came to light in 1872, after having been carried out for nearly 4 years of Grant's presidency and with the help of some of his administration's key people. In 1869, the first year of Grant's presidency, the notorious **Jay Gould**–Jim Fisk attempt to corner the gold market with the help of Grant's subordinates led to the "**Black Friday**" financial panic that cost both the country and Grant's reputation dearly. At the same time, American investors in the Caribbean island of Santo Domingo convinced Grant that annexing that land would benefit all parties concerned, when it would actually benefit themselves financially and create a host of new **foreign affairs** problems for the United States.

Grant was repeatedly and unwittingly used by crooked friends and associates although his motives were pure in all these scandals. Nor did this change in his second term. The so-called "Salary Grab" of 1873, which actually occurred on the last day of Grant's first term, set the tone for 4 more years of corruption, as congressmen voted themselves and the president (and Grant signed into law) large pay increases in an underhanded manner. The best known examples of corruption in Grant's second term were the "Tax Scandal," the "Whiskey Ring," and the "**Indian** Ring." The first involved the U.S. Treasury department appointing a tax collector named John D. Sanborn, who took money from corporations for himself in exchange for accepting smaller tax payments to the government. The second involved a tax collector named John McDonald, who took bribes from St. Louis area distillers to reduce their tax payments and colluded with Grant's personal secretary Orville Babcock to cover it up. The third involved Secretary of War William Belknap who awarded lucrative posts on Native American reservations in exchange for kickbacks.

Unfortunately, corruption was not merely a problem of the Grant administration or the federal government. It also permeated some state and local governments as well through political "machines" run by "bosses." In the South, these machines and bosses were concerned as much with white supremacy as with financial gain. White southern **Democrats** forced blacks and white carpetbagger **Republicans** out of office by either trumping up charges and stacking the juries against them, or by uncovering actual malfeasance when possible. Such methods ruined the careers, for example, of Mississippi Governor Adelbert Ames and South Carolina congressmen and legislators **Robert Smalls** and George Washington Murray, among many others. In the North, local corruption often involved industrial employers forcing their employees to vote for one party or candidate over another under threat of job termination in order to secure the most favorable legislation for their particular industry. The most notable abuser of state and local power was the "Tweed Ring," named for

William Marcy Tweed, who ran New York City's Democratic Party machine, **Tammany Hall**. Tweed colluded with contractors over a period of years to overcharge the city for building projects in order to skim the excess off the top for himself. He took perhaps as much as $25 million this way before being stopped by **Samuel Tilden** and fellow reformers. Meanwhile, the state of Pennsylvania became notorious for its corrupt Republican machine, run first by Simon Cameron, then by Matthew Quay. In the West, city and town governments often were plagued by corruption from all kinds of outlaws and miscreants—gamblers, rustlers, saloon keepers, brothel owners, shysters, and mining companies—colluding with mayors and lawmen.

Although the general tenor of the times made it appear that the American public was usually complacent about corruption, outrage eventually surfaced, once things had grown bad enough. Such outrage led to the rise of the reform-oriented **Liberal Republican** Party in 1872 and the **Mugwumps** in 1884, and to a movement to reform the civil service system. Although the Liberal Republicans failed, the movement prevailed, getting the **Pendleton Civil Service Act** passed in 1883. The Mugwumps succeeded at defeating the powerful-but-shady character **James G. Blaine** and getting the honest **Grover Cleveland** elected president. The anti-corruption mind set also contributed in part to the rise of the **People's Party** in the 1890s and the Progressive movement, which followed it going into the 1900s. **Theodore Roosevelt** came to prominence and power largely because the American public recognized his incorruptibility. *See also* WAITE, "BLOODY BRIDLES."

COWBOYS. The Gilded Age was the golden age of the cowboy in the American West. Several thousand men made their livelihoods by driving cows from Texas to stockyards in Kansas from the 1860s to the 1880s. In the days before the invention and widespread implementation of **barbed wire**, open grazing and herding was common, having evolved from the Mexican hacienda system in the early 1800s. Joseph McCoy, a cattleman from Illinois, is generally credited with starting the legendary cattle drives from the open ranges around the San Antonio area to Union Pacific **railroad** access points in Kansas, such as Abilene, Wichita, and Dodge City. His stockyards bought the hardy Longhorn cattle that others previously had spurned as an inferior breed and shipped them to slaughterhouses in Chicago. This created demand for cowboys to drive several million head of cattle north along the Chisholm Trail from 1867 to 1881, a job that lasted 2 or 3 months per drive.

The popular image of the cowboy of the "wild West" lore has some basis in fact. They were often small, wiry, and tough; they had to be in order to battle the elements and handle large animals on a daily basis. They dressed the way they did for practical reasons. For instance, the wide-brim hat shielded their heads from all-day exposure to the sun. The chaps protected their legs from briars, thorns, and all sorts of prickly brush as they rode horseback. Bandanas served as air filters in dust storms. Ropes were for lassoing runaway cows or rescuing them from dangerous predicaments.

The life of a cowboy could be exciting, as he traveled through American **Indian** territory, occasionally experiencing stampedes or trouble with rustlers. But day after day on the trail could also be extremely monotonous. Even so, because cowboys were itinerants— usually poor, young, unsettled bachelors with wild oats to sow—they tended to be a rowdy bunch. They, along with rustlers, greedy speculators, con artists, gamblers, gunslingers, and prostitutes, not to mention famous lawmen such as Wyatt Earp and Bat Masterson, turned towns like Dodge City into the epitome of the "wild West" in the 1870s.

By the mid-1880s, the need for cowboys had diminished drastically, for several reasons. One, as barbed wire began to cordon off the prairie, it became increasingly difficult to drive cows north to railroad loading/shipping points. Two, the development of windmills allowed water to be pumped from the otherwise arid plains, making it possible to do large-scale ranching anywhere in the West, such that cows did not have to be kept near or moved across rivers. Three, railroads were built running north and south from Texas to Kansas, making the old drives obsolete. Four, refrigerated cars made it possible to slaughter cattle wherever the cows already were, rather than having to drive them somewhere back east for slaughter. And finally, increased population in the West mitigated against driving cattle across private property. By the 1890s, the job of the cattle driver had largely been transformed into that of a stationary ranch hand, which lacked the sensational allure of the legendary cowboys. *See also* BUFFALO BILL; DALTON GANG; JAMES, JESSE; ROOSEVELT, THEODORE; HICKOK, "WILD BILL".

COXEY'S ARMY. Nicknamed for creator Jacob Coxey, a businessman, farmer, and Populist political spokesman from Ohio, Coxey's Army began as an organization called the "Commonwealth in Christ" in 1894. At the time, the **Panic of 1893** was wrecking the American economy, with the working class being hit the hardest. Coxey, like all Populists, favored strong federal government action to alleviate the misery. He proposed that Congress and the **Grover Cleveland** administration sell bonds to finance public works—especially new road projects—and thereby put thousands of the unemployed to work. Unable to get the attention of federal officials through conventional means, he and fellow Populist Carl Brown of California hatched the idea of presenting a "living petition" to them with "boots on." Thus, leaving Massillon, Ohio, on 25 March 1894 with 100 followers, Coxey and his "Industrial Army" staged the first "march on Washington." He picked up another 400 followers during the month-long trek, many from Philadelphia. The contingent of 500 Christian Socialist–Populists, though harmless and peaceful, scared Washingtonians. When Coxey tried to read a brief petition on the steps of the Capitol, police arrested him and the other leaders and had them jailed—with the blessing of President Cleveland. Although the march came to nothing, Coxey succeeded in raising awareness of the desperation of the working class, prompting other industrial "armies" to follow suit in marching on Washington later in 1894. Arguably, Coxey's Army had a negative impact on the Populist movement, as most Americans perceived the march on Washington as a far too radical measure. The march was the first big influence on Frank Baum's Populist novel, *The Wonderful Wizard of Oz* (1900). *See also* PEOPLE'S PARTY.

CRANE, STEPHEN (1871–1900). One of the few famous Americans to live his whole short life during the Gilded Age, Crane was born into a family of writers in Newark, New Jersey. Both parents died before he was grown, but he learned to support himself, if only meagerly, through journalism as a teenager. Moving to New York City in 1890, he lived among the poor and downtrodden in an overcrowded tenement neighborhood on the lower east side of Manhattan. There he gained a perspective on the harsh realities of life in an urban slum, which provoked him to become a pioneer of literary realism or naturalism. In 1893, he published his first novel, *Maggie: A Girl* *of the Streets*, which portrayed a good-hearted poor girl who fell on hard times and turned to the wretched, dead-end work of prostitution. The story proved too real and too ugly for publishers, and Crane was forced to self-publish it under an alias. Although the public generally ignored the book, it has since become a classic in the genre of realism.

In 1895, Crane published the novel that propelled him to instant fame, *The Red Badge of Courage*, which portrayed the angst of being a Civil War soldier gripped by fear and torn by his desire to escape the army, the battlefield, and death. So realistic was the novel that many readers mistook it for a memoir. Two years later, while working for the *New York Journal*, he ventured abroad to cover war stories. In an expedition to Cuba, his boat sank, leaving him stuck for a day-and-a-half in a small lifeboat off the coast of Florida. He recorded that harrowing experience in *The Open Boat and Other Tales* (1898). While covering the **Spanish–American War** in Cuba, he contracted malaria, which cut short his stay in the tropics. Moving to England, he came down with a terminal case of tuberculosis. Seeking treatment in Germany, he died at the tender age of 28, in the prime of his life and career. Some of his writings were published posthumously. *See also* LITERATURE.

CRAZY HORSE. *See* BATTLE OF LITTLE BIG HORN; INDIANS.

CREDIT MOBILIER SCANDAL. Among the worst cases of federal political **corruption** and financial chicanery in American history, the Credit Mobilier Scandal inspired **Mark Twain**, albeit indirectly, to dub his generation the "Gilded Age." The *New York Sun* first broke the story in 1872, just in time potentially to ruin **Ulysses S. Grant**'s presidential reelection bid. By that time, however, the complex money-making scheme had been going on for 5 years. The genesis of the scandal can be found in the United States government's desire to construct a **transcontinental railroad** at a time when few private sector **railroad** companies thought it a wise investment to build it. In the early 1860s, the Lincoln administration and the **Republican** Congress chartered two companies, the Union Pacific and the Central Pacific railroads, to carry out the enormous project. Congress gave each company generous land donations, mineral rights, loans to cover much of the building cost, and other incentives. Each company in turn sold public stocks and issued bonds to increase the corporate revenue, thus ensuring there would be enough money to complete the multimillion dollar job. The problem was that Union Pacific executives created another corporation with themselves as its directors to carry out the actual construction—the Credit Mobilier of America. Chartered in Pennsylvania as a private enterprise, it was named for the French company that had recently built the Suez Canal in Egypt. As a subcontractor, it could charge the Union Pacific, which received federal funds, with a higher tab for building than was actually necessary, and all the excess would go into the directors' pockets.

This was dirty business from the start, but complicating matters was the fact that in 1867, Oakes Ames, a Republican congressman from Massachusetts, took over as head of the Credit Mobilier. To ensure that the milking of the system continued unabated, and that no congressional investigation would be forthcoming into the fine details of where exactly the federal money was going in building the transcontinental railroad, Ames sold Credit Mobilier stock at a sharp discount to fellow Republican office holders. They profited handsomely and very quickly by reselling the stock on the open market at a tremendously increased price. Among those involved in this unsavory affair were the future president of the United States **James A. Garfield**, the current Vice President of the United States **Schuyler Colfax**, the current speaker of the House and future presidential nominee **James G. Blaine**, the current House Ways and Means Committee Chairman Henry L. **Dawes**, and about 25 others.

The *New York Sun* got the scoop on the case in September 1872 when an associate of Ames named Henry McComb turned him in after a disagreement. Although the negative publicity did not derail Grant's reelection bid, it did put the last nail in the coffin of Colfax's political career. It also prompted Congress to begin an investigation, which resulted in the creation of the Poland Committee in the House of Representatives, chaired by Luke Poland of Vermont. The Committee found that the Union Pacific's part of the railroad construction had cost less than $50 million, but it had received some $70 million in total compensation, with the extra $20 million-plus going to Credit Mobilier stockholders. It cleared Speaker Blaine quickly, found several others guilty of perjury (although none were ever prosecuted for it), found some guilty of naïveté (for lack of a better explanation), but censured only two house members for deliberate misconduct: James Brooks of New York and Oakes Ames himself. A later Senate investigation led to the censure of retiring Senator James Patterson of New Hampshire, but otherwise left no lasting scars on the others. **Democrats** made much political hay out of the affair, however, even bringing it up against Blaine in the presidential race of 1884.

CRIME OF '73. *See* FREE SILVER.

CURRENCY. *See* FREE SILVER.

CUSTER, GEORGE ARMSTRONG. *See* BATTLE OF LITTLE BIG HORN.

– D –

DALTON GANG. This band of outlaws grew up in Coffeyville, Kansas, in the 1870s and '80s. Although the oldest, Frank Dalton, died in the line of duty in law enforcement, the rest of the Dalton brothers—Grat, Bill, Bob, and Emmett—chose lives of crime. They started with stealing horses and selling whiskey in 1889–1890, but ended with robbing trains and a bank immediately thereafter. Along with a few unscrupulous friends, they formed the Dalton Gang in 1890–1891. They did most of their disreputable work in **Oklahoma**, the traditional **Indian** territory that was just opened to white settlement at the time. Their first planned, coordinated crime was staged in California, however, rather than Oklahoma. On 6 February 1891, they robbed a train on the Southern Pacific **Railroad**. Two of the brothers were caught and charged, while the others got away. Grat soon escaped, however, and headed back for Oklahoma. On 9 May, they robbed another train at a place that is now called Perry, Oklahoma. This time, gang member Charlie Bryant was caught and killed in a subsequent shoot-out with a deputy marshal. On 15 September 1891, the gang staged its most successful train robbery at Lelietta, Oklahoma, carting off some $10,000. They continued targeting trains in 1892, before foolishly deciding to switch to robbing banks. On 5 October 1892, under the leadership of Bob Dalton, the gang tried to rob two banks at once, in the broad daylight, in their hometown of Coffeyville, Kansas. The problem was that local townspeople knew who they were, and their reputation for crime. In the ensuing shootout, only Emmet survived, although he had 23 bullet holes in him. He was sentenced to life in prison, but was released after 14 years. Other members of the gang who were not present at the attempted bank robbery reorganized and continued their lives of crime.

DAVIS, JEFFERSON (1808–1889). Although primarily remembered as the President of the Confederate States of America during the Civil War, Jefferson Davis lived a long, notable life after the war, becoming perhaps the most controversial public figure of the Gilded Age. Born in Kentucky and reared in Mississippi, Davis graduated from the U.S. Military Academy at West Point, New York, in 1828. He served the United States in the Mexican War, the Franklin Pierce administration, and Congress, before launching into the disastrous Confederate government experiment. After the war, he was captured, imprisoned, and refused the rights afforded even common criminals. He was treated instead as the symbol of the defeated, treasonous South. Finally, after more than 2 years, he was allowed bail, which **Horace Greeley** and others sympathetic to his plight posted. The government subsequently dropped the case against Davis in 1869, and he walked away a free, if permanently tarnished, man at the start of the Gilded Age. He became the head of an insurance company in Memphis, Tennessee. He also traveled widely in the Americas and abroad. He was elected to the U.S. Senate again, but the 14th Amendment forbade his seating. General ill will from fellow congressmen, such as **James A. Garfield** and Zachariah Chandler, haunted him as well, preventing him from receiving a military pension.

In 1879, Davis moved to Biloxi, Mississippi, and took up residence at the Beauvoir plantation mansion. There he wrote his 1,200-page memoir, *The Rise and Fall of the Confederate Government* (1881), in which he defiantly continued to argue the constitutionality of secession and to defend the actions of the South in the 1860s. In the last year of his life, he wrote, *A Short History of the Confederate States of America* (1889). He died in New Orleans of unknown causes 2 months later.

His funeral procession from the Crescent City to Richmond, Virginia, where he was buried, was carried out with great fanfare and much media attention. Despite Davis's controversial life, he was eulogized as a man of great character and integrity by Americans on both sides of the Mason-Dixon line. *See also* LITERATURE.

DAWES SEVERALTY ACT. Also known as the General Allotment Act, this federal law named for Senator Henry Dawes of Massachusetts was designed to reform the largely dysfunctional **Indian** reservation system in the West by giving individual Native American families their own 160-acre homesteads and teaching them to live like whites. Congress passed it in 1887 after several years of agitation by white humanitarians, resulting largely from **Helen Hunt Jackson**'s books, *A Century of Dishonor* (1881) and *Ramona* (1883), which sharply criticized the federal government's abuse and neglect of the Indians. The assumption was that, given a choice, Native Americans would prefer to be homesteaders like whites and integrate into American society rather than be segregated on reservations. This assumption proved mostly false, because most Indians actually preferred to maintain their tribal heritage and identity, even if it meant living in communal squalor on a reservation, rather than imitate the ways of the white man. The bill's flaws notwithstanding, the Dawes Act represented a noble gesture and set the stage for Indians to become U.S. citizens later.

DEBS, EUGENE V. (1855–1926). Born in Terre Haute, Indiana, Eugene Victor Debs became the most prominent socialist in America in the 1890s and thereafter. His early career involved working on **railroads**, leading **trade unions**, and serving in the Indiana legislature as a **Democrat**. In 1893, he founded the American Railway Union, which staged the **Pullman Strike** in 1894. For his role in the strike, which shut down a large amount of the nation's railroad traffic for 3 months, Debs was arrested and prosecuted by the **Cleveland** administration for interfering with the delivery of the U.S. mail. The resulting court case, *In re Debs* (1895) became an important case in American history pertaining to labor union rights vis-à-vis government powers. Debs served a year in jail, during which time he read the works of Karl Marx and emerged in 1895 as a convert to socialism. The greater part of his public career occurred in the 20th century rather than in the Gilded Age, as he ran for president of the United States five times and tangled with the government over issues pertaining to World War I.

DELANY, MARTIN (1812–1885). Born to a free black family on the border of Virginia and West Virginia just below the Potomac River, Martin Robinson Delany grew to become one of the most important **African Americans** of the 19th century. He spent many of his antebellum years fighting for abolition of slavery and advocating emigration of his people out of the United States. He also published newspapers, authored notable books, and attended Harvard Medical School. In the Civil War he recruited for the Massachusetts 54th regiment and became the first black to earn the rank of major in the U.S. Army. During Reconstruction, he ran a Freedman's Bureau school in South Carolina, lost a bid for lieutenant governor there, then won appointment as a state judge in Charleston, but resigned amid a scandal. After the "redemption," however, new governor Wade Hampton reappointed him as a token black official.

Thereafter in the Gilded Age, Delany once again became an ardent emigrationist, serving as the financial chairman of the Liberia Exodus Joint Stock Steamship Company. He arranged the purchase of the *Azor*, but soon abandoned his role in this latest emigration scheme, deciding to stay in the United States, make his home in Ohio, and spend most of his last years writing. His last two works were entitled *Principles of Ethnology: The Origins of Races and Color* (1879) and *Search for a Place: Black Separatism and Africa* (1884). Like so many other black nationalists, his life was more tragedy than triumph. He left a legacy, however, as an advocate of black self-determination that now looms larger than his accomplishments appeared in his own lifetime. *See also* LITERATURE.

DEMOCRATIC PARTY. For most of the late 19th century, the **Republican Party** had majority control of the federal government while the Democratic Party tended to be in the minority. As a consequence of the Civil War and the unpopular presidency of Democrat Andrew Johnson from 1865–1868, the GOP controlled all three branches of the government and both houses of Congress at the beginning of the Gilded Age. The **corruption** of the **Ulysses S. Grant** administration, however, turned the House of Representatives over to the Democrats in 1874, and nearly turned the White House over in 1872 and 1876. The Democrats maintained their majority in the House for 16 out of the next 24 years. Democratic speakers of the House included Samuel J. Randall of Pennsylvania (45th and 46th Congresses), John G. Carlisle of Kentucky (48th through 50th Congresses), and Charles F. Crisp of Georgia (52nd and 53rd Congresses).

Democrats never had a majority in the Senate during the Gilded Age. Consequently, more often than not, they had difficulty passing meaningful legislation. In a strange way, this was not a bad thing for them, however, because they held such a strict, conservative, laissez-faire approach to governing that they likely would not have passed many laws that promoted change even if they had controlled the Senate.

As for the presidency, the Democrats were so weak in 1872 that they had fused with **Liberal Republicans** and nominated **Horace Greeley** (a man who had spent most of his career opposing the Democratic Party) to run unsuccessfully against the incumbent **Ulysses S. Grant**. Democratic candidate **Samuel J. Tilden** won the presidential sweepstakes of 1876 by their party's estimation, but allegations of fraud in four states kept the prize from them, as the **Compromise of 1877** awarded the victory to Republican **Rutherford B. Hayes**. In 1880, their candidate **Winfield S. Hancock** went down to defeat in another close race against **James A. Garfield**. Finally, in 1884, Democratic candidate **Grover Cleveland** captured the presidency, despite being accused just before the election of engaging in a sex scandal in which he allegedly fathered an illegitimate child. Although he enjoyed a prosperous and successful first term, he managed to defeat challenger **Benjamin Harrison** only in the popular vote in 1888, not in the Electoral College. He defeated Harrison in both counts in 1892, however, and suffered a tumultuous second term, which ensured the Democrats' defeat in 1896. In that year, the **Populists** fused with the Democrats and nominated **William Jennings Bryan** on a "**free silver**" platform, but lost to **William McKinley**.

Ideologically, most Democrats stood for several principles throughout the Gilded Age. They favored a small federal bureaucracy with few government programs, low taxes, low **tariffs**, and strong state and local governments, while they opposed suffrage and increased civil rights for **African Americans**, imperialistic **foreign** policy, and bimetallism (until Populist pressure forced free silver upon them in 1896). Their conservatism led to their being tagged with the moniker "Bourbons," because, ostensibly, like the French monarchs from whom the name derived, they had learned nothing from the people's revolution in which they lost their power (the Civil War). Southern anti-Reconstruction Democrats, meanwhile, called themselves "Redeemers," and their main concern from 1869 to 1877 lay in reclaiming their state and local governments from "carpetbaggers," "scalawags," and blacks, and thereafter in making sure they did not lose control again.

Some of the leaders of the party in the Gilded Age (besides those already mentioned) included Arthur Pue Gorman of Maryland, David Bennett Hill of New York, Thomas F. Bayard of Delaware, **James J. Hill** of Minnesota, **Thomas A. Hendricks** of Indiana, **Adlai E. Stevenson** of Illinois, Wade Hampton of South Carolina, Zebulon Vance of North Carolina, Lucius Q. C. Lamar of Mississippi, and Melville Fuller of Illinois. *See also* TAMMANY HALL; TWEED, WILLIAM MARCY.

DICKINSON, EMILY. *See* LITERATURE.

DOLE, SANFORD B. *See* HAWAII, ANNEXATION OF.

DONNELLY, IGNATIUS (1831–1901). One of the most colorful characters of the Gilded Age, Donnelly was born in Philadelphia to Irish immigrants. After studying and practicing law in Pennsylvania temporarily, he relocated to the frontier of the Minnesota territory in 1857. There he tried his hand at real estate speculating, unsuccessfully starting a cooperative, utopian farm community called Nininger just south of the state capital. He also joined the nascent **Republican Party** just in time to become its victorious candidate for lieutenant governor, a post he held for two terms (1859–1863). Elected to the U.S. House of Representatives thereafter for three consecutive terms (1863–1868), he took an extremely **liberal** stance on racial issues and **women**'s rights. After his ouster from Congress, he turned to supporting the **Grange**'s crusade against the **railroads**, he entered local politics, got involved in the Greenback movement, edited a newspaper, and began research on his first book. Long interested in esoteric knowledge about mysterious and controversial subjects, he published *Atlantis: The Antediluvian World* (1882), which gave us much of our current theoretical conception of Plato's legendary lost city of Atlantis. He treated the subject seriously and gave his opinions about it as facts, but much of his intriguing work was fabricated out of his own mind rather than supported by evidence. The following year he published another pseudo-scientific treatise about a comet hitting the earth during ancient times and destroying civilization. These books brought him great notoriety, and he seized the opportunity to make the national lecture circuit.

Donnelly's next contribution to American **literature** and conspiracy theory folklore came in 1887 and 1888 when he published *The Shakespeare Myth* and a sequel, which argued that Francis Bacon had been the actual author of Shakespeare's plays. Meanwhile, as he was stirring this literary controversy, he was simultaneously leading the Minnesota **Farmers' Alliance** toward its eventual political destination in the **People's Party**. In 1892, the new party considered nominating him for president or vice president of the United States, but the baggage of his literary and scientific quackery proved too heavy. Indeed, critics mocked him as the "Sage of Nininger" and the "Prince of Cranks," among other things. He did write the memorable preamble for the Omaha Platform, however. After the Populists had enjoyed their fleeting moment of near-glory and were then receding into the has-been category, they nominated Donnelly for U.S. Vice President in 1900, a fitting tribute perhaps to a man who had done so much to promote Populism. He died soon after this defeat.

DOUGLASS, FREDERICK (1818–1895). Born a slave in Maryland, Douglass had mixed racial ancestry, but was not sure of the identity of his father. Escaping north to freedom, he became the most prominent black abolitionist in the world. Although chiefly remembered for his crusade against slavery, after the Civil War he continued to hold the distinction of being the recognized leader of, or spokesman for, **African Americans**. He enjoyed associations with virtually every **Republican** president or congressman of importance, and most major Republican newspaper editors, which kept him almost constantly in the public eye throughout the Gilded Age. He made his living mainly as a lecturer, traveling the United States and the world.

He held several federal government appointments as well, such as foreign consul to Haiti, U.S. marshal for Washington, D.C., and recorder of deeds for Washington, D.C. In 1872, he was nominated for U.S. Vice President on the quixotic Equal Rights Party ticket with **Victoria Woodhull**, although he neither accepted nor officially declined the nomination. In 1874, he held the position of president of the soon-to-founder Freedman's Savings Bank.

At a time when so many Republicans began to back-pedal from civil rights for blacks, Douglass never wavered in his determination to uphold the standard of absolute equality for all Americans. He also championed **women**'s rights, which was even less popular than civil rights for blacks during the Gilded Age. His views, while generally accepted by today's standards as correct, were far ahead of their time. Most white Americans considered him eccentric at least, dangerous at worst. His marriage to a white woman in 1884 solidified that status. He remained active right up to his death, making stirring and quotable speeches. Thus, not until he died could another black leader, **Booker T. Washington**, earn the mantle of leader of African Americans, which he did coincidentally in the same year with his "**Atlanta Compromise**" speech.

DU BOIS, W. E. B. (1868–1963). Born in Massachusetts to parents who had been free blacks even before emancipation, William Edward Burghardt Du Bois grew up with as many advantages as an **African American** could have in the Gilded Age. A precocious student, he wanted to attend Harvard University, but was initially denied admission based on race. He thus trekked to Nashville, Tennessee, where he matriculated at the all-black Fisk **College** for 2 years. There he built an impressive transcript and soon managed to convince Harvard to admit him. In 1890, he became the first black to graduate from that prestigious institution. Thereafter, he studied abroad at the University of Berlin for a year, then returned to Massachusetts and earned a Ph.D. from Harvard, studying history and sociology. Harvard published his dissertation, *The Suppression of the African Slave Trade to the United States of America: 1638–1870* (1896), which became a classic in the historiography of American slavery. He took professorial teaching jobs first at Wilberforce University, then at the University of Pennsylvania. At the latter, he made his groundbreaking study in black sociology and criminology, *The Philadelphia Negro* (1899), in which he began to formulate a sweeping philosophy of American race relations, which he would hone and shape later as a professor at Atlanta University and in books such as *The Souls of Black Folks* (1903). Some of this philosophy, including his belief that the "talented tenth" of blacks must fight for the rights of the rest of the race, directly challenged that of the most influential race leader of the day, **Booker T. Washington**. Their rivalry would become legendary over time. Although much of his fame as a historical figure today results from his accomplishments in the 20th century, he had his start in the Gilded Age.

DUKE, BUCK (1856–1925). Born in central North Carolina near Durham, James Buchanan "Buck" Duke was the son of tobacco planter Washington Duke. Washington, a devout and progressive Methodist who opposed slavery and the Confederacy and favored **women**'s rights and the **Republican Party**, began the family tobacco business called Pro Bono Publico in 1859. After moving the company headquarters to Durham in 1874, he increasingly allowed his sons Benjamin and Buck to run the business. In 1878, the Dukes expanded the business and renamed it W. Duke, Sons and Company. Soon after, they began the transition from pipe and chewing tobacco to cigarettes; by that time Buck had emerged as the genius behind the company.

In 1884, Buck contracted with James Bonsack, inventor of the first cigarette-rolling machine, to use his new technology to get an advantage in the industry. The invention cut the cost of manufacturing cigarettes in half. Duke also improved the packaging of cigarettes, selling them in the kind of cardboard boxes that eventually became the familiar standard. At the same time, he moved his business headquarters to New York City and turned to new ways of advertising his product, using billboards as well as newspapers and periodicals, and spending far more money than not only his competition, but also just about any other company in the world. Indeed, his advertising strategy became a model for Madison Avenue in the 20th century. These innovations plus his willingness to undersell his competitors had given him the largest market share in the cigarette industry by 1890. In that year, he used his leverage to persuade his four primary rivals to join him in creating the American Tobacco Company (ATC), which became a trust modeled after **John D. Rockefeller**'s Standard Oil Company. Over the next decade, the ATC grabbed more than a 90 percent market share of the cigarette industry in the United States and raced toward world domination against its British rivals. In 1896, it became one of the founding members of the Dow Jones Industrial Average. Within another decade, an antitrust suit would force the breakup of the half-billion-dollar corporation.

In 1892, the Duke family began funding and influencing the small Methodist college called Trinity, which eventually became Duke University. Although Buck was generous in his philanthropy, leaving one of the largest endowments in American history, he was criticized for his ruthless business tactics. He also left his daughter a $100-million estate.

DUNNE, FINLEY PETER. *See* MR. DOOLEY.

– E –

EARP, WYATT. *See* GUNFIGHT AT THE O. K. CORRAL; TOMBSTONE, ARIZONA.

EDISON, THOMAS ALVA (1847–1931). Born in northern Ohio and brought up in southeastern Michigan, Thomas Edison grew up with a hearing problem. He was not a good student. As a teen, he learned the trade of a telegraph operator, which propelled him to invent better ways to transmit information artificially over long distances via wire. Moving to the suburbs of New York City on the New Jersey side, he first patented an electronic vote recorder, then in 1870, a stock market ticker tape machine. In 1876, he set up a research laboratory at Menlo Park, New Jersey, where he invented the phonograph a year later, raced to create a more functional telephone than **Alexander Graham Bell**'s, and developed the first incandescent light bulb in 1879. He financed the research on the latter through his Edison Electric Light Company, a corporation he founded in New York City with the backing of **J. P. Morgan** and the **Vanderbilt** family, among others. This company would evolve into the modern General Electric Company and would prove to be Edison's most financially successful business enterprise. In 1882 in lower Manhattan, Edison flipped the switch that turned on the first commercial electric lighting in the world. Although he would go on to invent many other gadgets and hold more than 1,000 patents in the United States alone, none of his later inventions had quite the same impact as his electric lighting. His experiments with motion picture cameras, however, paved the way for Hollywood and the whole movie industry.

Edison's prolific record of inventions and patents made the "Wizard of Menlo Park" by far the most famous and important inventor of the Gilded Age, but it also kept him embroiled in controversy. He conflicted with Bell and others over the rights to the telephone industry, William Sawyer and Joseph Swan over rights to the electric lighting industry, **George Westinghouse** and **Nikola Tesla** over the advantages of direct current (DC) as opposed to alternating current (AC), and general public opinion over the issue of capital punishment. His post–Gilded Age years brought him more fame, but his many unprofitable business ventures prevented him from becoming the tycoon that he should have been. He nonetheless ranks in history alongside the most influential people to have ever lived; a man who, more than any other individual, ushered in the second industrial revolution and pointed the way to the future. *See also* OAKLEY, ANNIE.

EDDY, MARY BAKER. *See* CHURCH OF CHRIST, SCIENTIST; WOMEN.

EDUCATION, ELEMENTARY AND SECONDARY. The American education system had been primitive and decentralized before the Gilded Age. Although a constantly evolving institution, the elementary public school system existed almost exclusively in the northeastern states prior to the Civil War. Private tutoring and study abroad were the main ways and means of formally educating children in the South, while apprenticing was still the primary type of education for the poor nationwide. Through the work of Horace Mann and other early education pioneers, professionalization and standardization of the teaching-learning process began in Massachusetts. In 1857, the National Teachers Association was formed in Philadelphia, Pennsylvania, to move the process along. In 1870, it merged with the National Association of School Superintendents and the American

Normal School Association to become the modern National Education Association (NEA). Despite the name, there was nothing "national" about it, because the South and West lagged terribly behind, generally considering formal education more of a luxury for the wealthy than a necessity for all citizens. In 1872, the NEA began advocating the establishment of preschools or kindergartens. Not until 1875, however, in Kalamazoo, Michigan, was the modern public school system born, when a state court ruling required all local taxpayers to support the local school. The idea spread rapidly around the nation. By the end of the Gilded Age, more than 3,000 such schools had opened. At the same time, another idea—that of compulsory education—began to spread as well, although not until the early 20th century would every state adopt it.

The type of education offered in Gilded Age schools tended to be "classical" Latin-Greek-academic. Vocational education was rare at first because apprenticing still filled that need. *McGuffey Readers* were the texts of choice. They evolved from the 1830s, when they contained Bible stories and moral lessons, to the 1880s, when in addition they contained more sophisticated readings and assignments covering the works of 111 different authors—largely to accommodate the growing number of secondary education schools and students. In 1892, the NEA established a "Committee of Ten" to develop a standard curriculum and a uniform system of grade levels. It decided that 12 years of education (excluding kindergarten) would be ideal—8 of which would be elementary and 4 secondary. Traditional academic courses would still be taught, but in addition to reading, writing, and arithmetic, other courses, such as history, civics, and science would be taught as well. Over time, vocational education was added. It first took hold in Freedmen's Bureau schools during Reconstruction as a type of education ideally suited for former slave children, who were widely considered intellectually unsuited for classical education but were not likely to get many apprenticing opportunities. In the 1880s and beyond, its success was made famous in **Booker T. Washington**'s Tuskegee Institute in Alabama. Meanwhile, in 1879, in St. Louis, Missouri, the first Manual Training School for white boys was opened. More often than not, however, whites did not have the option of attending an exclusively vocational school. Rather, they generally had a "shop" class added to the classical curriculum. By the end of the Gilded Age, about 100 American public schools offered some form of vocational or technical training. *See also* COLLEGES AND UNIVERSITIES.

ELLIS ISLAND. On 1 January 1892, the United States opened its largest **immigrant**-processing center on this island in New York harbor. Claimed by both New York and New Jersey in the 1700s, the island became federal property in 1808. As immigration reached a peak in the early Gilded Age, and as groups like the **American Protective Association** arose to complain about it, Congress and President **Benjamin Harrison** shifted immigration processing power from the states to the federal government. They decided a new federal facility was needed to process immigrants. Since most immigrants came into the port of New York anyway, Ellis Island seemed the perfect place for the new center. In its first year, it processed almost 450,000 people. Rather than merely run them through a rubber stamp naturalization process, however, Ellis Island administrators (from the U.S. Public Health Service and Bureau of Immigration) gave the poor prospective immigrants medical exams and other tests to determine their suitability for citizenship. In 1897, Ellis Island facilities burned to the ground and had to be rebuilt. *See also* CASTLE GARDEN.

EVARTS, WILLIAM M. (1818–1901). Born in Boston into one of the most distinguished families in American political history, William Maxwell Evarts was the grandson of a signer of the Declaration of Independence and U.S. Constitution and a cousin to U.S. Senator **George Frisbie Hoar** and erstwhile Attorney General Ebenezer Rockwood Hoar. He attended Yale University and Harvard Law School before moving to New York to practice law. His first claim to fame came in 1868 when President Andrew Johnson appointed him chief counsel in the impeachment trial. He proved an unusually gifted orator with a shrewd legal mind, and Johnson promoted him to attorney general for the remainder of his term. During the **Ulysses S. Grant** administration, Evarts successfully represented the United States in the *Alabama* **Claims Dispute** of 1871–1872. From then until 1886, he was engaged in practicing law off-and-on in New York City and in leading the fundraising effort to build the **Statue of Liberty**. Meanwhile, in 1875, he served as chief counsel for the Reverend **Henry Ward Beecher** in the infamous *Tilton v. Beecher* adultery case. In 1876–1877, he represented presidential candidate **Rutherford B. Hayes** and the **Republican Party** in the disputed election that led to the **Compromise of 1877**. Finally, he served one term as a U.S. Senator from New York, 1885–1891. With failing eyesight and poor health, he retired thereafter.

EXODUSTERS. It became apparent upon the **Compromise of 1877** that the U.S. Government would leave the freedmen to fend for themselves against racism in the South. Some **African Americans** weighed their options and decided their chances for happy lives were better outside the South than inside it. Aware that the federal government had encouraged settlement of the vast Great Plains since passage of the Homestead Act of 1862, some black leaders moved to Kansas, Colorado, and surrounding areas, acquired land, and began recruiting fellow black southerners to bring their families and start new lives there. The most famous of these leaders was Benjamin "Pap" Singleton of Tennessee, who became the "Moses" to lead the "exodus" out of "Egypt" (the South) to the "promised land" (Kansas). He and a few others managed to persuade at least 30,000 of these black "Exodusters" to take the offer. This mass migration of black workers leaving the cotton fields of some southern counties created labor shortages, which provoked some white pseudo-militia groups to stop them from leaving. Occasionally the Exodusters would make it all the way to the Mississippi River before being turned back by white patrols. Most of those who made it to Kansas found economic conditions just as abysmal there as where they came from. Moreover, they found nature harsher and whites not much better to them. Many stayed only a few months or years before returning to the South. Some Exoduster towns managed to survive, however, and are still alive today.

– F –

FALL RIVERS MURDERS. *See* BORDEN MURDERS CASE.

FARMERS' ALLIANCES. Several different organizations emerged on the national stage in the 1880s that joined farmers together into economic cooperative ventures and attempted political unity. The two largest came to be called the National Farmers' Alliance (NFA), founded in Illinois by Chicago newspaperman Milton George, and the National Farmers' Alliance and Industrial Union, founded partly by farmers in Lampasas County, Texas, and partly by farmers in Prairie County, Arkansas. Each group started locally under different names, growing and evolving into forces in the Midwest/Great Plains and the South, respectively, before loosely uniting into a single "National Farmers' Alliance" in 1889. Because of their sectional origins, the former has often been called the northern alliance and the latter the southern alliance. The South also had a Colored Farmers' Alliance, which, although segregated, was not totally cut off from the white organization.

These alliances were similar to the **National Grange**, an older, established fraternal organization of farmers, but they were less about fraternizing and more about collective economic and political action. In some cases, farmers joined both their local Grange and their local farmers' alliance concomitantly, but more often they chose one or the other. Whereas the Grange was mostly apolitical or nonpartisan and had a limited reform agenda, the alliances tended to work through their strongest local political party (**Republican** in the North, **Democrat** in the South) to accomplish their list of reform items, which grew longer every year. Their list began with a desire to obtain goods at cheaper prices and to sell their crops at higher prices. It ended with a call for **free silver** and a national income tax, among other things.

In 1889, at a meeting in St. Louis, Missouri, the northern and southern alliances began attempts to merge with each other and with the **Knights of Labor**, the largest industrial workers' **union** in the nation. Although achieving more of a loose confederation than a solid front, the NFA began making serious political inroads in 1890 in Kansas and Nebraska, and to a lesser extent enjoying political success in other states. This ultimately led to the formation of the **People's Party** nationally within 2 years. The move into third party politics doomed the NFA in the long run. Other causes of its demise include the lack of sectional and racial solidarity within the NFA, competition from the Grange and other farmers' fraternities, the introduction of the controversial sub-treasury plan of storing crops in warehouses until the optimal selling price arrived, and changing times in the 1890s.

FEDERAL ELECTIONS BILL OF 1890. Henry Cabot Lodge, a **Republican** from Massachusetts, introduced this bill in the House of Representatives in the **Billion Dollar Congress**. Its purpose was to enforce the 15th Amendment in the South and clean up the rampant **corruption** in northern city elections by stationing federal soldiers at the polls in precincts with a history of voting fraud. Opponents derisively called the plan the "Force Bill."

The bill indeed "forced" the civil rights issues of Reconstruction back to the fore after a 13-year break. Southerners, meanwhile, considered it an attempt to "force" black rule upon them. **Democrats** likewise considered it an ultrapartisan scheme to ensure Republican control of certain northern cities and districts that usually did not have a GOP majority. Although the bill passed in the House under the strong hand of Speaker **Thomas B. Reed**, it failed in the Senate as a result of one of the most dramatic filibusters in American history. The bill marked the last time the Republican Party took a leading role in attempting to enforce black voting rights. *See also* AFRICAN AMERICANS; HARRISON, BENJAMIN; MORTON, LEVI P.

FILIPINO INSURRECTION. *See* FOREIGN AFFAIRS; SPANISH-AMERICAN WAR.

FISH, HAMILTON (1808–1893). One of the few bright spots in President **Ulysses S. Grant**'s cabinet, Hamilton Fish was born into a family of privilege in New York City. After attending Columbia University, he practiced law, joined the Whig party, served in the U.S. House of Representatives, became lieutenant governor and then governor of New York, won election to the U.S. Senate, and helped found the **Republican Party**—all before he turned 50 years old. During the Civil War, he served the Abraham Lincoln administration and the New York GOP. In 1869, Grant tapped him to be secretary of state, a position he held for 8 turbulent years. During that time, Grant's cabinet changed frequently, as members retired, died, resigned in disgrace under allegations of **corruption**, or were replaced as they fell out of the president's good graces. Fish, however, managed to avoid all of those fates and distinguish himself as one of the best **foreign affairs** managers in American history. He helped settle the *Alabama Claims Dispute* through the Treaty of Washington in 1871, negotiated a settlement with Great Britain over where the border should be set between Canada and the United States on the West Coast at Vancouver Island, helped broker a peace treaty among several South American nations that were at war with one another, salvaged American pride after the execution of eight Americans by Spanish authorities in the *Virginius* affair in 1873, and initiated the economic relationship with the Hawaiian islands that eventually resulted in the **Annexation of Hawaii** two decades later. He advised against Grant's attempt to annex Santo Domingo, but he did not prevail upon the president on that issue—although the U.S. Senate ultimately did. After his tenure in the Grant administration, Fish retired to New York City and served in various public and private capacities, including working for the betterment of Columbia University and the New York public library system.

FISK, JAMES. *See* BLACK FRIDAY GOLD SCANDAL; GOULD, JAY; GRANT, ULYSSES S.

FLAGLER, HENRY M. (1830–1913). Born into a poor minister's family in New York, Henry Morrison Flagler moved to Ohio as a teenager to live with his half-brother. There he worked his way up from the bottom of the grain business to become a partner in D. M. Harkness and Company. During the Civil War, he founded a salt mining company in Saginaw, Michigan, but it failed after the war. Soon after, **John D. Rockefeller**, a young Ohio businessman, approached him about starting an oil company. Flagler then became a partner in what evolved into the Standard Oil Company, which made him fabulously wealthy. He then moved to the company's new headquarters in New York City. His wife became ill, and on her doctor's advice, in the winter of 1878, the couple vacationed in the warmer climate of Jacksonville, Florida, a town with few facilities to accommodate a wealthy New Yorker like himself. While north Florida was somewhat developed at the time, central and south Florida were little more than alligator-infested swamplands. Flagler immediately sensed that the Sunshine State was a diamond in the rough, just waiting to be cut and polished by some enterprising entrepreneur.

In 1885, Flagler began building the first facility in the area designed to attract tourists, the Hotel Ponce de Leon, in the oldest town in North America, St. Augustine. The region was so undeveloped, however, that getting building materials was difficult. To compensate, he purchased the local **railroad** line between Jacksonville and St. Augustine. Realizing there was money to be made in both railroads and hotels along Florida's Atlantic coast, he bought up several properties, from Daytona to Palm Beach, then expanded his rail lines all the way to the bottom of the state. The city of Miami has its origins here. Flagler turned the little community that was previously known as Fort Dallas into a bustling town that eventually became the biggest city in Florida. Local residents wanted to name the town for him, but he encouraged them to call it the old Ohio **Indian** tribal name, "Miami." They agreed, and thus it has been since 1896.

Still not satisfied with his accomplishments, Flagler next sought to extend his rail line and real estate holdings all the way to Key West. The result was the Florida Over-Sea Railroad, which was completed in 1912 and was hailed at the time as an engineering marvel in league with the Seven Wonders of the World. For each mile of track Flagler laid in Florida, the state gave him 8,000 acres. He ended up owning about 2.5 million acres, which made his estate worth multiple millions of dollars after his death. Yet, he also invested some $50 million in improvements in the state, including generous donations of land and buildings for schools, churches, museums, and various other civic and cultural sites.

FOREIGN AFFAIRS. The Gilded Age ranks among the least active, least important periods in American history for foreign affairs. Few world-changing events occurred during this time. The great exception was the **Spanish–American War** of 1898, which essentially put an end to the pre-imperialist Gilded Age and ushered in the United States' new era of involvement in world affairs. The lesser exceptions can each be noted briefly.

The most common foreign problems involved Great Britain. First, the *Alabama* **Claims Dispute**, an unresolved conflict between the United States and England resulting from the American Civil War, came to the fore at the beginning of the **Ulysses S. Grant** administration. In the war, British shipbuilders had constructed warships for the Confederate States of America, which sank U.S. vessels. The United States demanded reparations and ultimately got them in the

Treaty of Washington of 1871. While that issue was ongoing, another brewed on the Canadian border, also a carry-over from the Civil War. In 1870, Irish American "Fenians," who wanted Irish independence from Great Britain, foolishly launched raids into Canada—which was still part of the British Empire at the time—hoping to capture it and hold it hostage pending Ireland's liberation. Although not sanctioned by the U.S. Government, this ill-fated episode did nothing to help relations with England. Next, in 1878, the United States acquired the rights to Pago Pago in the Samoan Islands, which intensified an imperialist rivalry with England (as well as Germany) for control of the region. A controversy over fishing rights off the coast of Alaska in the late 1880s and American arbitration of the **Venezuelan Boundary Dispute** between England and Venezuela in the 1890s kept tensions high. "Twisting the lion's tail," a euphemism for saber-rattling against the United States' old mother country, became a popular pastime for some American political leaders, notably secretary of state and presidential candidate **James G. Blaine**.

The other nation that presented serious problems for the United States was Spain. In 1873, the first conflict arose when the Spanish navy captured a private American ship called the *Virginius* while on its way to deliver arms to anticolonial insurgents in Cuba. When eight Americans were executed for piracy, a few American jingoes called for war, but nothing came of it since those executed did not officially represent the U.S. Government and may indeed have been guilty of international impropriety. More than 20 years later, the Cubans were still trying to break free from Spain, and by then the tenor of the times had changed. Thanks to yellow press journalism, the jingoes became the loudest voices in America. The **William McKinley** administration tried to avoid directly aiding the Cubans against Spain, but the explosion of the U.S.S. *Maine* in Havana Harbor in 1898 ultimately led to war. Although a quick, easy war to win, it put the United States squarely in the role of the imperialist bully, which proved to have ramifications for the next century and beyond.

There were several isolated but noteworthy foreign affairs issues in the Gilded Age. One was the debate over the annexation of Santo Domingo, a Caribbean nation only recently liberated from Spanish control, which occurred during Grant's first term. American business interests there pushed for annexation and convinced Grant of the benefits: it would provide a place for oppressed southern **African Americans** to colonize, forcing white southerners to treat them better in order to prevent losing their labor force; it would give the U.S. Navy an important naval base; and it would secure another supplier of raw materials and another market for American finished goods. Charles Sumner of Massachusetts, head of the Senate Committee on Foreign Affairs, disagreed and led Congress to kill the proposal. Another was the 1891 **Valparaiso Incident** in Chili, in which some American sailors died, causing a temporary clamor for war that was quieted by payment of reparations to the United States. The **Annexation of Hawaii**, an issue that dragged on from 1887–1898, was more serious. It became the first case in American history of real imperialist expansion overseas, and was only finished as a part of the territorial acquisition of the Spanish–American War. The last two foreign issues of the Gilded Age were the beginning of the Filipino insurrection, a direct byproduct of the Spanish–American War, and the Open Door Policy, an indirect byproduct. In the latter, the United States asserted itself as a great world power for the first time, declaring itself the protector of China and threatening any nation that tried to take possession of it. *See also* FISH, HAMILTON; HAY, JOHN; TELLER AMENDMENT.

FREE SILVER. This rallying point for the Populists in the 1896 presidential election represented the culmination of more than two decades of national public debate over bimetallism. The origin of the issue dates to early U.S. history when the U.S. Treasury Department set the value of silver in relation to gold at 16 to 1, meaning 16 ounces of silver equaled 1 ounce of gold in terms of purchasing power. The problem was that this arbitrary standard did not always hold up to market forces. When the amount of silver being mined fell in the 1840s–1850s, the value of silver increased to the extent that mining companies sold their silver on the open market for a higher price rather than to the U.S. Treasury for minting. The government coined less of it, therefore, in the 1850s–1860s.

Meanwhile, the Abraham Lincoln administration ordered the printing of greenbacks in 1862 to finance the Civil War, and complicated the nation's monetary situation. After the war, the Andrew Johnson administration began calling for greenbacks to be cashed in for specie, but by then the amount the government would pay in exchange for them was less if paid in silver than in gold, and far below their face value. Those who cashed them in, therefore, wanted payment in gold rather than silver. That, plus the trend in leading nations such as England and France—to move away from bimetallism and toward the gold standard—further complicated the issue. The administration of **Ulysses S. Grant** and Congress felt pressure to demonetize silver dollars, which they did through the Coinage Act of 1873. The timing, however, could not have been worse, for two reasons. One, western miners struck a rich vein immediately after that, flooding the market with silver, decreasing its value, and causing public officials and newspaper editors in western states to demand resumption of government purchases and coinage of silver at the old 16 to 1 ratio. Two, it coincided with the **Panic of 1873**, which caused a 4-year economic depression that in popular perception was somehow tied to the currency issue. Opponents consequently called the Coinage Act the "Crime of '73."

Because of the public outcry to restore silver, which went against the wishes of eastern financial experts, in 1878 Congress passed the Bland-Allison Act over the veto of President **Rutherford B. Hayes**. It guaranteed that the U.S. Government would buy a certain amount of silver for coinage to assist western miners and appease their congressmen. A decade later, however, the National **Farmers' Alliance**, some industrial unions, and soon the **People's Party** began calling for an increase in the amount the government would purchase. In 1890, therefore, Senator **John Sherman**, working with the **Billion Dollar Congress** and President **Benjamin Harrison**, passed the Sherman Silver Purchase Act to quiet the critics, as well as to gain bipartisan support for other **Republican** legislation. Yet, the Populists would not be satisfied until the government coined silver in unlimited amounts, rather than in an arbitrarily determined quantity. This they dubbed "free silver." When the **Panic of 1893** hit, President **Grover Cleveland** tried to stabilize the economy by repealing the Sherman Act, which was a good economic idea but a bad political idea.

The combination of the depression and Cleveland's policies caused the Populists to grow in strength and number, and provoked many **Democrats** to become Populists or otherwise agree with them about free silver, which set up the final showdown in the "Battle of the

Standards," as it became known, in the presidential election of 1896. By the time **William Jennings Bryan** and the Democrats/Populists made free silver the main campaign issue of 1896, the economy was rebounding under the gold standard, and **William McKinley** and the Republicans were the beneficiaries. Whether American voters as a whole ever understood the financial and monetary theories and statistics behind the free silver issue is doubtful. But essentially, in retrospect, it appears that the "gold bugs" were right in declaring that free silver would have done the working class more harm than good in the long run, although that is certainly debatable.

FRICK, HENRY CLAY (1849–1919). Born in southwestern Pennsylvania, Frick did not venture far from his birthplace in launching a career in the coke and steel industries. In 1871, he founded Frick & Company to make coke—a type of fuel produced by refining raw coal, which steel plants used to stoke their blast furnaces. Getting in on the ground floor, Frick managed to develop a near-monopoly on the coke industry around Pittsburgh. In 1886, **Andrew Carnegie** bought a controlling interest in the company, incorporated it into his larger steel-making empire, and appointed Frick chairman. In 1891, they bought out one of their main rivals and created Carnegie Steel Company, Ltd. Although the two men did not always see eye-to-eye, they formed one of the most powerful and lucrative business partnerships of all time. In the arrangement, it was clear to all (except Frick himself sometimes) that Carnegie was the dominant partner. Carnegie typically served as the capitalist entrepreneur who brokered the deals and worked the financial negotiations, while Frick generally managed the hands-on affairs of the steel empire.

Frick's management style, like most Gilded Age industrialists, was ruthless and efficient—hard on workers, easy on stockholders, and indefatigable on the competition. This tough approach got him shot and stabbed nearly to death in 1892 during the **Homestead Strike** by an **anarchist** named Alexander Berkman. The assailant entered Frick's office in Pittsburgh, caught the unsuspecting Frick seated at his desk, and fired two shots at his head. Wounded severely and bleeding profusely from the neck, Frick, with the help of an assistant who happened to be in the room at the time, wrestled Berkman to the ground, then Berkman stabbed him several times in the leg. Frick recovered unusually quickly, and to the public eye seemed not to have been greatly affected by the incident. Indeed, Frick never changed his tactics in dealing harshly with his workers, and never expressed any remorse later in life about his methods. He simply continued thereafter to help Carnegie build the corporation, until 1898 when the two had an irreconcilable difference that resulted in their parting ways. Frick walked away with one of the largest fortunes in American history, although not nearly as large as Carnegie's. Like most of the Gilded Age tycoons, he left the bulk of his fortune to posterity through various philanthropic enterprises.

– G –

GARFIELD, JAMES A. (1831–1881). Born in northeastern Ohio, Garfield rose from humble birth to become a professor, college president, Ohio legislator, Civil War major general, ordained minister, congressional leader, and president of the United States. During the Gilded Age, he rose through the ranks of the **Republican Party** in the House of Representatives, surviving his implication in the **Credit Mobilier Scandal**, to become minority leader from 1877–1881. He earned the GOP's nomination for president in 1880 as a compromise among the party's various factions. He defeated **Democrat Winfield Scott Hancock** in the election, but served less than 4 months as president before being assassinated. After the Garfield administration repeatedly turned down office-seeker Charles Guiteau for a federal appointment, the mentally deranged Guiteau shot Garfield on 2 July 1881, as he stood at a train station in Washington, D.C. One bullet passed through Garfield's shoulder and out his back, while the other lodged in his chest. Garfield languished for more than 2 months before finally succumbing on 19 September. He was the second president to be assassinated in just 16 years. Ironically, he became greater after his death than he had been in life. His assassination prompted Congress and new President **Chester A. Arthur** to pass the **Pendleton Civil Service** Act in 1883, which reformed the spoils system that had led to his death.

GEORGE, HENRY. *See* "PROGRESS AND POVERTY."

GERONIMO (ca. 1823–1909). Born "Goyathlay" or "Goyahkla," this Apache warrior's name translates roughly to "one who yawns." The name "Geronimo" was a nickname, the origins and meaning of which are unclear. Although not born among the Chiricahua band of Apaches in Arizona, he allied with them early in life. In the 1870s, he emerged as the main leader of the band because of his cunning, stealth, and bravery in guerrilla warfare, and came to personify **Indian** resistance to both U.S. and Mexican authority. Seen by whites generally as a bandit and a bloody savage, he managed to elude capture throughout the early 1880s. His surrender to General Nelson Miles at Skeleton Canyon in Arizona on 4 September 1886 was/ is widely regarded as the end of the great Indian wars in American history, notwithstanding the fact that the **Wounded Knee Massacre** was yet to happen. Upon capture, government forces sent Geronimo to reservations in Florida, Alabama, and **Oklahoma**, in turn. He also received the honor of touring and appearing before white audiences at public events as the great Indian "chief," despite technically never having been a chief. He converted to Christianity in his old age and urged his people to follow its tenets. One of his final acts was to dictate his memoirs to a white writer, supplying posterity with valuable information about a fast-dying Native American culture. He died of natural causes on the reservation at Fort Sill, Oklahoma. *See also* TOMBSTONE, ARIZONA.

GILDED AGE, THE: A TALE OF TO-DAY. A satirical novel written by **Mark Twain** and Charles Dudley Warner in 1873, this 400-plus-page work of fiction pokes fun not only at government **corruption**, but also at American society in general in the post-Civil War period. It caricatures politicians from the highest senators to the lowest local judges, as ambitious, greedy, hypocritical, and shallow. Written in the wake of the infamous **Credit Mobilier** and **Tweed** Ring scandals of 1872–1873 (and some lesser scandals that have now been all-but-forgotten to history), it tells the interconnected stories of several unscrupulous congressmen and private citizens alike who plot and scheme to make their fame and fortunes by either breaking the law or twisting the democratic system to their own advantage. Some of the unsavory features of the system that it ridicules include graft, bribery, extortion, murder, land speculation, **railroad** kickbacks, discrimination against **women**, **religious** hypocrisy, racial problems in the South, land-grant colleges, abuses of American **Indians**, and, most important, lobbying and the pork-barrel process.

The title indicates the thesis: the United States in the 1870s was experiencing what people generally regarded as a "golden" age, when it was actually nothing more than a "gilded age"—a time when a thin veneer of material prosperity concealed the rot and decay of American society and government underneath. The book, which Twain cowrote early in his career, was his only non-solo novel. Eclipsed by his more famous books that followed, *The Gilded Age* would perhaps be almost totally forgotten today were it not for the use of the title to define an era of American history. Even so, it shows glimpses of Twain's literary genius and his astute ability for accurate, biting social and political commentary. *See also* LITERATURE.

GLADDEN, WASHINGTON (1836–1918). Born in east-central Pennsylvania, Solomon Washington Gladden grew up on a farm near Lake Ontario in New York. Ordained a minister in the Congregational Church in 1860, he served as pastor at various churches in New York and Massachusetts before accepting a pastoral position in Columbus, Ohio, in 1882, which he retained until his retirement in 1914. He spent his career advocating the **Social Gospel**, which meant he championed social justice, clean government, and urged Christians to embrace science and modernity rather than live with outdated traditions and notions. He published his first book in 1868 and would ultimately write more than 30 others. Among the most notable are *Working People and Their Employers* (1876), *Burning Questions* (1890), and *Who Wrote the Bible* (1891). He became the editor of the **religion** section of the *New York Independent* in 1871, which gave him an audience of perhaps a million readers. He used his editorial column to decry the **corruption** of the **Tweed** Ring and **Tammany Hall**, among other things. Although he supported workers' rights and **trade unions**, thus opposing the nearly unlimited power that many Gilded Age employers wielded under the laissez-faire mentality of that time, he drew the line at advocating socialism. Simple Christian principles, if applied to the social problems of the day, he believed, would be enough. He helped found the American Economic Association in 1885, served as vice president of the American Missionary

Association (AMA) from 1894–1901, and became president of the AMA thereafter until 1904. In his early years in Columbus, he fought for stricter blue laws and temperance reforms, and in his later years he fought against racial segregation and anti-Catholicism. Despite his own prejudices against religious and ethnic minorities, which were common in that generation, he believed everyone deserved equal protection under the law and equal opportunities to achieve the American dream. *See also* LITERATURE.

GLIDDEN, JOSEPH. *See* BARBED WIRE.

GOLD RUSH. *See* KLONDIKE GOLD RUSH.

GOLD STANDARD. *See* FREE SILVER.

GOMPERS, SAMUEL (1850–1924). Born in England, Gompers moved with his Jewish family to New York City in 1863, and became a U.S. citizen in 1872. His father was a cigar-maker, so Samuel apprenticed in that trade. Involved in the early struggles of the Cigar Makers' International Union, he became a leader and helped breathe new life into the organization after 1877. As is true for all **trade union** leaders, he fought for better wages and benefits for workers. In 1881, he founded the Federation of Organized Trades and Labor Unions, which 5 years later evolved into the larger American Federation of Labor (AFL). It encompassed a wide variety of industries and interests, but it primarily focused on skilled, rather than unskilled, labor. It became the main competitor of the older, more established **Knights of Labor** (KOL). When the KOL affiliated with radical socialists in the 1890s, the more moderate AFL siphoned off much of its membership and thus became the largest association of trade unions in the country by the turn of the century. Gompers steadfastly refused to wed the AFL to a national political party, preferring to work with whichever party held power at the time. There was, however, a natural predisposition to work with the **Democrats** at the local level in most cases. Because Gompers founded the AFL and served as its national president every year but one from 1886–1924, he and the AFL were virtually synonymous as long as he lived.

GOULD, JAY (1836–1892). Born to a poor family in the Catskills of southern New York, Jason Gould grew into a self-made man and ultimately became the most notorious tycoon-scoundrel of the Gilded Age. From humble beginnings on a farm, he progressed to hardware store clerk, land surveyor, tanner, stock speculator, author, and **railroad** magnate—all by the age of 30. His first claim to fame came in the late 1860s when Daniel Drew, in a well-publicized feud with **Cornelius Vanderbilt** over control of the Erie Railroad, brought him in as a corporate leader. Soon, Drew sold out to Gould and fellow businessman James Fisk. As director of the Erie, Gould managed to pry control from Vanderbilt by waging the "Erie War" against him, which involved arming workers to drive away Vanderbilt's people and watering the railroad stock to make it so worthless that the Commodore would no longer want it. When Vanderbilt prosecuted him for illegal business dealings, Gould bribed members of the New York legislature to get favorable treatment. He likewise kept a friendly and lucrative partnership going with the corrupt political boss of New York City, **William Marcy Tweed**.

Meanwhile, in 1869, Gould sought to make more money by manipulating the value of gold on the free market and influencing federal treasury policy. He and Fisk bought up as much gold as they could, hoping to inflate its price artificially, then convinced the **Ulysses S. Grant** administration to buy the gold from them. When Grant caught on to the scheme, however, he abruptly changed policy, selling off government gold supplies, flooding the market, and thus deflating the value. This caused a temporary economic crisis called **Black Friday**. Publicity about the scheme thereafter irreparably harmed Gould's reputation. Soon he was forced out as director of the Erie, but he merely started over by focusing on investments in western railroad lines. By 1882, he controlled 15 percent of all the rail lines in the United States. A year later he made a fortune when he sold his interest in the Union Pacific. In the meantime, he invested heavily in Western Union Telegraph Company, turning it into an extremely profitable monopoly. He also began investing in the elevated rail lines in New York City, which likewise proved a successful business strategy.

By all accounts, Gould was among the most shrewd and ruthless businessmen in an age known for them. **John D. Rockefeller**, for example, considered him the most astute player he had ever met in the money-making game. Vanderbilt was never beaten by anyone but Gould, which is a testament to both men's business acumen. He had no permanent friends, but he used people for personal gain, and seemed to relish in winning money games even while losing relationships and reputation. For this, he has generally been called the prototype for all other Gilded Age "Robber Barons," although, as with most of them, he was simultaneously an empire builder for the American economy. *See also* CORRUPTION.

GRADY, HENRY (1850–1889). Born in Athens, Georgia, Henry Woodfin Grady, matriculated at his hometown institution, the University of Georgia. Working as a newspaper reporter, he quickly built a reputation for his clear, thoughtful essays on the problems facing the South in the 1870s. After becoming part owner and managing editor of the *Atlanta Constitution* in 1880, he achieved national fame on 22 December 1886 when he gave an after-dinner speech to the New England Society at Delmonico's Restaurant in New York City. His speech focused on North-South reconciliation via the industrial development of the South. His ability to deliver this pro-business, pro-northern-investment-in-the-South message, while simultaneously discouraging his audience from heeding the call of racial reformers to try to solve the South's "Negro problem," elevated him to "spokesman of the New South." At 36, he became an instant celebrity, and had a bright future that even included a possible run for the vice presidency of the United States. Unfortunately for him, within 3 years he was dead. In December 1889, while suffering from pneumonia, he refused to cancel a speaking engagement at a Boston Merchants' Association banquet, the audience of which included **Grover Cleveland** and **Andrew Carnegie**, among other leading public figures. In this, his final speech, he moved the audience to a standing ovation and tears of sympathy for the beleaguered condition of the post-Civil War South, of which he seemed the embodiment—standing weakly, trembling with fever, voice shaking, nearing death. He died shortly after returning home to Atlanta. *See also* AFRICAN AMERICANS; PRESS, THE.

GRAND ARMY OF THE REPUBLIC (GAR). After the Civil War, Union veterans began organizing into fraternal groups to keep their military ties and war memories alive. The group that ultimately became the largest and most successful, the GAR, was formed in Illinois in 1866. In 1868, under the direction of John Logan, it began the practice of observing 30 May as "Decoration Day," a day to commemorate fallen soldiers, thus establishing what later became known as Memorial Day. From the election of 1868 to the turn of the century, the GAR became an arm of the **Republican Party**. It comprised such a large voting block that it determined the outcome of many GOP nominations and federal elections. It engaged in "waving the bloody shirt" to remind voters which party had fought to preserve the Union and which had fought to destroy it. Its other great impetus lay in lobbying for veterans' benefits and pensions, which it did successfully, except when the **Democratic** president and non-veteran **Grover Cleveland** was in the White House. The organization's zenith came in 1890 when it boasted more than 400,000 members and wielded great influence over the **Benjamin Harrison** administration and the **Billion Dollar Congress**, convincing them to spend down the national treasury surplus by increasing pensions for veterans. When Harrison appointed GAR member Corporal James Tanner, a double amputee, to run the pension bureau, Tanner remarked, "God help the surplus!" Not surprisingly, the number of pensioners doubled during the Harrison administration. The GAR spawned several auxiliary groups as well, such as Sons of the Union Veterans of the Civil War and the National Woman's Relief Corps. *See also* NATIONAL RIFLE ASSOCIATION.

GRAND OLD PARTY (GOP). *See* REPUBLICAN PARTY.

GRANGE, THE NATIONAL. Founded in 1867 by a Minnesota farmer and clerk in the U.S. Department of Agriculture named Oliver H. Kelley and a few others, the Grange, also called the Order of the Patrons of Husbandry, is still in operation today. It served two purposes originally: one, to be a fraternal order and social club for Midwestern farmers who were otherwise isolated on their rural farms, and two, to work for improvement of economic conditions for farmers through cooperative business ventures and nonpartisan state/local politics. Essentially, it was the first nationwide farmers' union. The Grange grew slowly until the **Panic of 1873** hit the economy and jolted farmers into action. It reached its peak around 1875 in membership, money, and political power, and the states most strongly affected were Illinois, Wisconsin, Minnesota, and Iowa, although it ultimately saw chapters spring up in 37 states. Its most important function historically came in battles against the railroads, as it sought government regulation of shipping rates. Its two great moments of glory came with the favorable ruling in the **U.S. Supreme Court** case *Munn v. Illinois* in 1877 and with the creation of the **Interstate Commerce Commission** in 1887. It was also instrumental in getting free rural delivery of the U.S. mail, among other things. By 1890, the **National Farmers' Alliance** had largely displaced it as the political voice of American farmers, although the Grange continued unabated serving its social and fraternal purpose. *See also* GRANGER CASES.

GRANGER CASES. The National **Grange** focused heavily on getting government regulation of **railroad** shipping rates and granary warehousing rates. Arguing that the railroads and granaries were charging exorbitant or discriminatory prices for Midwestern farmers to use their services, several important **U.S. Supreme Court** cases resulted. The most important initially was *Munn v. Illinois* (1877), in which the court ruled that the state of Illinois had a constitutional right to regulate the rates that private businesses charged when it was deemed in the general public welfare. However, when the Illinois state regulatory commission sought to regulate shipping rates for a railroad that crossed the state line, the court held such actions unconstitutional in *Wabash v. Illinois* (1886). Fortunately for farmers, the result of this ruling turned out favorable in the end, as the **Grover Cleveland** administration and Congress reacted immediately by creating the **Interstate Commerce Commission**, putting regulation of 75 percent of the nation's railroad traffic (the percent that crossed state lines) under federal regulatory control.

GRANT, ULYSSES S. (1822–1885). Born Hiram Ulysses Grant in southern Ohio, Grant achieved fame as a Union Civil War general, and particularly the one who finally succeeded in capturing Richmond and defeating Robert E. Lee. Although he had never involved himself in politics before, in 1868 his war hero status propelled him to the presidency of the United States on the **Republican** ticket. Considering that Reconstruction was the major issue facing the nation at the time, having a Union general in the White House seemed logical. Because of his lack of political experience, however, the duties of the office proved too great for him almost immediately. Surrounding himself with unscrupulous advisors, his administration quickly degenerated into the most corrupt one to that point in American history. The first major scandal to rock his presidency, the **Black Friday** gold scheme, occurred a mere 6 months into his first term and led to speculation about his honesty and competence. An equally damaging scandal, the **Credit Mobilier** railroad scheme, occurred in 1872 as Grant stood for reelection. Nearly costing him a second term, he won a narrow victory, thanks to the newly enfranchised **African American** voters of the South. Even so, the **corruption** of the administration, in part, inspired the **Mark Twain** and Charles Dudley Warner novel, *The Gilded Age* (1873).

Grant's second term suffered from even more scandals, including the Whiskey Ring, the **Indian** Ring, and the Sanborn Incident. Making matters worse, however, was the most serious economic crisis in American history to that point, the **Panic of 1873**, which precipitated a depression that lasted 4 years. Grant and the Republican Congress passed the Coinage Act in 1873, which Democrats berated as the "Crime of '73," setting off a 23-year public debate over bimetallism as a federal economic policy. In **foreign affairs**, Grant controversially supported the annexation of Cuba and Santo Domingo, and his secretary of state, **Hamilton Fish**, negotiated a settlement in the *Alabama Claims Dispute*. The combination of scandals and weak leadership on the issue of Reconstruction after 1874 (when Democrats took control of Congress for the first time since before the war) led to Grant's historic reputation as one of the worst American presidents.

Grant's post-presidential years were marked by his failure in a bid for a third term in 1880, his presidency of the **National Rifle Association**, his struggle with terminal cancer, and his writing of memoirs. Upon discovering that he would soon die of throat cancer, he contracted with Mark Twain's publishing company to write his memoirs while he still had time. He died in upstate New York, and his memoirs came out posthumously in two volumes in 1885 and 1886 respectively. *See also* COLFAX, SCHUYLER; GOULD, JAY; LITERATURE; WILSON, HENRY.

GREAT BLIZZARD OF 1888. Also known as the "Great White Hurricane," this "nor'easter" was the worst storm of the Gilded Age, and vies for the storm of the century. Striking the Atlantic coast from roughly the Canadian border to Washington, D.C., it centered around New York and lasted 3 days, from 12 to 14 March, 1888. Beginning as a rainstorm on Sunday, 11 March, a wall of cold wind blowing continuously around 40 miles per hour joined the precipitation to create a dangerous, destructive sleet storm, followed by a blinding snowstorm. Although some rural areas reported heavier snowfall and faster wind speeds, the great metropolises of New York City, Boston, Philadelphia, and Baltimore bore the brunt of the storm's fury. In Manhattan the first day, people tried to go about their business as usual, but by Monday afternoon, it had become obvious that this was no ordinary storm. Rather than letting up, it grew worse. By nightfall, ice caked and then snapped the telegraph lines, making communication with the outside world impossible. Rail lines and city streets alike were blanketed in ice before being covered in 3 to 4 feet of snow. By Tuesday afternoon, transportation services around the city had come to a standstill. Nor was it possible for pedestrians to travel even a few city blocks from home to work without extreme difficulty. Consequently, stores closed, and people had to make do with whatever provisions they already possessed. Meanwhile, the temperature outside hovered in the single digits Fahrenheit, and many horses froze to death on city streets. The East River between Manhattan and Brooklyn froze solid so that people could walk across. Snow continued falling throughout Wednesday, creating drifts that completely swallowed houses in some areas, particularly in upstate New York. By Thursday, 15 March, the storm had passed, and temperatures began to climb, melting the snow and creating widespread flooding. It took 8 days to clear the streets of debris in the major cities. When the final tally of the damages was totaled, more than 400 people had died and more than $1 billion (adjusted) in property damage had been recorded.

GREAT RAILROAD STRIKE OF 1877. The **Panic of 1873** led to a national economic downturn that affected the bottom lines of **railroad** corporations as much as any other industry. To cut costs, the various rail companies slashed wages. By 1877, the economy had suffered its fourth straight year of stagnation, during which time railroad employees had more often than not seen their wages decrease rather than increase. On 14 July, the Great Railroad Strike began in the small town of Martinsburg, West Virginia, as employees of the Baltimore and Ohio Railroad protested their second pay cut in a year. Within a week, the strike had spread to Baltimore, Maryland; Pittsburgh and Philadelphia, Pennsylvania; St. Louis, Missouri; and many smaller cities, as well as to other railroad companies that had made similar wage cuts to stay competitive in the industry. Within 2 weeks, the strike had not only reached Chicago but also had shut down most railroad traffic throughout the whole state of Illinois. The strike became most acute in Chicago when the Workingmen's Party, a minor Marxist organization, rallied the masses behind the strikers.

At each location, the initial reaction to the strike came from the railroad executives, who called first for local law enforcement to break the strike. Local police and sheriffs were generally ineffective, however, because they often feared the strikers or sympathized with their cause. The various state governors then sent in their state militias, but they also could not handle the problem alone. Ultimately, federal troops were needed to break the strike in the areas of strongest resistance. The strike became the first major problem for new President **Rutherford B. Hayes** to solve. He did not hesitate to send the troops, some of which had only recently been removed from the South at the end of Reconstruction. After more than 2 weeks of rioting and bloody clashes between strikers and federal troops, order was finally restored in most places. The final tally recorded more than 70 people killed, hundreds wounded and arrested, and untold millions of dollars of property damage.

Perhaps the most interesting fact about the strike in the larger context of American history is that it showed how the nation suffered from other problems just as serious as the racial problems of the South—which had consumed everyone's attention for so many years. Indeed, Reconstruction had separated the American people for 12 years along racial and sectional lines, but this strike showed that in the post-Reconstruction era Americans would be separated along class lines and, in a way, along railroad lines. *See also* HANCOCK, WINFIELD SCOTT; TRADE UNIONS.

GREELEY, HORACE (1811–1872). Born in New Hampshire, Greeley moved to New York City as an adult and started a career in the newspaper business. In 1841, he opened the *New York Tribune*, which quickly developed a reputation as one of the most unbiased and insightful papers in the country. Over the next two decades, Greeley evolved from a Whig to a **Republican**. During the Civil War, he was both an ardent supporter of the Union war effort and a frequently loud critic of the Abraham Lincoln administration. He identified with the Radical Republicans during and after the war, yet did an about-face after the election of **Ulysses Grant** as president. By 1872, he had turned completely against Grant and called for a new GOP nominee. In the first presidential election of the Gilded Age, a group of like-minded Republicans calling themselves **Liberals** nominated him to run against Grant. The **Democrats**, meanwhile, were in such a desperate state at the time that they threw their support behind Greeley, too, despite the fact that Greeley had made a career of opposing that party. In the midst of a poorly managed campaign, Greeley lost control of his newspaper to his friend and fellow editor **Whitelaw Reid**. This, combined with the death of his wife, his defeat in the election, and a penchant for eccentricity that he had been cultivating all his life, finally pushed him over the edge. He suffered a mental collapse, and on 29 November 1872, he died. He left a mixed legacy of good journalism, popular and unpopular editorial/political views, and strange social behaviors. *See also* PRESS, THE.

GREENBACKS. *See* BLACK FRIDAY GOLD SCANDAL; GOULD, JAY; GRANT, ULYSSES S.; SHERMAN, JOHN.

GUNFIGHT AT THE O. K. CORRAL. Around 3 p.m. on 26 October 1881, the most famous shootout between lawmen and outlaws in the history of the "wild West" occurred. The scene was in **Tombstone, Arizona**, a silver mining town that attracted all kinds of unsavory elements, including gamblers, alcoholics, barroom blowhards, genuine gunslingers, stagecoach robbers, and prostitutes. It also served as the local hub of commerce for cattle rustlers and law-abiding ranchers and cattle drivers alike, who were typically lumped together as "**cowboys**," and who were sometimes difficult to distinguish from one another. Among these cowboys were Ike and Billy Clanton, Frank and Tom McLaury, Billy Claiborne, and West Fuller. The job of distinguishing between the good guys and bad guys fell to local law enforcement officials. In Tombstone, they included Virgil Earp, the official "city marshal," his brothers Wyatt and Morgan, who served as deputies when necessary, and sheriff Johnny Behan. Two complicating factors were added to this mix, however. One, Doc Holliday, a gambler and gunslinger with a checkered past, allied himself with the Earp brothers against his foes, the Clantons; and two, the Earps and Behan were rivals for power in town, and Behan wanted to protect the cowboys from the Earps and Holliday.

Several minor disputes between various members of these law-men and cowboy factions had occurred in recent weeks leading up to the fateful day of the shootout, and each side accused the other of stagecoach holdups and attempted murder. The immediate cause of the gunfight, however, was a barroom altercation between Doc Holliday and Ike Clanton the day before. Finally, on 26 October, the Earps and Holliday decided to rid the town of the Clantons and their cohorts once and for all. The four walked in unison down Fremont Street with loaded weapons (one shotgun and three pistols) toward the O. K. Corral where the Clanton and McLaury brothers had converged. The plan was supposedly to disarm and arrest the cow-boys, but words exchanged between the two groups at close range led immediately to the lawmen opening fire on the cowboys, some of whom were not armed. For the next 30 seconds, each side tried to empty their weapons on the other. In the fracas, Frank and Tom McLaury and Billy Clanton were killed, while Ike Clanton safely ran for his life. On the other side, Virgil and Morgan Earp and Doc Holliday were wounded. Neither Behan nor Claiborne and Fuller had arrived on the scene in time to participate or stop the fight.

Thereafter, the three dead cowboys were put on display in town in open caskets before being buried in Boothill Cemetery. The Earps and Holliday, meanwhile, stood trial for murder. The trial lasted through most of November and became a media sensation, as newspapers in San Francisco picked up the story. In the end, the defendants walked away scot-free, but not without controversy. The question of who were the good guys and who were the bad guys in this affair persisted not only through the rest of the Gilded Age but also remains to the present.

– H –

HANCOCK, WINFIELD SCOTT (1824–1886). Born near Philadelphia, Pennsylvania, he was named for the famous American general Winfield Scott, with whom he would later have the honor of serving in the Mexican War and the Civil War. Between the two wars, he fought in the 1855 Seminole War in Florida, where he had his first exposure to American **Indian** affairs. During the Civil War, he fought in several important battles, but his role at Gettysburg was most notable. There he was wounded, but survived and was promoted to major general by war's end. After the war, he conducted the executions of the conspirators in the assassination of Abraham Lincoln. He was then assigned to the West, where he had more dealings with Native Americans. In 1867, he wrote a memoir expressing his thoughts on Indian affairs. As military Reconstruction began, he was assigned to oversee the Texas-Louisiana district, where he developed political opinions favorable to the **Democrats**. Consequently, in 1868, his name was seriously mentioned for the presidential nomination of that party. This put him at odds with the winning candidate, **Ulysses S. Grant**, and the **Republican Party**. Grant thus removed him from his post in the former Confederacy, sending him back west again, then finally stationing him in New York City. He saw important action in both places, dealing with the Indians yet again in the Dakotas and commanding troops in the East during the **Great Railroad Strike of 1877**. Although his name came up again for the Democratic nomination in 1876, he did not win it until 1880. He lost the popular vote to **James A. Garfield** by only 2,000 votes, but was soundly defeated in the Electoral College, 214 to 155. The following year, he became president of the **National Rifle Association**. After his death, his widow published his biography in 1887. Although he chose to affiliate himself with the minority party and to espouse unpopular political views, Hancock was universally esteemed as a man of the highest integrity and character. Remembered primarily for his Civil War service, he became an important, if largely forgotten, political leader of the Gilded Age.

HANNA, MARK (1837–1904). Born in northeastern Ohio, Marcus Alonzo Hanna attended high school and **college** in the Cleveland area before serving in the Union army in the Civil War, then going into the grocery business for several years. From there, he invested in iron and coal, bought a newspaper and a theater, became president of a bank, grew quite wealthy, and evolved into a **Republican** boss in Cleveland politics. He worked his way up in the GOP in Ohio by supporting various successful candidates for president or Congress, such as **James Garfield**, **John Sherman**, and **William McKinley**. His association with McKinley made him a national figure. After McKinley lost his seat in Congress in 1890, Hanna helped him win the gubernatorial races of 1891 and 1893. Sensing an opportunity to play king maker in 1896, Hanna successfully pushed for McKinley's nomination for president at the Republican National Convention. He then won the job of chair of the Republican National Committee, in which capacity he basically served as McKinley's campaign manager. His strategy for raising money from his fellow millionaires by milking their fear of **Democrat/Populist** opponent **William Jennings Bryan**'s radical economic ideas worked amazingly well. Likewise, his strategy of shipping voters to the doorstep of McKinley's Akron home to listen to prepared speeches and rehearsed questions and answers, was equally brilliant. Hanna's management of the campaign of 1896 served as a "how-to" guide for all future presidential campaigns going into the 20th century. In 1897, the Ohio legislature sent Hanna to the U.S. Senate, where he served until his death. During that time, his most notable distinction was the mutual antagonism he shared with the newest star in the Republican Party, **Theodore Roosevelt**.

HARDIN, JOHN WESLEY (1853–1895). Born a few miles north of modern Dallas, Texas, John Wesley Hardin was the son of a Methodist minister who named him for the English founder of Methodism, John Wesley. Reared in southeastern Texas, less than 100 miles from Houston, he had a problem controlling his temper and soon found himself in trouble with the law while just a young teenager. Not following in his father's footsteps, he lived a wild and hazardous life. He first became a **cowboy** on the Chisholm Trail, driving cattle from Texas to Abilene, Kansas. In Abilene, he befriended Sheriff **"Wild Bill" Hickok**, who took a liking to the youngster, despite his reportedly having killed a black man, several Mexicans, and perhaps three Union soldiers in Texas. Some time around 1871, Hardin committed the only completely indefensible cold blooded murder on his resume when he shot a man in an Abilene hotel for snoring too loudly. He immediately skipped town to avoid arrest by Hickok, heading back to Texas. There he moved around frequently—from Gonzales to Trinity, DeWitt, Wilson, and Brown Counties, among others—running with gangs of fellow outlaws at times, and staying with family at other times, all the while shooting those who got in his way. In 1874, Hardin killed a man (a deputy sheriff in Brown County) who made him a public enemy worthy of being captured by the Texas Rangers. To escape, Hardin fled to Alabama and Florida, took on an alias, and tried to settle down with his wife and children. Tipped off by an intercepted letter intended for one of Hardin's Texas relatives, the Rangers finally tracked him down in 1877 and, after a shootout, arrested him on a train near Pensacola, Florida. Tried in Austin, Texas, he was sentenced to 25 years. Oddly, in prison, he earned a law degree, and was released after 15 years, supposedly a reformed man. Once out, he opened a law practice in El Paso, but returned to his old ways—associating with prostitutes, gamblers, and other miscreants. In 1895, while sitting in a saloon playing cards, he was abruptly shot dead by one of his associates—a fate strangely similar to that of his former friend, Wild Bill Hickok.

HARLAN, JOHN MARSHALL (1833–1911). Born near Danville, Kentucky, to a wealthy, slaveholding family, Harlan grew up around influential Whig politicians with a federalist/nationalist view of the Constitution. After practicing law and trying his hand at politics, he enlisted in the Union army in the Civil War. Joining the **Republican Party** thereafter, he helped secure the presidential nomination of **Rutherford B. Hayes**, who, upon the **Compromise of 1877**, in turn appointed him to the **U.S. Supreme Court**. For the next 34 years, he had the dubious distinction of holding the minority opinion, and sometimes being the lone dissenter, on key cases involving civil rights and other issues designed to expand the power of the federal government at the expense of the states. His first major dissent came in the *Civil Rights Cases* in 1883, when he upheld the constitutionality of the Civil Rights Act of 1875. More dramatically, however, he stood as the lone dissenter in the infamous ***Plessy v. Ferguson*** ruling of 1896, in which he sought to protect the rights of **African Americans** against the capriciousness of both southern state law and his colleagues on the bench. He also dissented in *Pollock v. Farmers' Loan & Trust Co.* in 1895 to uphold the constitutionality of Congress levying a federal income tax. Although often despised in his own generation for his dissenting opinions, history has largely vindicated him on these issues. Harlan's service on the court transcended the Gilded Age; he served until his death, leaving a legacy of courageous, if often unpopular, opinions. He also fathered a future Supreme Court Justice, John Marshall Harlan II.

HARRIS, JOEL CHANDLER (1848–1908). Born an illegitimate child in rural Putnam County, in central Georgia, Harris first apprenticed as a newspaperman at age 13. As an adult, this talented but shy stutterer worked in the newspaper business in New Orleans and Savannah before joining the staff of the *Atlanta Constitution* in the late 1870s. There he developed his "Uncle Remus" children's tales, which launched his fame. The lead character was a slave on a Georgia plantation who spoke with a thick black southern accent and had a knack for dramatic storytelling. The most famous tale involves Br'er (Brother) Rabbit outsmarting Br'er Fox by using reverse psychology, feigning terror at the thought of being thrown into the briar patch when that is actually the very thing that would allow him to escape. Such tales were neither new nor original. They derived from experiences of actual slaves whom Harris encountered while growing up. Robert Roosevelt, the uncle of **Theodore Roosevelt**, who also had family roots in Georgia, published some of the first tales. Roosevelt's version lacked the endearing development of Harris's, however, and thus had little literary impact. In 1880, Harris published his first book, *Uncle Remus: His Songs and Sayings*, which he followed with several more Uncle Remus collections and some books and articles on other subjects as well.

Harris has been criticized in the late 20th century for basically stealing black folklore and profiting from it. In his defense, however, there was no mechanism in place during the Gilded Age for copyrighting such material. Besides, Harris clearly felt sympathetic toward **African Americans** in real life, taking a more liberal position on race relations than most of his peers in an era when the common view held that blacks were inferior and should be treated as such. Interestingly, once he ascended to the presidency, Theodore Roosevelt congratulated Harris for his success in publishing the tales that both men had heard as children, and called him a literary genius. *See also* LITERATURE.

HARRISON, BENJAMIN (1833–1901). Born in southwestern Ohio, Harrison was the grandson of former President William Henry Harrison and the great grandson of the "Benjamin Harrison" who had signed the U.S. Declaration of Independence in 1776. A lawyer by training, he set up practice in Indianapolis, Indiana, in 1854. He attained the rank of colonel (and temporarily the rank of general) in the Civil War, in which he served honorably, but without any great distinction. From the war's end to 1881, he likewise did nothing extraordinary to distinguish himself, but he stayed active in the **Republican Party** and benefited from his famous name. He served one term in the U.S. Senate from 1881–1888, again without any notable accomplishments to show for it. His lackluster credentials actually helped him gain the Republican nomination for president in 1888, because he had no record that offended any faction. He defeated **Grover Cleveland** by winning the Electoral College vote only, not the popular vote, and became the 23rd U.S. president.

Harrison's one term in the White House is memorable for several important pieces of legislation and one major legislative defeat by filibuster. Working with the **Billion Dollar Congress**, Harrison passed the **McKinley Tariff**, the **Sherman** Anti-Trust Act, and the Sherman Silver Purchase Act, all in 1890. In that same year, he failed to get the **Federal Elections Bill** passed, because the **Democrats** staged the most dramatic filibuster in American history to that point. His administration was considered highly partisan at the time, a perspective that historians have done little to change in subsequent years. Once he left office, Harrison returned to Indiana, where he again did nothing particularly noteworthy for the rest of his life. *See also* MORTON, LEVI P.; REED, THOMAS B.; REID, WHITELAW.

HATFIELDS AND MCCOYS. The most notorious family feud of the Gilded Age took place in rural Appalachia near Pikeville, Kentucky, but made it all the way to the **U.S. Supreme Court** before it was over. It pitted the Hatfield clan of Logan County, West Virginia, against the McCoy clan of Pike County, Kentucky. The patriarchs of the clans were "Devil Anse" Hatfield and "Ole Ran'l" McCoy, each of whom had 13 children, but also had extended family and friends who were drawn into the feud. The families knew each other well, had done business with one another, and were even kin by marriage. Their feud began with tensions created during the Civil War, when the Hatfields sided with the Confederacy and the McCoys with the Union. When wounded Union veteran Harmon McCoy was found murdered after coming home from the war, a relative of the Hatfield clan named Jim Vance, a Confederate, became the prime suspect, although he could not be proven guilty.

In 1873, the two brothers-in-law, Floyd Hatfield and Randolph McCoy, who had married sisters, argued over who owned a particular hog. They went to the local court, where a Hatfield presided as judge. Various family members testified along strict clan lines, until Bill Staton, who was related to both, sided with the Hatfields. Floyd Hatfield thus got the hog, but the McCoys eventually got revenge, killing Staton several months later after numerous heated arguments and fights. Two McCoy brothers, Paris and Sam, were charged with his murder, tried, and acquitted on grounds of self-defense. In 1880, Johnse Hatfield, the family playboy, retaliated by wooing the young and pretty Roseanna McCoy to run off with him. This act hit the McCoy clan in their most vulnerable spot and raised the stakes in the feud considerably. The McCoys struck back by capturing Johnse and taking him to the local jail to be held pending a hearing. Roseanna, however, alerted Devil Anse Hatfield of the situation, and he rounded up a posse and freed his son.

The feud stalled until an election day rolled around in 1882, and members of both families showed up at the polls in Kentucky at the same time. A fight broke out in which three McCoys attacked one Hatfield and killed him, provoking the Hatfield clan to kill the three McCoys in return. By this point, the infamy of the feud had spread throughout Appalachia, and the governors of both West Virginia and Kentucky got involved. Since the dispute was of the interstate variety, complications arose that made the wheels of justice turn slowly. Five years passed with no progress made. By 1887, however, the

Hatfields began to fear that they would soon be called to account for the events in 1882, so they plotted to eliminate the witnesses, which led to their murdering two more McCoys in 1888. This action finally forced the case out of local and into federal jurisdiction. Nine Hatfields were tried for murder, four were given life in prison, and one named Ellison Mounts was sentenced to death. He was publicly hanged in 1890. Thereafter, each side wearied of the feud, and neither pursued vengeance anymore.

HAWAII, ANNEXATION OF. Hawaii had been the jewel of the Pacific from its discovery by the English explorer Captain Cook in the 1770s until the 1890s. Like England, the United States began cultivating a close relationship with the native Hawaiians in the early 1800s for economic and **religious** reasons. At the time the natives lived in warring tribes, all competing for control of a unified government for the islands. In the mid-1800s, many diverse ethnic groups came to inhabit the islands, including Chinese and Portuguese, and, in the late 1800s, Japanese. American missionaries and businessmen dominated this ethnic milieu, however, and put the United States in the best position among the various imperialist nations in the 1880s–1890s to take complete control of the islands.

In 1887, Americans already living in Hawaii took the first important steps toward making the islands a territory of the United States. Lorrin A. Thurston, a newspaper publisher born to missionaries in Hawaii took charge of a small group of fellow Americans that came to be called the Committee of Public Safety and threateningly forced the "Bayonet Constitution" on the native King Kalakaua. This new constitution gave more power to the whites and less to the natives. Six years later, when Queen Liluokalani tried to restore the old system of government, the Committee of Public Safety (with the help of some U.S. marines sent by U.S. Minister to Hawaii John L. Stevens) staged a *coup*, deposed the queen, and appointed Sanford Dole as provisional president of Hawaii.

In 1893–1894, Dole and Thurston tried to persuade President **Grover Cleveland** and Congress to annex Hawaii. Cleveland, after an investigation, declared the new government illegitimate, however, and refused to support annexation. On 4 July 1894, therefore, the Dole government declared itself the independent and sovereign Republic of Hawaii.

Within three years, **William McKinley** had been elected president, and the annexationists had hope once again. Events during and after the **Spanish–American War** in 1898, in which the U.S. Navy traversed the Pacific Ocean to fight in the Philippines, brought the annexation of Hawaii back to the fore. It allowed annexationists to explain more easily why the United States needed to possess the islands for strategic national defense reasons, rather than for merely economic and racial reasons. On 7 July 1898, the United States formally annexed Hawaii, giving it "Territory" status. *See also* AMERICAN ANTI-IMPERIALIST LEAGUE; FOREIGN AFFAIRS.

HAY, JOHN (1838–1905). Born in south-central Indiana, John Milton Hay grew up in Illinois, attending school in Springfield, before moving to Rhode Island to matriculate at Brown University. He then studied law in Illinois, becoming a friend of Abraham Lincoln just in time for Lincoln's presidential election in 1860. He moved with the Lincolns to Washington, D.C., where he served as the president's personal secretary until the 1865 assassination. He also served a short stint in the Union army during the Civil War, attaining the rank of colonel. His intimacy with Lincoln allowed Hay to coauthor two authoritative books on him—*Abraham Lincoln: A History* (10 volumes, 1890), and *Abraham Lincoln: Complete Works* (1894). Between the war and his publication of these books, Hay became a notable writer of newspaper editorials for the *New York Tribune* and of original works of poetry. Upon marrying into a wealthy family from Cleveland, Ohio, he moved there and pursued a leisurely literary career for most of the Gilded Age. He served 2 years in the **Rutherford B. Hayes** administration, however, as assistant secretary of state. For the next 16 years, he was out of public office, more because he backed the wrong **Republican** candidates during those years than by choice.

In 1896, Hay finally chose the right candidate, **William McKinley**, who promptly awarded him the post of ambassador to Great Britain for 1 year, before elevating him to secretary of state. That important position was all the more so at this critical time, as the **Spanish–American War** was just ending and the administration was ready to embark upon its path toward control of overseas territories via an imperialist **foreign** policy. He famously called that 2-month military conflict "a splendid little war." Hay made two of the greatest contributions to not only American but also world history by formulating the Open Door Policy with regard to China in 1900 and then negotiating three treaties to secure the right of the United States to build the Panama Canal. He continued to serve as secretary of state in the **Theodore Roosevelt** administration until his death. *See also* LITERATURE; PRESS, THE.

HAYES, RUTHERFORD B. (1822–1893). Born in central Ohio, Rutherford Birchard Hayes attended Harvard Law School in Massachusetts, started a practice in Cincinnati, entered politics as a Whig, and helped organize the **Republican Party** in Ohio in 1855. In the Civil War, he attained the rank of major general temporarily, was nearly fatally wounded, and won a seat in the U.S. House of Representatives without even leaving the battlefield or campaigning. Elected governor of Ohio in 1867, 1869, and 1875, he developed a reputation as an honest and moderate leader at a time of Republican excess and radicalism. In the presidential election of 1876, he and **Democrat Samuel J. Tilden** became embroiled in the most serious vote-counting dispute in American history, as both sides claimed three southern states' and one western state's electoral votes. Congress had to set up a special Joint Electoral Commission to resolve the dispute. Reaching an agreement on 26 February 1877, the election was certified in Hayes's favor just 2 days before the 4 March inauguration, and the **Compromise of 1877** was accomplished. Hayes's term as president thereafter consisted of carrying out the conditions of the compromise, pushing for civil service reform, breaking the **Great Railroad Strike of 1877**, and vetoing the Bland-Allison Act. After leaving office, he spent the rest of his life working for various humanitarian causes, notably serving as chair of the two **Mohonk Conferences on the Negro Question** in 1890–1891. *See also* WHEELER, WILLIAM A.

HAYMARKET INCIDENT. On 1 May 1886, various **trade unions** and political factions staged strikes and rallies simultaneously in several cities around the United States to promote the 8-hour workday. This was the first observance of what became known as "May Day" around the world. Chicago, Illinois, hosted the largest strike, with nearly 100,000 workers participating. At the McCormick Harvester factory in the Windy City, the strike continued for 2 more days. A small fracas broke out there on 3 May among strikers, replacement workers, and police, which turned deadly. The following day, 4 May, at Chicago's Haymarket Square, local labor leaders and political agitators rallied the masses to decry the previous day's trouble. Police were there for crowd control. The rally proceeded without incident for quite a while before some anonymous person in the mob threw a bomb that killed seven policemen. The police then opened fire on the crowd, killing four workers. Perhaps 100 or more people were wounded in the melee.

The next day the police began rounding up local labor leaders and agitators, lumping them all together as supposed **anarchists**. When authorities could not identify the bomber, they took eight men into custody as conspirators guilty of inciting the bombing and riot through their incendiary speeches and **literature**. Most of the defendants were German **immigrants**, and there was a touch of xenophobia among the prosecutors, judge, and jury. Mainly, however, there was generally a bias against organized labor and Marxist ideology in Gilded Age America. Not surprisingly, the jury found all eight men guilty, issuing seven death sentences and sentencing one to 15 years. Three eventually received pardons from the German-American governor of Illinois, **John Peter Altgeld**. Five were sentenced to hang, but one of them committed suicide in prison the day before the hanging. The others went to the gallows together in a very public execution on 11 November 1887.

The verdict was controversial from the beginning, but the **U.S. Supreme Court** upheld it. Yet, over the decades, it came to be seen by most observers as a grave miscarriage of justice. The case was a setback for organized labor in the United States, but, ironically, it became a major catalyst for socialist labor movements in Europe. May Day became institutionalized in countries around the world as a commemoration to the victims of the Haymarket incident.

HEARST, WILLIAM RANDOLPH (1863–1951). Born in San Francisco to a millionaire miner and rancher father, he was sent to New Hampshire for private schooling before enrolling in Harvard University in Massachusetts in 1885. Expelled from Harvard for bad behavior, he took over one of his father's holdings, the *San Francisco Examiner* in 1887, soon turning it into the premier paper in the American West by imitating

Joseph Pulitzer's successful formula of excellent investigative reporting on political and business **corruption**, with colorful human interest stories and illustrations thrown in for entertainment. In 1895, he expanded his operations nationally by buying the struggling *New York Morning Journal* and doing more of the same right in Pulitzer's back yard. With his family fortune, he ultimately managed to hire some of the best writers in America, including **Mark Twain**, **Stephen Crane**, Ambrose Bierce, and Jack London. Hearst also lured "Yellow Kid" comic strip creator Richard F. Outcault away from Pulitzer's *New York World*, and sought to siphon off the *World*'s circulation by making the *Journal* more sensational in news coverage and presenting more tabloid topics.

The Cuban Revolution of 1895–1898 furnished a perfect opportunity for Hearst to gain market share for his new paper. He sent correspondents to cover the colonial problem between Spain and Cuba, basically with instructions to find a story or make up one. This led to Pulitzer's rival paper, the *New York World*, doing the same to keep pace, and soon the two media giants were banging the drum for American intervention to help the Cubans. This jingoism made an impact on the reading public, Congress, and President **William McKinley**, who conceded to send a U.S. warship to Cuba in February 1898. When the American ship mysteriously exploded in Havana Harbor, Hearst impetuously blamed Spain and called for war. Although Pulitzer followed suit, Hearst almost single-handedly created the **Spanish–American War** by printing falsehoods, exaggerations, distortions, and half-truths—a practice that soon came to be known as "yellow" journalism.

Hearst lived a long, materially prosperous life after the Gilded Age, winning election to the U.S. House of Representatives as a **Democrat**, amassing a publishing empire and a fortune larger than his father's. He built a world-famous mansion in California, kept company with Hollywood celebrities, and became the chief subject of the unflattering composite character Charles Foster Kane in Orson Welles's classic film *Citizen Kane*. He is speculated to have been a murderer as well, although he was never prosecuted for it. *See also* PRESS, THE.

HEINZ, HENRY J. (1844–1919). Born to German **immigrant** parents in Pittsburgh, Henry John Heinz began gardening and selling produce to local merchants around Sharpsburg, Pennsylvania, while still a child. He continually expanded his enterprise until 1869, when, at the age of 25, he founded the Anchor Pickle and Vinegar Works, which he renamed Heinz, Noble & Company in 1872. The company's first specialty was horseradish bottled in transparent jars to show off its freshness and purity. Heinz quickly added several types of pickles, mustard, sauerkraut, and vinegar to his list of products. Reorganizing the company with his brothers in 1875, he called it F & J Heinz, which it remained until its final name change in 1888 to the H. J. Heinz Company. In 1876, Heinz put a previously little-used condiment on the market: tomato ketchup. It ultimately became the company's most profitable and legendary product. In 1886, Heinz began selling his merchandise abroad and within 10 years had opened a European branch in London. In 1893, he sold his wares at the **Columbian Exposition** in Chicago, which popularized the Heinz brand nationwide and even internationally. In 1896, Heinz decided to make his company slogan "57 Varieties" to emphasize the diversity of his product line. The company was actually selling more than 57 separate types of goods at the time, but Heinz just liked the sound of "57 Varieties" and thought it a lucky number. He must have been right, because the H. J. Heinz Company, which came from humble beginnings in the Gilded Age, grew to be one of the largest food processing businesses in the world in the 20th century. *See also* HERSHEY, MILTON S.

HENDRICKS, THOMAS A. (1819–1885). Born in southeastern Ohio to a politically prominent family, Thomas Andrew Hendricks grew up in central Indiana. After studying law in Pennsylvania, he returned to Indiana to practice. Joining the **Democratic Party**, he served in the state legislature before being elected to the U.S. House of Representatives in 1850. After two terms, he was turned out of office, and then served in the Indiana state government and as postmaster of New York City. Elected to the U.S. Senate in 1862, he served one term before being elected governor of Indiana. The national Democratic Party was in such bad shape following the Civil War that it had few good choices to nominate for president in 1868 or 1872. Consequently, Hendricks received some votes for the nomination. In 1876, he received the nomination for the vice presidency as **Samuel Tilden**'s running mate. Failing in that election due to the **Compromise of 1877**, he returned to practicing law until the presidential election of 1884, when he finally won as the vice presidential running mate of **Grover Cleveland**. Unfortunately, he did not live long thereafter. Before the end of just 1 year on the job, he died, leaving behind little more than his name as a footnote in Gilded Age history.

HERSHEY, MILTON S. (1857–1945). Born into a Mennonite family near Harrisburg, Pennsylvania, Milton Snavely Hershey apprenticed as a confectioner before starting his own candy business in 1876 in Philadelphia. Marginally successful, he tried the same in New York and Chicago, but did not enjoy the same results. In 1883, he opened the profitable Lancaster Caramel Company, whose featured products were caramel-based, as the name implied. While visiting the **Columbian Exposition** in Chicago in 1893, he was impressed with an exhibit of German chocolate manufacturing equipment and bought it. He then experimented with recipes for making milk chocolate (as opposed to traditional water-based chocolate) and opened the Hershey Chocolate Company in 1894 in his small hometown. It took 5 years to perfect his recipe, but once accomplished, he put a better-tasting product on the American market than any other that could be commonly found at the time. Selling his caramel business, he focused on chocolate almost exclusively thereafter. By the end of the Gilded Age, his enterprise was large enough that he could begin to build a company town for his employees, which still bears his name today. Although Hershey's did not become the world's largest chocolate business until the 20th century, it had its start, as did so many other food-producing companies, in the Gilded Age. *See also* HEINZ, HENRY J.

HICKOK, "WILD BILL" (1837–1876). Born in north-central Illinois to an abolitionist family that participated in the Underground Railroad, James Butler Hickok became one of the most famous frontiersmen of his era. At age 18 he began driving stagecoaches along the Santa Fe and Oregon Trails. He then had brief stints as the local lawman in towns in Kansas and Nebraska, the latter offering his first occasion to kill an outlaw. His reputation for no-nonsense law enforcement made him regionally famous while he was in his early 20s and earned him the nickname "Wild Bill." During the Civil War, he joined the Union army as a scout and thereafter served temporarily as a U.S. Marshal. In

1865, he killed a former friend in a quick-draw duel in an open street in Springfield, Missouri, which almost single-handedly created the myth of such duels being common in the "Wild West."

Hickok's fame became national in 1867 when *Harper's Monthly* ran a story about him. He then became the prototype for the rugged western gunslinger that dime novelists made into a legend. He reveled in the attention, adding to his legend by exaggerating his exploits to news reporters. His flamboyant persona often made his tales credible to people who normally would have known better. For example, he liked to wear matching Colt .36 pistols with ivory handles and no triggers, which he placed backward in their holsters. He would draw them underhanded and sling them forward for maximum speed, or draw them with crossed arms, cocking them on the way up, and firing them accurately without aiming.

In the early 1870s, he befriended **Buffalo Bill** Cody, who was younger than he and in some ways his imitator, dressing and wearing his hair like Wild Bill. The two had many of the same frontiersman qualities, but Buffalo Bill's reputation would soon outgrow Hickok's, partly because he lived so much longer. Hickok, a frequenter of saloons and an avid poker player, finally played one too many hands. On 2 August 1876, while sitting at a table in a saloon in the town of Deadwood, in the Black Hills of South Dakota, a disgruntled drunk man named Jack McCall shot him in the back of the head. Hickok died holding what has since become known as the "Dead Man's Hand"—a pair of aces and a pair of eights, with the fifth card unaccounted for. In an unofficial public hearing, McCall was found not guilty, because he claimed that he was merely avenging the death of his brother at the hands of Hickok years earlier. In a later official trial, however, McCall was found guilty and hanged. Meanwhile, Hickok was buried in Deadwood, soon to be joined by the most famous wild woman of the West, **Calamity Jane**, who loved him despite his lack of reciprocation of those feelings. *See also* HARDIN, JOHN WESLEY.

HILL, JAMES J. (1838–1916). Born in Ontario, Canada, James Jerome Hill suffered an accident in childhood that put out his right eye. When he was a young teen his father died, and he was forced into a life of self-reliance. With a modicum of education and an exceptionally sharp mind for business, he moved to St. Paul, Minnesota, in 1856, where he dabbled in various jobs from bookkeeping to wholesaling, retailing, and shipping. The beginning of his fortune, however, came from supplying coal to the **railroads** of the Northwest in the late 1860s. Not content to do just one thing at a time, he branched out into banking and railroads in the 1870s. The **Panic of 1873** provided him a perfect opportunity to grab a struggling railroad, the St. Paul and Pacific. With his business partners, he turned it into the St. Paul, Minneapolis, and Manitoba Railway Company in 1879 and immediately began laying plans for expanding it into a transcontinental line. With no government subsidies, his plan seemed unrealistic to most observers. He ingeniously figured out other ways to offset the cost and guarantee quick returns on his investment. He gave discounts to **immigrants** to ride his trains in exchange for their agreeing to build homes and businesses along his line. In this way, he became the only one of the great railroad moguls of the Gilded Age to apply successfully the "if you build it, they will come" concept. By 1893, his Great Northern Railway, which stretched from Minnesota to Washington, was both complete and profitable. This was again, just in time for another national economic depression, the **Panic of 1893**, which, unlike so many of his competitors, he weathered successfully. Although he was often seen as a ruthless millionaire in his day, he was generous in his philanthropy, and came by the moniker "empire builder" of the great Northwest honestly.

HOAR, GEORGE FRISBIE (1826–1904). Born in Massachusetts to a distinguished Unitarian family that included a grandfather who had signed the Declaration of Independence and the U.S. Constitution, a father who had served in Congress, a brother who became attorney general in the **Ulysses S. Grant** administration, and a cousin— **William Evarts**—who served in various capacities in public service, George Frisbie Hoar attended Harvard University and Harvard Law School before entering politics. Elected to the U.S. House of Representatives in 1868 as a **Republican**, he gained promotion to the U.S. Senate 8 years later. He distinguished himself as one of the most incorruptible public servants in Washington during an age noted for **corruption**. A progressive thinker, he favored civil rights for **African Americans**, better treatment of American **Indians**, and **women**'s suffrage. He was one of the few Republicans in the Senate to consistently oppose the anti-Chinese **immigrant** policy that became fashionable during the Gilded Age. He likewise stood adamantly against the imperialist **foreign** policies of the **William McKinley** and **Theodore Roosevelt** administrations. Outside of politics, he served as president of the American Historical Society and sat on the board of the Smithsonian Institution and Harvard University, among other important organizations and agencies. *See also* AMERICAN ANTI-IMPERIALIST LEAGUE; CHINESE EXCLUSION ACT; SPANISH–AMERICAN WAR.

HOLLIDAY, DOC. *See* GUNFIGHT AT THE O. K. CORRAL; TOMBSTONE, ARIZONA.

HOMER, WINSLOW (1836–1910). Born in Boston, Massachusetts, Homer grew up with natural artistic talent. Apprenticed at age 19 to a lithographer, he developed skills as a sketch artist, which ushered him into the art world. He found employment with *Harper's Weekly* during the Civil War, drawing illustrations straight from the battlefront. After the war, he traveled abroad and further honed his skills by studying new styles and techniques. In the 1870s, he began experimenting with watercolors, which ultimately became his artistic forte. He exhibited some of his early paintings at the 1876 **U.S. Centennial** Exposition in Philadelphia. The realism with which he portrayed man and nature immediately caught the eye of art critics and the general public alike. Residing on the coast of Maine and making trips to Florida and the West Indies, Homer created his most famous paintings of fishing village scenes, beaches and boats, shorelines and storms at sea. His most enduring piece was called "The Gulf Stream" (1899), which depicted a lone **African American** man on a small boat at sea surrounded by hungry sharks. Among his other great works are "Snap the Whip" (1872), "Breezing Up" (1876), and "Eight Bells" (1886).

HOMESTEAD STRIKE. One of the most important labor disputes of the Gilded Age, this strike occurred at **Andrew Carnegie**'s Homestead, Pennsylvania, steel mill from 30 June to 20 November 1892. Carnegie had acquired this Pittsburgh-area mill a decade earlier, and had already experienced run-ins with the Amalgamated Association of Iron and Steel Workers Union—the largest **trade union** in the United States at the time—which organized the labor for the plant. In 1889, Carnegie, working through his manager, **Henry Clay Frick**, negotiated a three-year contract with the union that kept wages stable, but a downturn in the market value of steel began nationwide immediately thereafter, which cut into Carnegie's profits. In 1892, just as the contract was about to expire, the union began demanding wage increases. Carnegie and Frick determined to give them just the opposite, however—a wage cut. When the two sides could not come to terms, Frick announced that he would no longer recognize the union's legitimacy.

Knowing the workers would strike, Frick struck first. On 30 June, he locked the doors of the mill, erected a fence around the property, topped it with **barbed wire**, and had guard towers constructed on the perimeter to keep the workers out. Frick then began advertising for scabs to replace the union workers. Union members, their families, and local sympathizers kept a round-the-clock vigil going for the next week around the town to keep out the scabs. Frick called local law enforcement to the scene, but the angry unionists numbered about 5,000 and the sheriff and deputies easily backed down. Thus, on 5 July, some 300 **Pinkertons**—the nation's premier private law enforcement agency—arrived on the scene to secure the mill for the Carnegie company in one of the most bizarre episodes in American history. The Pinkertons attempted to sneak in by cover of darkness and by way of the Monongahela River on barges, but the unionists were waiting for them. In the wee hours of the morning of 6 July, a battle ensued that lasted off-and-on for about 13 hours, in which more than a dozen people were killed or wounded. In the end, the Pinkertons surrendered, and the lockdown continued.

Next, Frick sought the help of the governor and the Pennsylvania militia. A force of more than 8,000 militiamen arrived in town on 12 July, and easily secured the area. The next day, the first scabs showed up for work, and more violence erupted. The strikers were beaten, however, as the power of the state bore down upon them. After the 23 July attempted assassination of Frick by an anarchist, all public sympathy for the strike evaporated. By the middle of August, the mill was back to operating at near-half capacity with 1,700 scabs. By the middle of October, the militia pulled out. By 20 November, what was left of the union voted to end the strike. Frick then made good on his vow to slash wages, and added insult to injury by downsizing the workforce and increasing the workday.

HOWARD, O. O. Born in Leeds, Maine, in 1830, Oliver Otis Howard grew up on a farm where his father employed an **African American** helper. His acquaintance with this black man gave him a perspective on race relations that most of his northern contemporaries would never know. This became a major factor in determining his destiny and life's work. After attending Bowdoin **College** in Maine, he graduated from the U.S. Military Academy at West Point, New York, and had a **religious** conversion experience in the Congregationalist faith that would forever alter his character and earn him nicknames such as the "Christian Soldier," "Christian General," and "Bible General." He served honorably in the Union army during the Civil War, and by the end he commanded the Army of the Tennessee. Immediately after the war, President Andrew Johnson appointed him the first and only head of the Freedmen's Bureau, a position in which he could focus on one of his passions—promoting racial equality. Besides protection of the former slaves from angry white southerners, he considered **education** the most important thing he could give them. Consequently, he encouraged Congress to reinstate military occupation of the South from 1867–1870, while he focused on creating schools. By 1870, he had overseen the opening of some 4,000 freedmen schools, which employed some 9,000 teachers, and enrolled some 240,000 students. The most lasting of his education legacies was and is his namesake, Howard University, in Washington, D.C., which was intended to provide blacks with the highest-quality education in fields such as medicine and law. He served as the school's president from 1872–1874.

Meanwhile, the **Ulysses S. Grant** administration tapped Howard for help in subduing the American **Indians** in the West. In 1872, Howard worked out a treaty with Apache Chief Cochise, which helped speed the end of the Apache wars. Soon after, he moved to Portland, Oregon, and began trying to do the same with the Nez Perce Indians of the Pacific Northwest. Although he sympathized with Chief Joseph in his desire to allow the tribe to stay in its traditional territory, he ultimately enforced the will of the U.S. Government and forced their removal to a reservation in Idaho. Unable to stay in one place very long, Howard then accepted a position as head of his old alma mater at West Point, where he served from 1880–1882. After several more moves, he finally settled in Burlington, Vermont, where he retired and eventually died. His last public service kept him busy from 1895–1901 when he created Lincoln Memorial University in Tennessee as a school for poor Appalachia whites.

He also left a legacy in books he wrote. As the author of eight books, four for adults and four for children, he is primarily remembered for his documentation of the history and culture of the western Indians of the Gilded Age.

HOWELLS, WILLIAM DEAN (1837–1920). Born in Ohio to an editor who moved often from town-to-town, William followed in his father's footsteps, ultimately becoming the most important fiction writer of the Gilded Age besides his friend **Mark Twain**. Getting his start in newspapers, he wrote for the *Ohio State Journal* prior to the Civil War. He supported Abraham Lincoln enthusiastically in print in 1860, which earned him the post of consul to Venice, a position he kept for nearly 4 years. His new status also enabled him to meet and fraternize with some of the most famous American literary figures alive at the time, including Nathaniel Hawthorne, Henry David Thoreau, and Ralph Waldo Emerson. Upon returning to the United States, he began writing for *Atlantic Monthly*, becoming assistant editor in 1866 and editor in 1871, an exalted position in American literary circles that he kept for a decade. During and after his stint there, he began writing and publishing his own works of fiction in the new genre of "realism," of which he was a pioneer. The most famous of his books, *The Rise of Silas Lapham* (1885), is about the complexities of the intersection of the business world and personal problems in Gilded Age America. Although he wrote more than 100 novels, collections of poems, short stories, and assorted essays, all of which were well-received in the 19th century, much of his work fell into disrepute by the time of his death and thereafter. Critics charged that his realism did not seem so realistic in the modern world of the 1920s. Ironically, it was as a literary critic that he made the most enduring contribution to American letters. He read the work of many upstart writers, and his positive reviews put them on the road to success. In this category were American authors **Stephen Crane**, Hamlin Garland, Emily Dickinson, Henry James, and Sarah Orne Jewett, and foreigners Emile Zola and Leo Tolstoy, among others. In the early 20th century, Howells became a charter member of the American Academy of Arts and Letters, as well as its first president. Although much of his work seems dated and dry to modern readers, William Dean Howells was considered the "Dean" of all American writers in his own day. *See also* LITERATURE; PERIODICALS.

HOW THE OTHER HALF LIVES. Subtitled *Studies Among the Tenements of New York*, this 1890 book by Danish **immigrant**-journalist Jacob Riis helped usher in the Progressive Era and the modern, practical, study of sociology. Influenced by Charles Dickens's novels about the plight of the poor in London, Riis set out in 1877 to document the real-life conditions of New York City's poverty-stricken neighborhoods. Although he wrote well-researched and factually accurate newspaper and magazine pieces to that effect over the years, it was his illustrations rather than his words that ultimately captured the public's attention. Using the new invention of flash photography, he took some unposed night-time photos, as well as some daytime and staged photos, of the deplorable overcrowding and unsanitary living conditions that plagued the tenements of the Lower East Side and Brooklyn. Originally published serially in 1889 in *Scribner's Magazine*, the collection of essays and photos was published in book form the following year.

The book led to the abolition of some of the worst settlement houses in New York, helped generate a reform movement for improving city living conditions in America generally, and served as a prototype for later muckraker *exposés* of the Progressive Era. It also made an impact on a young author of realism/naturalism fiction named **Stephen Crane**. Along with the work of Jane Addams at **Hull House** in Chicago, Riis's book brought desperately needed, better-late-than-never attention to one of the most serious social problems of the Gilded Age. The only major criticism of the book has been Riis's prejudice toward Jews and Catholics, groups that comprised the majority of his subject matter, and which, while trying to help ease their condition, he nevertheless portrayed with negative stereotyping. *See also* LITERATURE; PERIODICALS.

HULL HOUSE. Chicago, Illinois, grew faster than any other American city during the Gilded Age. Its population reached more than one million by 1890. Overcrowding among the working poor and **immigrants** was a rampant problem. The difficulties of assimilation into the mainstream of American society compounded the problem and fostered many urban social ills. In 1889, Jane Addams and Ellen Gates Starr decided to do something about it, opening Hull House, a "settlement house," on Chicago's Halsted Street as a haven for needy immigrants. Hull House ran primarily on charity and philanthropic good will rather than government funding. It operated as an outreach program, similar to a **foreign, religious** mission but in a domestic setting. Those who worked there were missionaries in a sense, but with a secular rather than religious mission. Hull House offered a variety of services—basically anything and everything necessary to sustain life and health, as well as **education**, entertainment, and community activities. It also served as a permanent residence for Addams, and a semi-permanent one for Florence Kelley, who joined Addams as one of the premier **women**'s and children's advocates in the United States. Thanks to Addams's high profile as a lecturer and author, Hull House enjoyed adequate funding and national recognition for several decades beyond the Gilded Age, and was perhaps the most successful operation of its kind in American history. It provided a model for various government social service agencies that arose in the 20th century.

HUNT, RICHARD M. (1827–1895). Born in Vermont to a prominent New England family, Richard Morris Hunt moved with his mother to Europe when he was 15. In Paris, France, he was honored to be the first American to attend the prestigious School of Fine Arts, where he studied architecture for a decade. Impressing his teachers, he won the school's highest honor and went on to work temporarily for the government of Napoleon III on the Louvre before returning to the United States in 1855. In New York City, he started the country's first professional architectural school and later helped establish the American Institute of Architects, of which he became president in 1888. His influence garnered recognition for the field of architecture as a true profession in America, worthy of the most rigorous academic study, and requiring the technical skills of an engineer and the eye of an artist. The "beaux-arts" style that he acquired from Paris but which imitated ancient Greek architecture, became his hallmark. Among the many public buildings, monuments, and private homes he designed were the *New York Tribune* office, which was a semi-skyscraper and contained one of the first modern elevators; the pedestal for the **Statue of Liberty**; the **Biltmore Estate** mansion and outbuildings in North Carolina; the **Vanderbilt** Mausoleum on Staten Island, New York; the Central Park front of New York's Metropolitan Museum of Art; the main administrative building at the **Columbian Exposition of 1893** in Chicago; the American Revolutionary Battle of Yorktown monument in Virginia; various buildings on the campuses of Harvard, Princeton, and Yale Universities; and mansions for several Gilded Age millionaires. *See also* OLMSTED, FREDERICK LAW.

HUNTINGTON, COLLIS P. (1821–1900). Born into a large working-class family in Connecticut, he left home at age 14 to make his own way in the world. First becoming a successful retailer in the Northeast, he moved to California in 1849 to get in on the gold rush. Settling in Sacramento, he opened a general store that catered to miners and proved lucrative. He formed a partnership with local merchant Mark Hopkins in 1855, helped establish the **Republican Party** in California in 1856, and joined with **Leland Stanford** and Charles Crocker in 1860 to form the corporation for building the western half of the first **transcontinental railroad**. Huntington and his three partners in the Central Pacific **Railroad** Corporation formed the "Big Four," which became a virtual synonym for western "Robber Barons." Unquestionably the leader of the big four, Huntington developed a reputation for ruthlessness matched only by the most notorious business moguls of the Gilded Age. In 1868, he helped create the Southern Pacific Railroad, which built the western portions of the second and third transcontinental lines. In 1871, he branched out back to his eastern roots, forming railroad and shipping enterprises from coastal Virginia to the Ohio River. His work resulted in the development of new cities on each end of the line—Newport News, Virginia, and Huntington, West Virginia. By the late 1890s, Huntington owned the largest private shipbuilding facility in the world in Newport News. In 1884, he built a gaudy mansion in New York City and became part of the American "royalty" that was the Gilded Age millionaire set. At his death, he left his substantial art collection to the Metropolitan Museum of Art in New York, and part of his fortune eventually went to build one of the finest libraries in the world, the Huntington Library in southern California.

– I –

IMMIGRANTS. At the beginning of the Gilded Age, the population of the United States stood at about 38.6 million. By the end, in the census of 1900, it stood at a little more than 76 million. Much of that growth came from procreation, but a large part came from immigration. In the 1870s and '80s, the bulk of immigrants came from Germany, Ireland, and Scandinavia. In the 1890s, Italy provided the largest number, followed by Russia, Poland, and Austria-Hungary. In most cases, immigrants came to America to escape poverty in Europe or to increase their fortunes, but some were fleeing political upheaval or **religious** persecution. In the latter category were millions of Jews from eastern Europe, where persecution ran the gamut from mild discrimination to official pogroms. Likewise, Roman Catholics sometimes suffered discrimination in Great Britain or in one of the Germanic nations, and they found a similar anti-Catholic sentiment waiting to greet them in the United States. Although a large number of Irish immigrants settled in Boston, New York, and in the industrial Midwest, they tended to spread out generally over the nation, as did Germans and Scandinavians.

Wherever the immigrants came from, they were expected to learn English and assimilate into the broader Anglo-American culture. Most did so with no qualms, but the propensity of certain ethnic groups to congregate with their own kind in localized areas often made it appear that they favored retaining their old world heritage to acculturating into the American mainstream. Generally, Jews settled in New York City and other large metropolises, where there was relative safety in numbers, with few seeking rural, isolated living arrangements in America. Italians, Irish, and other Catholics often banded together in communities for the same reason. One result of these ethnic neighborhoods was the creation of slums and ghettos, where squalid conditions prevailed. Jacob Riis's groundbreaking study *How the Other Half Lives* (1890) documented such problems in New York. Another result was frequent territorial disputes and gang activity. A third result was that they sometimes voted for one party or the other en masse, making them the de facto political enemy of the opposing party.

Germans were unique among immigrant groups in that they were the most heterogeneous. They might be Protestant, Catholic, Jewish, or something else. They might come from a rural or urban background, they might be from the northern lowlands or the southern highlands, and they might become **Democrats** or **Republicans** once in America. They had large enough numbers spread through the Northeast, Midwest, and Great Plains that they often deliberately retained many aspects of their old world culture—language, **education**, food, and music—including printing newspapers in German. At the height of the Germans' influence in the 1880s and '90s, they published some 800 non-English newspapers and held controlling votes in Milwaukee, Wisconsin; Cincinnati, Ohio; and St. Louis, Missouri; among other major cities. There were hundreds of *kleindeutschlands* (little Germanies) spread all over the country. **Samuel Gompers's**

American Federation of Labor had so many German-speaking members that it was once officially a bilingual organization. The stereotype of Germans as **anarchists** and labor organizers occasionally put them in conflict with Anglo-Americans, as happened in the **Haymarket Incident** in Illinois in 1886. The Irish, similarly, had problems stemming from labor activities, as the saga of the **Mollie Maguires** in Pennsylvania in 1877 illustrates.

Prior to the Gilded Age, the U.S. Government had done little to discourage any particular type of immigration, but beginning in 1875 with the Page Act, Congress wrote the first law barring what was commonly considered "undesirable" immigrants. The Page Act prohibited those who trafficked in slave labor, prostitution, or other criminal activity, and was largely aimed at stopping importation of Chinese immigrants. This law did not put a stop to the rampant xenophobia against the Chinese in California, however, and in 1878, Irish labor leader Dennis Kearney led an attack against them in San Francisco. Consequently, in 1882, Congress passed the **Chinese Exclusion Act**, which prevented all Chinese immigration for the next 10 years.

In 1892, **Ellis Island** in New York harbor was opened to process effectively all the non-English speaking immigrants from so many different backgrounds. At the same time, Anglo-American "WASPs" (White Anglo-Saxon Protestants) began calling for a prohibition against various kinds of "undesirable" immigration, including Catholics, Jews, anarchists, socialists, communists, the mentally ill, the physically disabled, polygamists, illiterates, and paupers. In 1893, the **American Protective Association** was founded to lobby for keeping out non-Protestants, and in 1894 the **Immigration Restriction League** was founded for keeping out the rest. Their efforts convinced Congress in 1896 to pass a bill requiring a literacy test for immigrants, but President **Grover Cleveland** vetoed it. Cleveland and the Democratic Party owed their political fortunes far more to the new immigrants than did the Republican Party. Such efforts came to naught until the 20th century, when world events increased the perceived need for immigration reform. Meanwhile, in the last decade of the Gilded Age, **foreign** birth accounted for 90 percent of Chicago's population; 88 percent of New York City's; 83 percent of Cleveland, Ohio's; 63 percent of Boston's; and 62 percent of Cincinnati, Ohio's. This fact made true Emma Lazarus's famous poem inscribed on the **Statue** of **Liberty**, which said the United States had an open, golden door of opportunity for the tired, huddled masses who yearned to breathe free. *See also* CASTLE GARDEN; TRADE UNIONS.

IMMIGRATION RESTRICTION LEAGUE (IRL). Created in 1894 in the midst of the avalanche of new immigration from eastern Europe, the IRL was founded by some Boston elites from Harvard University named Prescott Hall, Robert Ward, and Charles Warren. It quickly picked up supporters in Congress, including Henry Cabot Lodge of Massachusetts and George Edmunds of Vermont. It also gained support from some influential scholars, including historian John Fiske, geologist and paleontologist Nathaniel Shaler, and racial theorist Madison Grant. Within 2 years, it had developed branches in several major cities. Its modus operandi consisted of educating the public about the ills of unrestricted immigration and lobbying Congress to pass a law to keep certain types of people from entering the United States. It was not without precedent, since in 1882 Congress had passed the **Chinese Exclusion Act**. The League primarily asked for and got a literacy test bill that required all **immigrants** to prove that they could read a few words, but not necessarily in English. The thought was that literate immigrants were less likely to become a public nuisance. This mattered greatly to many Americans at the time because the new eastern European immigrants appeared to have a higher rate of crime, vice, and poverty than old stock immigrants, and these negative demographics seemed to correlate to the prevalence of illiteracy among the different groups. Congress passed the bill in 1896, but President **Grover Cleveland** summarily vetoed it as contrary to the American spirit of equal opportunity for all. The organization survived the veto and lived to see its wishes fulfilled 20 years later during the presidency of Woodrow Wilson. Although the IRL tried to avoid the appearance of being racist, it seemed to people many at the time, as it does to most observers today, to have been just that. *See also* AMERICAN PROTECTIVE ASSOCIATION.

IMPERIALISM. *See* AMERICAN ANTI-IMPERIALIST LEAGUE; FOREIGN AFFAIRS; SPANISH–AMERICAN WAR.

INDIAN RING. *See* CORRUPTION; GRANT, ULYSSES S.

INDIANS, AMERICAN. The Gilded Age marked the end of traditional Indian culture and self-determination. It represents one of the most tragic periods for any racial group in American history. Decades before the Gilded Age, the eastern tribes had been subjugated by the U.S. government and/or white Americans in general. By the time of the **Ulysses S. Grant** administration, the focus was on rounding up the many free western tribes and corralling them on reservations. **Corruption** and incompetence plagued the Bureau of Indian Affairs during these years. Federal policy and the typical white attitude were summed up by General Philip Sheridan's infamous paraphrase, "The only good Indian is a dead Indian."

With treaties already in place for dealing with various tribes, Congress decided in 1871 to stop the practice of treating tribes as independent powers. Essentially, that meant they would now be dealt with as criminals if they did not immediately surrender to their fate. Of course, many tribes fought to keep their sovereignty and their ancestral land, to their peril. The Indian group that constituted the most immediate and persistent threat under this new policy was the Apaches of the desert Southwest. Actually composed of seven different tribes and other subtribes, including the Chiricahua, Jicarilla, Kiowa, and Mescalero, the Apaches were considered such a problem that the Mexican government put a bounty on their scalps. Cochise, the chief of the Chiricahua, led the resistance until General George Crook captured him in 1871. He escaped, however, and fought another year before surrendering to General **O. O. Howard** and going quietly to a reservation. **Geronimo** took over the Apache resistance at that point, and fought until 1886, when he was finally captured by General Nelson Miles.

Meanwhile, the Comanche tribe of the west Texas region had a similar experience. Mixed-race Chief Quanah Parker led a coalition of Comanche, Cheyenne, Kiowa, and Arapaho to defeat at the Second Battle of Adobe Walls in 1874. The U.S. Army retaliated by waging the Red River War in 1874–1875, which effectively ended the Indian resistance in the region. Once on the reservation, Parker bridged the gap between the Indians and whites, starting the Native American Church movement, which blended Christianity with the use of traditional Indian drugs, and encouraged his tribe to assimilate and modernize. At the same time, a thousand miles to the west, the government sought to subjugate the tribes of the Pacific Northwest, including the Modocs and the Nez Perce. Several battles occurred in each case in the 1870s. Most notably, Chief Joseph of the Nez Perce led his people on a 1,400-mile retreat from Oregon to Montana to avoid being sent to a reservation in Idaho. Despite the valiant effort, he surrendered in 1877 with the famous words, "From where the sun now stands, I will fight no more forever."

In the meantime, the Lakota (Sioux) tribes of the northern Great Plains became the next target for subjugation. They comprised several bands, including Minneconjou, Teton, Oglala, and Hunkpapa. When gold was discovered on their sacred lands in the Black Hills in 1874, their rights to the land were abrogated by an influx of prospectors and by indifference or hostility on the part of the government. Chiefs **Sitting Bull** and Crazy Horse tried nobly to defend their land, but were forced off by the U.S. Cavalry, which pursued the Indians relentlessly as they fled westward. The greatest victory for any of the western tribes came during this flight, when, in the summer of 1876, Crazy Horse's forces annihilated Colonel George Custer's troops at the **Battle of Little Big Horn**. Other cavalry units took over at that point and captured Crazy Horse and forced Sitting Bull to lead his people to Canada. In time, he returned, surrendered, and went peaceably to a reservation in South Dakota. There in 1890, after lending his support to the Ghost Dance craze, he was killed by Indians working for the government. Two weeks later and a few miles away, the most tragic episode of Gilded Age Indian history occurred, when the cavalry massacred at least 300 Ghost Dancers at **Wounded Knee**.

In the midst of this suffering and bloodletting, some white reformers lobbied the government to adopt a more humane approach toward the Indians. **Helen Hunt Jackson** wrote books and lectured on their behalf, Massachusetts Senator Henry Dawes wrote the **Dawes Severalty Act** to try to help them assimilate into white culture, bureaucrats such as **Carl Schurz** tried to encourage better treatment, and missionaries and educators opened schools and churches for them. General white sentiment, however, and the Indians' reluctance to embrace such change worked against reform. With the **Benjamin Harrison** administration's opening of **Oklahoma** to white settlers in 1889 and the Wounded Knee tragedy of 1890, the fate of the western tribes was sealed.

INFLUENCE OF SEA POWER ON HISTORY, 1660–1783, THE.
Published in 1890, this book contained a series of lectures by the
president of the U.S. Naval War **College**, Captain Alfred Thayer
Mahan. Its thesis was simply that in modern international warfare, the
nation with the strongest navy would likely win. Using the wars of
empire between England and France in the 17th and 18th centuries as
a model, it showed that the former ultimately defeated the latter not
by superiority in land forces but by naval strength. From this historical
example, Mahan drew conclusions that greatly affected contemporary
American military policy and **foreign affairs** in the 1890s. He argued
that a modernized navy that employed state-of-the-art technology
would be paramount to waging war successfully in the near future. He
added that more naval bases were needed in strategic locations around
the world (Great Britain already had them). Although the United
States had already begun a naval buildup and upgrade before publication of the book, the ultimate impact of *The Influence of Sea Power
on History* cannot be overstated. It heightened both the American
public's and federal policy makers' awareness of the need for a stronger navy at a critical time in the nation's history. The book influenced
events leading up to and throughout the **Spanish–American War**,
affected the decisions of President **Theodore Roosevelt** and Secretar-
ies of State **John Hay** and Elihu Root, and, most importantly, laid the
foundation for naval strategy in World War I, not only for the United
States but also, in fact, for all the major belligerents.

INTERSTATE COMMERCE COMMISSION (ICC). Created by
Congress and President **Grover Cleveland** in 1887, the ICC, as it
was always known popularly, regulated **railroad** shipping in the late
Gilded Age. Calls for federal regulation of railroads that crossed state
lines began with the **Grange** in 1867. Farmers in the Midwest, South,
and Great Plains complained that the railroad companies were goug-
ing them with high shipping rates. Indeed, the charge was accurate in
many cases. Rail lines running through rural America had a natural,
as opposed to artificial, monopoly in their respective regions of service. Consequently, railroad companies could charge the highest price
the market would sustain. Since most farmers and small townspeople
depended on rail transportation for their livelihoods, they protested to
both state and federal authorities. Other related complaints included
that railroads gave rebates to certain corporations which the average

folks could not get for the same service, and that they often gave free tickets to influential politicians and newspaper editors to win their favor. Some states passed laws regulating railroad rates within their borders early in the 1870s. The federal government dragged its feet on the issue, however, and did not create the ICC until 20 years after the Grange first called for such an agency.

The delay resulted largely from the fact that the U.S. Government had never previously established any such regulatory agency. The first of its kind, the ICC would signal a highly controversial move away from traditional laissez-faire capitalism toward a socialistic policy. After the 1886 **U.S. Supreme Court** case *Wabash Railroad v. Illinois*, however, the move was almost unavoidable. Once created, the five-man agency proved partly ineffective, mainly because railroad corporations had plenty of money to fight the ICC in court, and its powers were not clearly defined in the Interstate Commerce Act that created it. Not until subsequent legislation strengthened it in the 20th century did it become really effective.

– J –

JACKSON, HELEN HUNT (1830–1885). Born Helen Fiske in Massachusetts, this white writer of American **Indian** history and novels suffered through her early years, as both parents, her first husband (E. B. Hunt), and her two sons died. A friend of Emily Dickinson and other famous poets of the Northeast, she began seriously writing poetry in the mid-1860s to ease the pain of losing loved ones. She might have gone on to become one of the great poets of the age had she not been diverted toward the cause of helping the Indians. In 1875, she married W. S. Jackson of Colorado, whose wealth as a **railroad** mogul afforded her the luxury of spending her time in research, writing, and humanitarianism. Living in Colorado put her in the vicinity of the Indians, but, ironically, a visit to Boston in 1879, where she heard a lecture by Ponca Indian Chief Standing Bear, first drew her attention to the problem. From then until her death, she focused exclusively on helping the western Indians, who had no notable white advocates at the time. Her book, *A Century of Dishonor* (1881), detailed the relations of the U.S. Government with the Indians for the first 100 years of the nation's history, and indicted the government and most white Americans as liars, thieves, and murderers. She sent a copy to every member of Congress, hoping it would lead to reform of national Indian policy. Although it did not spark an immediate reaction, she was not deterred.

Jackson next went to southern California to investigate the problems with the so-called "Mission" Indians, who had suffered under the Mexican, as well as the U.S., government. For her efforts, she won appointment from President **Chester A. Arthur** as special agent to the Indians for the U.S. Department of the Interior. As such, she was commissioned to write a report and recommend a solution for the problems facing the Indians of California. The individuals she met while on this assignment spurred her to write her most commercially successful novel, *Ramona* (1883). Congress also gave serious consideration to her report on the Mission Indians, but passed no legislation with regard to it. Soon after she died, however, Congress posthumously rewarded her work with passage of the **Dawes Severalty Act**. Like many reformers, therefore, Jackson never saw the fruit of her efforts in her lifetime, but she laid the basis for reform in future generations. In the end, her two books taken jointly had roughly the same effect on Indian policy as Harriet Beecher Stowe's *Uncle Tom's Cabin* (1852) had on American slavery. *See also* LITERATURE.

JAMES, JESSE (1847–1882). Born to a Baptist minister father near Kansas City, Missouri, Jesse Woodson James grew up in a slaveholding family that sided with the Confederacy during the Civil War. A Union raid on the family home in 1863 resulted in the beating of the 16-year-old James and the hanging of his stepfather. Thereafter, Jesse and his brother Frank joined the Confederate guerrilla force of Bloody Bill Anderson and William Quantrill and became enemies of the United States. After the war, when Jesse tried to surrender, Union soldiers shot him. As he recovered from his wound, he joined other former Confederates who refused to let the war end and continued attacking business interests, usually in the form of banks and trains. In 1869, James struck out on his own as the leader of an outlaw group, and was elevated to a southern cult hero by a pro-Confederate Kansas City newspaper editor. Over the course of his career as a bandit, James committed robberies from Alabama to Minnesota, and from Kentucky to Kansas, hitting half of the states in between, resulting in the murder of perhaps 16 people, and making him the most notorious outlaw of the Gilded Age. As his status grew, the **Pinkerton Detective Agency** of Chicago, Illinois, got involved in trying to catch him. A Pinkerton raid on his mother's home in Missouri in 1875 that severely injured his mother and burned down the house created sympathy for James among the general public. A bank robbery gone bad in Northfield, Minnesota, the following year resulted in the James gang's decimation. Jesse then reconstituted his gang with inferior younger men, one of whom, Bob Ford, soon turned against him. When the governor of Missouri put a $10,000 price on his head—dead or alive—Ford shot James in the back at his home in St. Joseph on 3 April 1882. This ignoble death did nothing to end the legend of this outlaw with a "Robin Hood" image, but rather kept it alive among his admirers for decades to come.

JIM CROW. *See* AFRICAN AMERICANS; *CIVIL RIGHTS CASES*; *PLESSY V. FERGUSON*; SOCIAL DARWINISM.

JOHNSTOWN FLOOD. Located about 30 miles east of Pittsburgh, the city of Johnstown had a population of more than 25,000 and was one of many iron and steel mill towns in western Pennsylvania in the Gilded Age. In 1889, it suffered one of the worst catastrophes in American history, when the dam holding back the 2-mile long and 1-mile wide Lake Conemaugh broke. At the time, a local hunting and fishing club owned the lake, which was nestled in the mountains 14 miles north of town, and used it as a resort. Famous club members included **Andrew Carnegie**, **Henry Clay Frick**, and Andrew Mellon. Originally constructed during the canal-building craze that swept the country in the early 1800s, the dam that formed the lake was completed in 1853. It broke in 1862 but was not fully repaired to its final form until 1881. By 1889, it was still strong enough to hold under normal conditions.

In late May, however, rainfall had drenched the mountains of western Pennsylvania, and the lake soon filled to capacity. On 31 May, area residents worked hard to dig a new overflow spillway and to build up the height of the dam, but to no avail. Water began to pour over the top, and at 3:15 p.m., the dam gave way. Some 20 million tons of water flooded the valley below where, 450 feet lower in altitude, Johnstown sat. It took about 45 minutes for the full force of the flood waters to reach the city. Along the way, the flood picked up trees, animals, buildings, **barbed wire**, steel mills, telegraph lines, **railroads**, a small town of 250 homes, and everything else that stood in its path. It wiped out Johnstown in a mere 10 minutes, killing approximately 2,200 people—some of whose bodies were never found. Thousands more were left homeless and destitute. They were ministered to by the **American Red Cross**, among other charitable groups and government agencies. It took 5 years to clean up and to get the town back to its antediluvian condition. Not surprisingly, the lake bed was left dry, and the dam was not rebuilt.

JONES, "GOLDEN RULE" (1846–1904). Born in Wales, Samuel Milton Jones immigrated to the United States at the age of three with his family. Settling in New York, the family was poor, and Samuel received little **education** before going to work 12 hours per day in a sawmill as a young teen. At 19, he moved to Titusville, Pennsylvania, and began working in the oil fields. Within 5 years, he had learned enough to form his own oil company. In 1885, he moved to Lima, Ohio, and helped found another oil company, which subsequently became part of **John D. Rockefeller**'s Standard Oil trust. In 1892, he relocated to Toledo, Ohio, and started yet another business, the Acme Sucker Rod Company, which sold Jones's own invention, the "sucker rod," used for deep well drilling, to oil companies everywhere. His greatest contribution to Gilded Age America, however, came in his innovative business management plan. He developed the most magnanimous policy toward his employees of any of the great industrialists of this era. His policy was based on the Christian "Golden Rule." He told his workers that if they would do their best work every day, always be honest, and follow the Golden Rule, he would treat them with respect, pay them a higher-than-average wage; institute a profit-sharing plan; give them an 8-hour workday, 40-hour workweek, and a 5-percent Christmas bonus; and not make them punch a clock. Although this generous policy cut into his bottom line, he still made a healthy profit and incurred the good will of not only his employees but also the people of Toledo.

With the fortune he earned from his business and the notoriety he garnered from his management style, "Golden Rule" Jones, as he was now known, ran for mayor of Toledo in 1897 as a **Republican**. Once in office, he engaged in one of the most impressive reform programs of any city administration in American history, utilizing his Golden Rule approach there as well. He created a cooperative insurance program for city employees, built free city parks, playgrounds, kindergartens, and a community center, as well as showed more mercy to criminal suspects in municipal court than was common at the time. For all such reforms, he fell into disfavor with the local Republican Party. In 1899, he was forced to run for reelection as an Independent. He won easily, and was twice more elected, before dying in office. Although his political agenda had many of the hallmarks of socialism, he rejected the socialist label and refused to allow his opponents to categorize him. He was his own man and did things his own way, and his "way" helped usher in the Progressive Era. In retrospect, he was clearly one of the first Progressives, and may properly be dubbed a "Christian Socialist" as well.

JOURNALISM. *See* LITERATURE; PERIODICALS; PRESS, THE.

– K –

KEARNEY, DENNIS. *See* CHINESE EXCLUSION ACT; IMMIGRANTS.

KELLY, OLIVER H. *See* GRANGE, THE NATIONAL.

KLONDIKE GOLD RUSH. On 16 August 1896, George Carmack and a small group of American **Indians** discovered gold in the Yukon Territory of western Canada, in a tributary of the Klondike River dubbed "Bonanza Creek." Despite the strike occurring on **foreign** soil, some 100,000 Americans flooded northwestern port cities such as Seattle, Washington, and San Francisco, California, becoming "stampeders" (a nickname equivalent to the 49ers of the California gold rush of 1849). The gold fields were in an extremely remote region, approximately 1,000 miles northeast of Seattle. Gaining access to the region was difficult at best and impossible for most. Stampeders had three choices of routes to get there, none of which was much better than the others. The overland trek from the interior of Canada and the American Northwest proved to be the hardest and deadliest. Fortunately, few took it. Most chose to sail from Seattle to Skagway or Dyea, Alaska—small ports that turned into boom towns for miners. Either amounted to the last stop before embarking into the rugged wilderness of the interior. Full of con men and outlaws, these towns were no place for greenhorns. Once there, stampeders chose between the White Pass Trail leaving Skagway or the Chilkoot Trail leaving Dyea. Depending on the exact point of departure, these narrow, winding, steep, slippery trails were 25–35 miles long. Some stampeders had horses and others had dog teams to carry their supplies. The White Pass Trail proved deadly for man and animal alike. So many horses died on it that folks began calling it the "Dead Horse Trail." Some humans died on it from malnutrition or disease. Yet, this grueling journey was just the beginning.

Once the stampeders reached the Canadian border, they were met by the Mounted Police, who turned away any who had not brought enough supplies to last a year. This meant perhaps a half-ton of food and another half-ton of clothes, blankets, tools, utensils, etc. Those allowed to enter then proceeded to one of the lakes at the headwaters of the Klondike River, where the first arrivals usually built their own rafts to carry them 500 miles down the dangerous, rapid-infested river to Dawson City, the nearest town to the gold fields. Of the 100,000 who began the journey in Seattle or San Francisco, only 35,000 made it all the way to Dawson City. Although the first prospectors did strike it rich and became known as the "Klondike Kings," almost none of the late-arriving stampeders found their fortune there. The roughly 4,000 who made any money at all prospecting got the nickname "Sourdoughs." Most simply lost what they had invested to get there—an average of $1,200 at the time (about $20,000 today). Some went to work as day laborers, but none had endured the harsh trip or invested their lives and savings for that; they wanted to strike it rich, but most never did. Businessmen in Seattle, Skagway, and Dawson City who sold supplies for the prospectors were the main recipients of the gold rush's bounty.

The outbreak of the **Spanish–American War** in 1898 and the discovery of gold further away in Canada and later in Nome, Alaska, ended the stampede. By then, some $50 million (or $1 billion today) in gold had been taken from the Klondike. Some notable Americans who participated in the rush included Jack London, author of *Call of the Wild*; Augusta Mack, founder of the Mack Truck company; Sid Grauman, owner of Grauman's Chinese Theater in Los Angeles, California; Wilson Mizner, owner of the Brown Derby restaurant in Los Angeles; and Tex Rickard, builder of Madison Square Garden in New York City.

KNIGHTS OF LABOR (KOL). Founded in 1869 by Uriah Stephens, the Noble and Holy Order of the Knights of Labor was originally a fraternal organization that catered to the needs of the urban working class in Philadelphia, Pennsylvania. Borrowing rituals, terminology, and symbolism from Freemasonry, the KOL operated in secrecy as a private club until after Stephens resigned. During that time, it expanded its base, opening more than 1,000 local chapters. In 1879, Terence Powderly became the group's leader—the Grand Master Workman. On his watch, the KOL grew to more than 700,000 members over the next decade, including both **women** and **African Americans**. It advocated the standardization of the 8-hour workday and the abolition of child labor, among other things. At its peak in the early 1890s, the KOL developed a powerful political voice by joining with the National **Farmers' Alliance** to form the **People's Party**. Internal discord, competition from more radical **trade unions** composed of socialists and **anarchists**, and the demise of the People's Party led to the decline of the national organization by the end of the century, although local chapters continued to function for some years thereafter. *See also* GOMPERS, SAMUEL.

– L –

LABOR DAY. *See* PULLMAN STRIKE; TRADE UNIONS.

LABOR UNIONS. See TRADE UNIONS.

LANGSTON, JOHN MERCER (1829–1897). Widely regarded as second only to **Frederick Douglass** in importance among **African Americans** of the 19th century, John Mercer Langston was born in Virginia to a wealthy white planter and a free black mother. When he was only 4 years old, both parents died, and friends from Ohio adopted him. There he grew up among free blacks in Chillicothe and Cincinnati. In 1849, he graduated from Oberlin **College**, where 3 years later he earned a master's degree in theology. Studying law thereafter, he became the first black attorney in Ohio, as well as a founding father of the **Republican Party**. When the Civil War broke out, he organized the now-famous black 54th Regiment of Massachusetts. After the war, he got involved in the Freedmen's

Bureau, before becoming the first dean of **Howard** University Law School in Washington, D.C., a position he held until 1871. He later served as vice president and interim president of the university. In 1877, **Rutherford B. Hayes** appointed him U.S. Consul to Haiti. He continued at that post through the **Garfield** and **Arthur** administrations. In 1885, he accepted a job as president of Virginia Normal and Collegiate Institute. Three years later, he ran for the U.S. House of Representatives from the Fourth District of Virginia. State Republican boss William Mahone refused to allow this black man to run on the GOP ticket, however, forcing Langston to run instead as an Independent. The **Democratic** candidate won the election, but Langston accused the Democrats of voting fraud, a charge that the Republican-controlled **Billion Dollar Congress** upheld. Langston was belatedly awarded his seat, but he lost his bid for reelection in 1890. He then retired and wrote his memoirs, *From the Virginia Plantation to the National Capital*, which is a valuable primary source of information about race relations and politics in the Gilded Age. The town of Langston, **Oklahoma**, and its local university are named in his honor. *See also* LITERATURE; REED, THOMAS B.

LIBERAL REPUBLICANS. In 1872, a faction of the **Republican Party** broke from supporting President **Ulysses S. Grant** for a second term because of the **corruption** that had plagued his first term. They called themselves the "Liberals" because they favored change, not only in the oval office but also in federal civil service positions generally. They also wanted to end Reconstruction (which they viewed as a quagmire) so the federal government could focus on other issues. The leaders of these liberals included senators **Carl Schurz** of Missouri, Charles Sumner of Massachusetts, and Lyman Trumbull of Illinois, as well as editors **Horace Greeley** and **Whitelaw Reid** of the *New York Tribune*, Henry Watterson of the *Louisville Courier-Journal*, and Murat Halstead of the *Cincinnati Commercial Gazette*. At the formative meeting of the potential new party, which was held in Cincinnati, Ohio, delegates drew up a 12-point platform and nominated Greeley for president and Benjamin Gratz Brown, the governor of Missouri, for vice president. Greeley, an eccentric editor, had no experience in elected office and had a history of lambasting **Democrats** in his paper. Gratz had a reputation as a public drunkard. Even so, the ticket garnered the support of the Democratic Party, which had been in disarray since the Civil War. Democrats threw their support behind the ticket as their best hope for attaining some measure of power in the federal government. Certainly, a Liberal victory would have been better for them than having Grant in office for 4 more years, but it was not to be. Grant easily defeated Greeley, who died after the election but before the official vote could be counted. By 1876, the rest of the Liberal leaders had either died or returned to the regular Republican fold. *See also* PRESS, THE.

LITERATURE. Book writing, publishing, and selling was a multimillion dollar industry in Gilded Age America. Since literacy rates had reached more than 90 percent by this time and no electronic media existed yet, books played an important role in the **education** and entertainment of most Americans. Improved technology and mass production lowered costs and allowed ever-increasing numbers of households, as well as libraries and schools, to fill their shelves. Most book sales to individuals occurred through mail order advertisements and catalogues rather than through bookstores, but the main source of literature for the reading public, at least in the densely populated eastern United States, was the local library. The number of local and regional public libraries with a minimum stock of 300 books grew to about 5,000 by the end of the 19th century. **Andrew Carnegie**'s philanthropy was partly responsible for this growth, but grassroots fund-raising and municipal taxation contributed just as much. By 1876, there was enough demand for professionalization of the library system that the American Library Association was formed. Book clubs, in which groups of people would read the same books in succession so they could converse about them, also abounded.

Literature came in two basic types then, as today: fiction and nonfiction. Fiction comprised the overwhelming majority of book sales. Authors such as **Mark Twain**, Louisa May Alcott, and Sarah Orne Jewett ranked among the best-selling American fiction writers of the day, while Lew Wallace's *Ben Hur: A Tale of the Christ* (1880) became the single best-selling book in American history to that time. Readers eagerly followed the works of British writers such as Arthur Conan Doyle and Rudyard Kipling, and there was still a large market for the old classics written by Shakespeare, Dante, Milton, and Sir Walter Scott, as well. Yet, dime novels, which were of a lower literary quality, outsold all of these authors whose work has stood the test of time. Western adventure dime novels by **Ned Buntline** and eastern rags-to-riches stories by **Horatio Alger** were widely popular.

Much of the literature of the day was regional in scope. **Joel Chandler Harris**, **George Washington Cable**, and Kate Chopin were some of the most famous southern writers, while Bret Harte and Ned Buntline wrote about the West. **William Dean Howells** and Henry James had a more northeastern orientation, while Mark Twain was the one author who could write authoritatively about, and thus appeal to, every part of the country. Twain's *The Adventures of Huckleberry Finn* (1884) was hailed at the time as a national treasure, a designation that it still enjoys. Of course, his book ***The Gilded Age*** (1873), which he coauthored with Charles Dudley Warner, captured the essence of American life so well that it lent its name to this whole era of history.

The fictional genres of the day that made the most pronounced and lasting contributions to American literature were realism and naturalism. Naturalism was the great innovation of the 1890s that originated mainly with **Stephen Crane** but was quickly copied by many others. Bleak, pessimistic, and tragic tales with unhappy endings, such as Crane's *Maggie: A Girl of the Streets* (1893), Kate Chopin's *The Awakening* (1899), and Theodore Dreiser's *Sister Carrie* (1900) are exemplary of this style. Novels that explored human psychology without judging it, were also popular at this time. Among them were Crane's *The Red Badge of Courage* (1895) and Howells's *The Rise of Silas Lapham* (1885).

Poetry continued to be an important form of literature in the Gilded Age, but it did not have as much popular appeal as in previous generations. Walt Whitman and John Greenleaf Whittier continued to publish critically acclaimed, if not commercially lucrative, volumes right up to their deaths in the 1890s. Emily Dickinson, meanwhile, achieved fame posthumously in the 1890s for her unorthodox poetic style. Perhaps the closest thing to a "popular" poem at the time was "The Pledge of Allegiance," written in 1892 by Francis Bellamy and published in the *Youth's Companion* magazine to inspire children toward patriotism and civic duty.

Among nonfiction works, the best sellers of this era were often self-help and/or **religious** books. In the former category, Orison Marden and Samuel Smiles made their living encouraging and inspiring people to greatness with revealing titles like *Pushing to the Front, How to Succeed, Character, Thrift*, and *Duty*. Charles Sheldon's self-explanatory *In His Steps: What Would Jesus Do?* (1897) became one of the most important, if largely forgotten, books in American history. Although not exactly self-help authors, Andrew Carnegie, **Booker T.**

Washington, and **John Mercer Langston** all wrote books conveying the message that people who work hard enough and are persistent enough will eventually succeed.

As for history books, **Henry Adams** wrote *The History of the United States of America (1801–1817)*, meticulously chronicling the important Jeffersonian era. **Ulysses S. Grant**'s *Personal Memoirs* (1885–1886) provided valuable first-hand information about the Civil War and Reconstruction, while his second vice president, **Henry Wilson**'s three-volume *History of the Rise and Fall of the Slave Power in America* (1872–1877) became a masterpiece on antebellum sectional issues. **Jefferson Davis**, however, countered Wilson with *The Rise and Fall of the Confederate Government* (1881), which proved just as historically important. **Theodore Roosevelt**'s writings, which included histories of the western frontier and the **Spanish–American War** made lasting impressions on how Americans perceived both of those topics. Future President Woodrow Wilson made his foray into history and political science at this time, too, with the publication of his dissertation on the workings of the U.S. Government. George Washington Williams and **W. E. B. Du Bois**, meanwhile, wrote some of the earliest histories of **African Americans**, and **Elizabeth Cady Stanton**, **Susan B. Anthony**, and Matilda Joslyn Gage wrote the first comprehensive **women**'s histories.

Politically important works of the day included Alfred Thayer Mahan's *The Influence of Sea Power on History* (1890), which helped cause and justify the huge naval buildup and acquisition of overseas territories in the coming age of imperialistic **foreign** policy; Henry George's *Progress and Poverty* (1879), which argued in favor of socialistic ideas for spreading the wealth in this age when the excesses of unbridled capitalism ran rampant; **Helen Hunt Jackson**'s *A Century of Dishonor* (1881), which created enough white guilt over the treatment of the American **Indians** that Congress was goaded into reforming federal policy in dealing with this oppressed minority group; and **Ida B. Wells-Barnett**'s *Southern Horrors* (1891) tried to do the same for blacks, but without success, while **Nellie Bly**'s *Ten Days in a Mad-House* (1890) succeeded at getting reform in the treatment of the mentally ill. Edward Bellamy's ***Looking Backward*** (1888), although a work of science fiction because it involved time travel, painted a portrait of what life in America would be like a century later, and it turned out that the United States had converted to a version of socialism—a reaction to and critique of late 19th century industrial society.

Children's literature sold well during the Gilded Age. Frances Hodgson Burnett's *Little Lord Fauntleroy* (1886), Anna Sewell's *Black Beauty* (1877), and Robert Louis Stevenson's *Treasure Island* (1883) and *Dr. Jekyll and Mr. Hyde* (1885) became classics. Alger and Buntline's dime novels were largely read by children rather than adults, as were Doyle's *Sherlock Holmes* books and Kipling's *The Jungle Book. See also HOW THE OTHER HALF LIVES*; MR. DOOLEY; TOURGEE, ALBION.

LOOKING BACKWARD. Published in 1888, this Edward Bellamy novel is one of the most important American books ever written. It fits neatly in the genre of science fiction made popular by French writer Jules Verne and English writer H. G. Wells in the late 1800s. It portrays a futuristic American society based on "Nationalism," a term that Bellamy used to describe what is normally called "socialism" in modern parlance. The subtitle, *2000–1887*, indicates that the central character, a Boston man named Julian West, who falls into a hypnotic sleep in 1887, awakens to find a radically new United States in which every American shares equally in the bounty of the nation. He is thus fascinated by "looking backward" from the beginning of the 21st century to learn the evolutionary process that brought these changes about. Starting from real life economic issues of the Gilded Age, such as industrial monopolies and corporate combinations, Bellamy envisioned the federal government eventually expropriating such efficient business operations and putting them to use for the benefit of the whole country. The book offered a vision that looked much the same as what the **People's Party** would soon come to espouse, which focused on government takeover of national transportation and communication systems. The book sparked the rise of "Nationalist Clubs" devoted to bringing this imaginary, benevolent, nearly omnipotent federal government into existence. Socialists such as **Eugene V. Debs**, educators such as John Dewey, and many Progressives in the 20th century also embraced the book and were heavily influenced by it long after the Gilded Age had ended.

– M –

MAHAN, ALFRED THAYER. *See* INFLUENCE OF SEA POWER ON HISTORY, 1660–1783, THE.

MCCOY, JOSEPH. *See* COWBOYS.

MCKINLEY, WILLIAM (1843–1901). Born in northeastern Ohio, William McKinley served as a school teacher on the eve of the Civil War. The 18-year-old then enlisted in the Union army and over the next 4 years worked his way up to the rank of major. After the war he attended law school in New York before opening a practice in Canton, Ohio. A **Republican**, he won his first seat in the U.S. House of Representatives in 1876. After winning his next two congressional races, he lost his seat in the contested 1882 election. He went on to serve three more terms before being booted out along with the Republican majority after the illustrious **Billion Dollar Congress** of 1890, in which the **tariff** bearing his name became law. Undaunted, he developed a friendship with party boss, millionaire industrialist, and campaign manager **Mark Hanna**, and won terms as governor of Ohio in 1891 and 1893. Hanna's packaging of McKinley in the presidential election of 1896 against **Democrat**/Populist challenger **William Jennings Bryan** became legendary for its Machiavellian characterization and helped rewrite the rules for running a national campaign.

McKinley's 1896 platform put him squarely on the side of maintaining the gold standard against the relentless onslaught of the **free silver** advocates, and Congress concurred with a law to that effect in the new president's first term. McKinley also pushed for a higher tariff, and Congress gave him that, too, in the Dingley Act. By far the most important occurrence of the new administration, however, was the **Spanish–American War** of 1898. Although McKinley was an imperialist and is generally credited with beginning the United States' push for world power, he was in fact reluctant to go to war with Spain. Goaded into it by public opinion, the "yellow press," questions about his manhood, the sinking of the U.S.S. *Maine*, and his own humanitarian desire to liberate oppressed people around the world, he became the first president since Abraham Lincoln to lead the nation to war.

The main result of winning the war for McKinley personally and politically was that he gained in popularity. He easily won reelection in 1900, this time with **Theodore Roosevelt** as his running mate. Less than a year later, however, he was dead, the victim of an assassin's bullet. While he attended the Pan-American Exposition at Buffalo, New York, an **anarchist** named Leon Czolgosz shot him at close range with a pistol concealed in a handkerchief. Although a tragedy, in an ironic twist of fate, the death of McKinley elevated a greater man, Roosevelt, to the White House. *See also* HEARST, WILLIAM RANDOLPH; PULITZER, JOSEPH.

MEAT PACKING INDUSTRY. *See* ARMOUR, PHILIP; SWIFT, GUSTAVUS; UNION STOCK YARDS.

MOHONK CONFERENCES ON THE NEGRO QUESTION. These two assemblies convened at the Lake Mohonk Mountain House, a Quaker **Chautauqua**, in the Shawangunk range of Ulster County, New York, in 1890 and 1891. Chaired by former U.S. President **Rutherford B. Hayes**, the purpose of the conferences was to discuss ways to deal with the sad reality of the **African Americans'** difficult plight in the Jim Crow era. The speakers and attendees included some of the most prominent, influential, and **liberal** intellectuals of the day. Among them were **Albion Tourgee**, novelist, political pundit, and former judge of Chicago, Illinois; **O. O. Howard**, author, educator, and former Civil War general; Dr. Lyman Abbott and Dr. James Buckley, reverends of New York City; Edward H. McGill, president of Swarthmore **College** in Pennsylvania; Dr. Merrill E. Gates, president of Rutgers College in New Jersey; Andrew White, former president of Cornell University in New York; Dr. A. F. Beard, corresponding secretary for the American Missionary Association; Dr. William Hayes Ward, editor of the *New York Independent*; and W. T. Harris, the U.S. Commissioner of Education. They discussed what to do for, to, and about blacks in a white-dominated, racially discriminatory country in the pivotal transition period between Reconstruction and the turn of the 20th century.

The participants agreed on very little. Some even denied there was such a thing as a "Negro Question," contending that the only question was that which is common to all humanity: are all men really created equal? If so, they said, all men should have the same opportunities and receive the same treatment legally and socially, regardless of race. Most rejected such egalitarian idealism and rhetoric, however, saying blacks had never been treated equally, they had always held a special status in the United States, and the "Negro Question" was merely what to do about it. After determining that political equality for blacks was not in the foreseeable future, they ultimately decided that the best hope for betterment of the race lay in **education**. They mostly agreed to promote the type of education that **Booker T. Washington** was already proffering at Tuskegee Institute, which relied heavily on white sympathy, patience, and philanthropy. The conferences thus achieved almost nothing and served indirectly to lend credence to the accommodationist approach to race relations, which seems in hindsight to have been a retardant of progress in the long struggle for African American civil rights.

MOLLIE MAGUIRES. A clandestine fraternal organization and **trade union** of Irish American coal miners in northeastern Pennsylvania in the early Gilded Age, the "Mollies" originated in Ireland in the 1840s as a result of the infamous potato famine. The nativist, anti-Catholic bias that existed in the United States in mid-1800s led these Irish **immigrants** to band together for their own protection. Over time, they developed a tendency to go far beyond mere self-defense, however, to engage in terrorist activities against employers and/or other nativists. Operating in absolute secrecy and silence, they would pick a person they believed had done them wrong or posed a threat to them, and assassinate him or threaten to do so hoping to drive him out of town. They also managed to control the public offices of some towns and counties in Pennsylvania in the 1870s, where they typified the **corruption** of Gilded Age politics. They were **Democrats** who, like their southern counterparts during Reconstruction, were radically partisan and localist in ideology.

In the mid-1870s, the president of the Philadelphia and Reading **Railroad**, Frank Gowan, who was also a coal mine owner and a county district attorney, hired **Pinkerton** detective James McParlan to infiltrate the group and bring it to justice. As a result, 20 leaders of the Mollies went to trial and eventually to the gallows. The most publicized hangings occurred en masse on 21 June 1877, in Carbon County. Thereafter, the organization soon ceased to be newsworthy. Its reputation has been largely rehabilitated in history as modern advocates for the working class, as well as Irish Americans interested in their heritage, have succeeded at raising doubts about who were the bad guys in this saga. These revisionists blame capitalist-industrialist business leaders and **Republicans** for framing the Mollies, who were really just poor workers fighting for their rights.

MOODY, D. L. (1837–1899). Born in Northfield, Massachusetts, to a poor family, Dwight Lyman Moody was brought up a Unitarian but converted to evangelical Christianity by way of a Boston Congregational Church at age 17. His conversion experience affected him profoundly, and, although a novice, he immediately began a lay ministry while working in a shoe store. He moved to Chicago, Illinois, a year later, where he continued as both a shoe salesman and a lay minister. So effective was he at street corner evangelism that, within three years, he was conducting the largest set of Sunday School meetings anywhere in the world. Word of his exciting new way of teaching and leading by example soon spread throughout the Midwest. In 1860, President-elect Abraham Lincoln even visited one of his meetings. During the Civil War, he ministered to wounded soldiers, and after the war became president of the Chicago Young Men's Christian Association and built a new church edifice to house his growing Sunday School classes. Unfortunately, in 1871, the **Great Chicago Fire** destroyed the building. Although he managed to rebuild, he soon moved his ministry headquarters back to Massachusetts and began evangelizing abroad.

Moody's first trip to England, Scotland, and Ireland in 1872 resulted in revival meetings unlike any seen since the Great Awakening of the 1730s-1740s, with thousands of conversions. Returning to the United States, he began holding similar revivals around his own country. In 1875, he drew crowds estimated between 10,000 and 20,000 in Brooklyn, New York, and Philadelphia, Pennsylvania. President **Ulysses S. Grant** and several members of his cabinet attended one of the meetings in Philadelphia. The next year, a revival in Manhattan, New York, drew crowds of up to 60,000 per day for 10 straight weeks. Similar results came from his crusades in Chicago; Boston, Massachusetts; Baltimore, Maryland; St. Louis, Missouri; San Francisco, California; and Buffalo, New York. Moody's finest moment came in 1893 at the **Columbian Exposition** in Chicago, where almost two million visitors signed the register at his Bible School. He continued holding revival meetings until the very day he died.

Although Moody was a member of a Congregational church, one of the reasons for his success was his refusal to be hemmed in by a denominational name. He preached a version of Protestant theology that could be embraced by Methodists and Baptists, among others, which would become the most common type of Christianity to be found in America in the 20th century. Moody left several legacies that are still fixtures of American evangelical Christianity today. The most notable was his Chicago Evangelization Society (now called the Moody Bible Institute), which opened in 1889 and still trains ministers today. While accurate records are impossible, it is estimated that Moody's preaching resulted in approximately one million conversions over the course of his life. *See also* RELIGION.

MORGAN, J. P. (1837–1913). Born in Hartford, Connecticut, to a wealthy banking family, John Pierpont Morgan enjoyed all the advantages of his father's fortune. He attended school first in Hartford, then in Boston, Massachusetts, where he studied business mathematics. Later, studying in Europe, he mastered the French and German languages. All of his **education** was custom tailored to prepare him for a career in international finance. At age 20, he settled in New York City and began a career that put him in the global cotton trade (and indirectly on the side of the South) during the bumper crop years of the late 1850s just before the outbreak of the Civil War. Although he publicly backed the Union during the war, he actually used the conflict as an opportunity for personal profit, regardless of which side his commercial transactions helped or hurt. In 1871, he co-founded his own banking firm called "Drexel, Morgan," which helped finance some of the largest corporate growth in world history, mainly focusing on steel and **railroads**. Yet, his best days were still to come.

In 1895, Morgan launched his own banking firm, J. P. Morgan and Company, which ultimately became the largest financial conglomerate in America, if not the world, in the early 20th century. His status made him appear to be in some ways more powerful than either the president of the United States or Congress. Fortunately, he tended to help the U.S. Government in times of national financial distress rather than try to undermine it, although his every move was calculated to make a personal profit. He seemed mostly apolitical, working with either party when it suited his interests. He worked, for example, with the **Democratic Grover Cleveland** administration to bail out the government by supplying it with gold during the **Panic of 1893**, and then supported the **Republican William McKinley** against the **free silver** Democrats and Populists in the campaign of 1896. Likewise, he sometimes worked with famous industrialists and inventors, such as **Andrew Carnegie**, **Thomas Edison**, and the **Vanderbilts**, and sometimes against them, as in the cases of **Jay Gould**, Jim Fiske, Jay

Cooke, and E. H. Harriman. Ultimately, regardless of the situation, he was in it for himself. He arranged corporate mergers that skirted the antitrust law successfully for more than a decade. Morgan, therefore, as much as any other individual of the Gilded Age, personified what critics have called the "Robber Baron" stereotype, although in his defense, it can be argued that his reorganization and streamlining of the railroad and steel industries were positive actions for the nation as a whole.

In addition to his financial dealings, Morgan became noteworthy as a patron of the arts, donating his world-class collection of paintings, sculptures, books, and miscellaneous other treasures to various New York museums and repositories. His personal life was marred by a facial deformity that grew with age. Although he did not let it force him into seclusion, he did not like publicity—especially having his picture taken, except when he authorized it and could have the photographs retouched. *See also* MORTON, LEVI P.

MORGAN, JOHN TYLER (1824–1907). Born in the eastern hills of Tennessee, Morgan moved with his family to central Alabama as a youth. He practiced law in Talladega and Selma before becoming a leading secessionist and brigadier general in the Civil War. During the Alabama "Redemption" in 1876, he was sent by the **Democratic** state legislature to the U.S. Senate. He served continuously until his death, building a reputation as one of the best orators in the history of that august body. More often than not, he voted with the minority on any given issue, since **Republicans** usually controlled the Senate in the Gilded Age. He thus became adept at filibustering, and in fact led the memorable debate over the **Federal Elections Bill** in 1890 for the Democrats. He consistently espoused a racist point of view that few other southern leaders of the Gilded Age could match, rejecting racial equality as impossible by nature. He favored disfranchising **African Americans**, repealing their U.S. citizenship, colonizing them in the Congo or the Philippines, and basically reducing them in other ways to the status of slaves or something close to it. Despite the starring role this Alabamian played in formulating the ideology of white supremacy of the Jim Crow era, he has mainly been forgotten to American history except for his leadership in making the United States a global imperialist power around the turn of the 20th century. Indeed, he strongly supported the **Spanish–American War**; argued for the **Annexation of Hawaii**, Cuba, and the Philippines; and pushed for the building of an isthmian canal in Central America as forcefully as anyone. Although he favored Nicaragua rather than Panama as the place to put the canal, he is still linked to the construction of the Panama Canal as much as any other member of Congress, and perhaps second only to **Theodore Roosevelt**. *See also* FOREIGN AFFAIRS.

MORTON, LEVI P. (1824–1920). Born Levi Parsons Morton into a Congregationalist minister's family in Vermont, "L. P.," as he eventually became known, grew up too poor to go to **college**. He made his living in the business world by starting small and working his way up. He lived and worked in New Hampshire, Massachusetts, and New York, doing everything from teaching school to operating a dry goods store to engaging in international trade and Wall Street banking. Ultimately, banking would be his ticket to fortune and power. His New York firm, working with his London branch, arranged the $15 million financial transaction between England and the United States for the *Alabama* **Claims** settlement of 1871. After Jay Cooke's Philadelphia banking firm collapsed, setting off the **Panic of 1873**, Morton's New York bank became one of the strongest, if not *the* strongest, in the nation.

Morton joined the **Republican Party** and aligned himself with **Roscoe Conkling**'s **Stalwart** faction in the 1870s. He lost his bid for a seat in Congress in 1876, but won on his second attempt in 1878. In 1880, he almost became vice president for **James A. Garfield**, which would have made him president upon Garfield's assassination. The Conkling machine installed **Chester A. Arthur** instead, and Morton accepted the post of ambassador to France. While in Paris, he assisted in the completion of the **Statue of Liberty** project. In 1888, he was nominated for vice president on a ticket with **Benjamin Harrison**. The Harrison administration proved short, exciting, and turbulent, and it ended badly for both Morton and the GOP. His role in presiding over the U.S. Senate during the climactic **Federal Elections Bill** filibuster of 1890–1891 without taking a partisan stand on the bill incurred the anger of both Harrison and party bosses, causing them to jettison him from the ticket in 1892 and replace him with **Whitelaw Reid**. Morton still controlled New York, however, and won the governor's race there in 1894. After one term, he retired to a long life of banking and investing in real estate. His final notable act came in merging his banking firm with **J. P. Morgan**'s in the early 20th century. In the end, Levi P. Morton ranks among the most influential people of the Gilded Age, but is one with whom modern Americans are generally unfamiliar.

MR. DOOLEY. The literary creation of journalist Finley Peter Dunne (1867–1936), this Irish bartender-philosopher in south Chicago, Illinois, burst onto the scene in 1898 and became an immediate cultural icon. Known for their wit and wisdom on contemporary political and social issues, Mr. Dooley's best aphorisms would have been literary gems under any circumstances, but the delivery of them with a thick Irish brogue greatly enhanced their appeal at the time. Mr. Dooley soon went into national syndication after publication of his popular commentary on the **Spanish–American War** in the *Chicago Post*. Dunne then collected Mr. Dooley's newspaper pieces into a book called *Mr. Dooley in Peace and War* (1898), capitalizing on the public fascination with American global imperialism. For his effort, Dunne earned a place in the most influential circle of politicians and writers of his day, which included **Theodore Roosevelt** and **Mark Twain**, among others. Mr. Dooley continued to have a wide audience for more than a decade, as Dunne published several additional books in his name.

Some of Mr. Dooley's most famous sayings (paraphrased in modern English) include: *Trust everybody, but cut the cards; A fanatic is a man who does what he thinks the Lord would do if He knew all the facts; A newspaper's job is to comfort the afflicted and afflict the comfortable. See also* LITERATURE; PRESS, THE.

MUGWUMPS. A **Republican** faction that arose during the presidential campaign of 1884, the Mugwumps were mainly the old **Liberals** and Half-Breeds of earlier election seasons. They favored abolition of the spoils system, even after the **Pendleton Civil Service Act** of 1883 had started reforming it. They opposed the **Stalwart** faction of their own party, which favored keeping the status quo and held power out of proportion to its size. The irony of the Mugwumps was that the man who had formerly been the leader of the Half-Breeds, **James G. Blaine**, became the Republican nominee whom they so strongly opposed in 1884. Basically, Blaine had so soiled his reputation as a reformer through scandals that fellow reformers in the GOP could not bring themselves to support his candidacy. Mugwumps thus turned to supporting the **Democratic** candidate **Grover Cleveland** in that election, which helped Cleveland become the first Democrat elected president since before the Civil War. The name "Mugwump" derives from New York editor Charles Dana's description of this faction as traitors to their party—men with their "mug" on one side of the fence and their "wump" on the other. *See also* CORRUPTION; NAST, THOMAS; SCHURZ, CARL.

MUIR, JOHN. *See* SIERRA CLUB.

MULLIGAN LETTERS. *See* BLAINE, JAMES G.

– N –

NAST, THOMAS (1840–1902). Born in Germany, Thomas Nast immigrated to New York City with his family when he was a small child. As a teenager he studied art, and his drawings impressed one of the most important publishers in America at the time, Frank Leslie. He worked his way to the top of the New York publishing world as an illustrator during the Civil War. By the time of the Gilded Age, he had settled into a career with *Harper's Weekly* as a political cartoonist. His genius lay in taking ideas associated with political issues and bringing them to life in sketches that dramatized and often exaggerated them for effect. His ability to capture what the reading public was thinking and put it into picture form in **periodicals** allowed him to convey the news to the poor, illiterate masses of New York. It is said that his caricatures of the **corruption** of Boss **William Marcy Tweed** did more to bring the Tweed Ring to justice than any other factor. He stood on the side of the **Republican Party** for most of his career, and Abraham Lincoln considered him a powerful propagandist for the Union during the war. Thereafter, he strongly supported his friend **Ulysses S. Grant** as president, but he did not like **James G. Blaine**, and thus became a **Mugwump** in 1884. He was **liberal** in his views of race relations for the time, except that he held a strong prejudice against Irish Catholics. Undoubtedly, Nast's most enduring legacy has been his invention of the donkey as the symbol of the **Democratic Party** and the elephant as the symbol of the GOP. *See also* PRESS, THE.

NATIONAL FARMERS' ALLIANCE. *See* FARMERS' ALLIANCES.

NATIONAL RIFLE ASSOCIATION (NRA). The NRA, an organization that is currently among the most powerful special interest groups in the United States, began as a small marksmanship training center for National Guardsmen in Gilded Age New York. Founded in 1871 by Union veterans William Church and George Wingate, it was modeled after the British NRA, which had been founded a decade earlier. During the Civil War, Union military officers found that their troops, before enlisting or being drafted, all too often did not know anything about firearms usage, handling, or care, much less about marksmanship. After the war, Church, the editor of the *United States Army and Navy Journal*, and Wingate, a captain in the New York National Guard, decided to change that. They recruited the head of the **Grand Army of the Republic (GAR)**, General Ambrose Burnside of Rhode Island, as their first president, and they received a charter and a $25,000 grant from the state of New York to begin operations. They bought 70 acres on Long Island and named the property Creedmoor; in 1873, it opened as a shooting range and training ground. It proved both popular and successful, and other shooting clubs sprang up around the nation in the following years. Several other famous Union generals followed in Burnside's footsteps, serving as president of the NRA. They included Philip Sheridan, **Winfield Scott Hancock**, and former U.S. President **Ulysses S. Grant**, who served from 1883 to 1885.

In the early 1880s, the NRA came under fire from New York Governor Alonzo Cornell, who was not a strong supporter of the Second Amendment right to keep and bear arms. Around the same time, the GAR began rifle training apart from the NRA. Thus, state support of the NRA ended, and the NRA had competition from the largest private organization in America, the GAR. In 1892, the NRA left New York, moved to New Jersey, and practically ceased to operate until after the **Spanish–American War** of 1898, when the postwar Filipino insurrection renewed interest in marksmanship.

NATIONAL WEATHER SERVICE (NWS). Created by a joint resolution of Congress and President **Ulysses S. Grant** in 1870, the NWS started out under the jurisdiction of the War Department, falling specifically within the purview of the U.S. Army Signal Corps. Prior to its creation, little official meteorological research infrastructure existed in the United States. A few professors and individual weather-hounds had kept records of weather patterns in their local areas, but it was not until the Union army discovered the benefits of accurate forecasting during the Civil War that the need for a national meteorological research organization came to the fore. One of these professors, Increase A. Lapham of Wisconsin, working with his congressional representative from Milwaukee, Halbert E. Payne, lobbied for the creation of the NWS. Initially, the Signal Corps, under the direction of General Albert J. Myer, set up 24 posts along the Atlantic coast, the Gulf coast, and the Great Lakes, for tracking the weather nationally. The first official, coordinated reports were taken in the 7 a.m. hour on 1 November 1870. They were then transmitted by telegram to the main office in Washington, D.C. The collections of these regular transmittals were labeled "Telegrams and Reports for the Benefit of Commerce" and were issued by the "Division" of the same.

In 1872, Congress increased the size and scope of the NWS, adding stations throughout the United States, but the sparsely populated West lagged behind for several years. Meanwhile, the War Department added meteorology courses to its Signal Corps training curriculum. In 1873, the official local forecasts were distributed to area post offices for the benefit of the citizenry. In the 1880s, the NWS experienced turmoil, as **corruption** was found in its ranks. In 1890, new President **Benjamin Harrison** and the **Billion Dollar Congress** converted it into a civilian agency, placing it under the Department of Agriculture. Officials of the NWS were responsible for making reports pertaining to major events of the Gilded Age, such as the **Great Chicago Fire** of 1871, the **Rocky Mountain Locust Plague** of 1875–1876, and the **Great Blizzard** of 1888.

NATIONAL WOMAN SUFFRAGE ASSOCIATION. *See* ANTHONY, SUSAN B.; STANTON, ELIZABETH CADY; WOMEN.

NATIVE AMERICANS. *See* INDIANS, AMERICAN.

NEWSPAPERS. *See* PRESS, THE.

– O –

OAKLEY, ANNIE (1860–1926). Born Phoebe Ann Mosey to poor Quaker parents on a farm in rural Ohio, Annie Oakley—or "Little Sure Shot," as **Sitting Bull** would later dub her—began hunting to help feed her family when she was only 8 years old. She quickly developed shooting accuracy rivaling that of the best adult male marksmen. She learned to handle a rifle, shotgun, and pistol with equal skill. Her first claim to fame came from beating traveling side-show shooter Frank Butler in a $100 match in Cincinnati, Ohio, in 1881. Butler may have let her win, because he missed only the last shot of 25 attempts, whereas she missed none. He was immediately smitten with her beauty and talent, and she with his charm and business acumen. They married and began touring together, with her taking the stage name "Annie Oakley," supposedly from the name of the neighborhood (Oakley) where they resided in Cincinnati. In 1885, **Buffalo Bill** discovered the 5-foot-tall female phenomenon and launched her to national, and even international, fame and fortune. She became the main attraction in Buffalo Bill's "Wild West" show for most of the next 17 years, performing for the crowned heads of Europe and the American public alike. In 1894, she also appeared in one of **Thomas Edison**'s early experimental kinetoscope films, making her one of the first "movie stars" and one of the most recognizable celebrities of the Gilded Age.

OKLAHOMA LAND RUSHES. Except for the panhandle, the land composing the modern state of Oklahoma had been designated officially as **Indian** territory from the 1830s to 1889. The so-called Five Civilized Tribes (Choctaw, Chickasaw, Cherokee, Creek, and Seminole) held millions of acres there, as did the Cheyenne, Arapahoe, Iowa, Sac and Fox, Kaw, Pottawatomie, Shawnee, and Kickapoo. In the 1880s, as a result of pressure from **railroad** interests, federal politicians, and some white citizens, the U.S. government began laying the foundation for a coerced set of agreements through which these tribes would sell all their "surplus" or "unassigned" lands. Congress and President **Benjamin Harrison** passed the Indian Appropriations Bill of 1889, and on 22 April of that year, the land was to be sold on a first-come basis through a "race," "rush," or "run." Approximately 50,000 men, women, and children arrived to take part in the race. Two million acres were to be divided into 160-acre parcels. At high noon that day, with the firing of a rifle, the race began, and pandemonium ensued as pedestrians, equestrians, wagoners, and train passengers scattered across the terrain to stake their claims. Most got their land, but many disputes arose over who had rightful claims and who did not because thousands of "Sooners" had sneaked into Oklahoma and laid wait in hiding in order to beat the rush. By the end of the day, towns made up of tents housing about 10,000 people had sprung up at Guthrie, which became the first territorial capital, and at Oklahoma City.

The initial land rush was so successful that over the next 6 years, 6 additional land sales days were held that carved up the rest of the modern state. The largest came on 16 September 1893, when some 7 million acres were claimed by roughly 100,000 takers. Rarely in human history has a region become so populated and been developed so quickly as Oklahoma, as a result of these land rushes. The negative side of the story, of course, was that the Native Americans experienced yet another betrayal at the hands of the white man's government.

OLMSTED, FREDERICK LAW (1822–1903). Born in Hartford, Connecticut, to a wealthy family, Frederick Law Olmstead became a student of life, traveling around the world as a seaman before settling temporarily on Staten Island, New York, as a farmer. He studied civil engineering and agricultural sciences, mostly informally rather than in **college**, although he did attend some classes at Yale University. At age 30, he began working for the *New York Times* as a tourist observer of the South. He penned three books dealing with antebellum life in the South, and his observations strengthened his resolve as an abolitionist. On the eve of the Civil War, he secured a contract to design Central Park in New York City, and the field for which he is chiefly remembered—"landscape architecture" (a term of his own making)—

was born. Meanwhile, he became one of the earliest members of the **Republican Party**, supported the Abraham Lincoln administration, and worked for the Union cause in the Civil War as head of the U.S. Sanitary Commission. After the war, he co-founded the *Nation* news magazine in 1865, before resuming landscape architecture. Thereafter, he designed some of the most important grounds in America, including those of the **Biltmore Estate** in Asheville, North Carolina; **Stanford** University in Palo Alto, California; the **Columbian Exposition of 1893** in Chicago, Illinois; the first complete city park system in America in Buffalo, New York; and the U.S. Capitol grounds in Washington, D. C.—all in the 1880s and 1890s. In Boston, Massachusetts, in 1883, he started the first professional landscape design firm in America. Olmsted, more than any other individual, was responsible for the development of the modern style of city parks in America, as well as the greening of city streets and the synthesizing of nature with concrete and asphalt surroundings. *See also* HUNT, RICHARD M.

OLNEY, RICHARD. *See* CLEVELAND, GROVER; PULLMAN STRIKE.

OPEN DOOR POLICY. *See* FOREIGN AFFAIRS; HAY, JOHN.

– P –

PANIC OF 1873. The banking panic of 1873, the major economic crisis of the 1870s, led to a nationwide depression that lasted roughly 4 years. It began with the 18 September bankruptcy of the nation's most notable banking firm, Jay Cooke and Company of Philadelphia, which had been the principal financier of U.S. government **railroad** projects since the Civil War. Cooke had overextended his reach by financing the building of the nation's second **transcontinental railroad**, the Northern Pacific, at a time when the western states and territories were already saturated with unprofitable lines. When this banking giant went down, a chain reaction resulted that led to 89 railroad companies declaring bankruptcy, some 18,000 other businesses going under, the New York Stock Exchange closing for 10 days, and unemployment reaching 14 percent nationwide by 1877. It precipitated the **Great Railroad Strike of 1877**, hastened the demise of Reconstruction in the South, and put the last permanent scars on **Ulysses S. Grant**'s presidency. The only large sector of the American economy that did not suffer depression as a result of the panic was farm and crop prices. The **Grange**, in fact, boomed at this time, while similar industrial groups plummeted from 30 national **trade unions** to 9, with membership decreasing from 300,000 to 50,000. Time and the natural business cycle brought the nation out of the depression by 1878.

PANIC OF 1893. Twenty years after the **Panic of 1873**, another banking panic hit, devastating the U.S. economy again. It began just 10 days before **Grover Cleveland** was sworn into office in March. The bankruptcy of the Philadelphia and Reading **Railroad**, one of the largest companies in America, and the failure of the National Cordage Company, which previously had owned the most heavily traded stock in the country, precipitated a chain reaction of collapses. In the summer of 1893, the Erie; the Northern Pacific; and the Atchison, Topeka, and Santa Fe Railroads all went under. Over the next 4 years, 70 additional railroads collapsed, some 15,000 other businesses failed, 500 banks folded, and unemployment nationwide reached a peak of over 20 percent. The unemployment rate was as high as 50 percent in some states, such as Ohio, causing Jacob Coxey to lead "**Coxey's Army**" in a march on Washington, and setting off the Tompkins Square Riot in New York City in 1894. The **Pullman Strike** in Chicago made an already bad situation much worse, as it shut down even more railroads. Added into this volatile mix of problems were the **People's Party** and the **free silver** issue, which combined with the depression to cause a major upheaval in Washington, of which the **Republican Party** was the main beneficiary. Unlike in the 1870s, agriculture did not go unaffected, as crop prices fell hard. As with the Panic of 1873, the Panic of 1893 ended only after the natural business cycle had run its course. *See also* DEBS, EUGENE V.; PINGREE, HAZEN; TRADE UNIONS.

PENDLETON CIVIL SERVICE ACT. On 16 January 1883, in the wake of the assassination of President **James A. Garfield** by a disappointed federal office seeker, new President **Chester A. Arthur** signed the Pendleton Act into law. Named for **Democratic** congressman George Pendleton of Ohio, and supported by Half-Breed **Republicans**, it reformed the federal patronage system. It created a merit-based system for government job applicants. The problem it corrected was the old "spoils system," in which the president appointed friends, relatives, and monied supporters to low-level federal jobs, such as tax collectors, postmasters, and **foreign** consuls. Many appointees were unqualified for their positions, and those who were qualified owed favors to the president and party faction that gave them their jobs. **Corruption** of various types resulted from this system. Although the U.S. Civil Service Commission had been created in 1871, it immediately proved ineffective at ending the corruption in the **Ulysses S. Grant** administration. In fact, corruption reached an all-time high under Grant and the **Stalwarts**. Under the Pendleton Act and its new merit system, however, real reform began as candidates for government jobs had to pass a civil service exam administered by a reconstituted, bipartisan Civil Service Commission. The commission then, in theory, chose the most qualified person for the job regardless of party affiliation. Although the Pendleton Act reformed patronage at the federal level, it did not affect the machine politics so common at the state and local levels. *See also* ROOSEVELT, THEODORE.

PEOPLE'S PARTY. The largest and most notable third party of the Gilded Age, the People's Party, traced its beginnings primarily to the National **Farmers' Alliance** (NFA) and the **Knights of Labor** (KOL). In 1890, these "Populist" rural farmers of the South and West united with urban industrial workers of the Northeast and Midwest to form a third party that would represent the interests of the working class. This was a major change from the "bloody shirt" politics that had kept northerners and southerners divided and westerners largely ignored. The groups' initial unifying issue was the belief that inflation of the nation's money supply would benefit the poor. A majority of neither **Democrats** nor **Republicans** was disposed to agree, favoring the continuation of the tight money policy that had been in effect for most of the years since the Civil War. The NFA and KOL believed, along with western silver miners and their political representatives, that a "**free silver**" policy would be the best way to achieve the desired inflation. By 1892, the People's Party, which had already been operating in Kansas at the state level for 2 years, was ready to go national.

At a conference in St. Louis, Missouri, on 22 February, the national party was launched, with **Leonidas Polk** of North Carolina as its foremost leader and expected presidential nominee, and with plans to hold its formal national convention on 4 July in Omaha, Nebraska. When Polk died on 11 June, however, the party turned to the uninspiring **James B. Weaver** of Iowa as its nominee. The party's great accomplishment at the convention was to draw up the Omaha Platform, a collection of all the various special interest reform issues on which working class people could agree. Reading much like a socialist manifesto, the platform laid on the national political table some of the main ideas that would later be incorporated into the federal system in the Progressive movement of the early 20th century. In the meantime, the Populists drew more than a million popular votes and 22 electoral votes in the presidential election of 1892, but these votes were far too few to come close to winning. The party did capture some congressional seats and state offices, however. When the **Panic of 1893** hit, the Populists claimed a moral victory over the major parties and seemed to be in a good position to capture the White House in 1896.

In 1894, two events that national public perception associated with Populism occurred and damaged the party—the **Pullman Strike** in Chicago, Illinois, and the march on Washington, D.C., by **Coxey's Army** of unemployed industrial workers. Both made Populism appear too radical, bordering on **anarchism**. By 1896, the fragile coalition of sectionalists, industrialists, and agrarians that comprised the party had already begun to lose its cohesion. Many southern Populists returned to the Democratic fold in order to keep a "solid South" of white power. Many northern Populists returned to the Republican ranks. The party remained a force in national politics nonetheless. Unable to agree on a platform and a presidential candidate, however, the Populists chose to fuse with the Democrats, who had co-opted many of the Populists' ideas and who had nominated the fiery young **William Jennings Bryan** of Nebraska—a free silver advocate whose views on several issues were compatible with their own. Bryan lost the election, however, and the economy recovered, the nation soon went to war with Spain, America's attention turned to **foreign affairs**, and Populism faded into obscurity. Although a shell of the People's Party survived for several more years, it would never again be a force in national politics. Its influence, however, can still be felt today in that many of its issues were adopted by Progressives who succeeded where Populists had failed. *See also* DEBS, EUGENE V.; DONNELLY, IGNATIUS; TILLMAN, "PITCHFORK" BEN; WAITE, "BLOODY BRIDLES."

PERIODICALS. In the era of pre-electronic media, reading was an extremely important leisure activity as well as the main way to acquire news. Periodicals—magazines and similar printed materials that were neither newspapers nor books—provided some of the most popular forms of entertainment and sources for conversation and news. During the Gilded Age, the market for periodicals grew in proportion to the U.S. population, until by the turn of the 20th century, there was one magazine in circulation for every literate adult American, or about 65 million. Improved technology that allowed for mass production at lower costs made this giant increase possible, but so did new marketing and advertising strategies that placed the burden of cost on advertisers rather than on consumers. In the early part of the Gilded Age, *Century*, *Harper's*, *Scribner's*, and *Atlantic Monthly* were the best-selling magazines, with a combined circulation of more than a half-million per month. By the mid-1890s, *McClure's*, *Munsey's*, and the *National Police Gazette* each had a circulation that large, as did the most notable children's magazine, the *Youth's Companion*. This and similar children's periodicals were designed to instill moral **education** as much as to entertain, teaching the Victorian values that dominated the age: belief in God, reverence for the Founding Fathers and the U.S. government, respect for parents and elders, sharing, forgiving, and playing nice. There was, however, a separate and gigantic industry devoted to publishing **religious** tracts and Sunday School materials, with Methodists and Catholics leading the way in publications. Serialization of some of the most popular books of the day by the most famous authors attracted large audiences. **Mark Twain**, **William Dean Howells**, Rudyard Kipling, and Henry James, among many others, published this way.

In addition to periodicals that dealt mainly in human interest stories, some focused on hard news or political satire. *The Nation*, cofounded by E. L. Godkin and Frederick Law Olmsted in 1865 in New York, provided fairly balanced coverage of the major news topics of the day, albeit from a **Liberal/Mugwump**/Anti-Imperialist point of view. *North American Review*, a Boston, Massachusetts, intellectual's journal with a small circulation, provided some of the most thorough and balanced coverage of serious political issues in the Gilded Age. *Puck*, founded by Joseph Keppler in 1871, was known more for its political cartoons lampooning **Republicans**, **Tammany Hall**, the Irish, and the Catholic Church than for its social commentary. Taking its name from William Shakespeare's impish character in *A Midsummer Night's Dream*, it had as its motto, "What fools these mortals be." It took the basic idea that **Thomas Nast** had successfully employed for *Harper's Weekly* and made it into a new journalistic genre. A competitor, *Judge* magazine, came out in 1881 but rarely put out the quality of work or enjoyed the success of *Puck*. Although not exactly periodicals, the **Sears and Roebuck** and Montgomery Ward catalogues ranked as the most prolific publications of the late Gilded Age. *See also* LITERATURE; PRESS, THE.

PILLSBURY, CHARLES A. (1842–1899). Born in New Hampshire, Charles Alfred Pillsbury attended Dartmouth **College** before moving to Montreal, Canada, to begin a business career. Preceded by his uncle, John Sargent Pillsbury, he moved to Minneapolis, Minnesota, in 1869, and the two built a flour milling operation on the falls of the Mississippi River. Later that year, with chief competitor Cadwallader Washburn, the Pillsburys created the Minneapolis Millers' Association to supervise quality control of the grain coming into the mills. Using traditional water power to turn the grinding wheels, Charles discovered that steel rollers were more efficient than old fashioned stones at milling the hard wheat of the northern Midwest and Great Plains. Within 3 years, he had assumed control of the company, reorganizing it as C. A. Pillsbury and Company and introducing "Pillsbury's Best XXXX Flour," which he claimed was the finest quality baking flour in the world. In 1882, he opened his "A" mill, which was the largest in the nation. Meanwhile, John left the company to serve as the **Republican** governor of Minnesota for 6 years.

With powerful political connections to go along with an ambitious and innovative industrial mind, Charles built his company into a Gilded Age powerhouse, vertically integrating it into a near-monopoly by building his own grain elevators along the rails and rivers that supplied the wheat to Minneapolis. In 1889, however, he and his competitor Washburn sold out to an English syndicate, which put one of America's largest food processing industries largely in **foreign** hands, although Pillsbury himself continued on as director of the "Pillsbury-Washburn Flour Mills Company, LTD." This combination of foreign ownership, monopolistic tendencies, and ties to the GOP at high levels of government contributed to Minnesota's Populist revolt of the early 1890s, under the leadership of **Ignatius Donnelly**. Yet, the company continued on, virtually unaffected by such discontent, producing more than 10,000 barrels of flour per day at the end of the 19th century.

PINCHOT, GIFFORD. *See* SIERRA CLUB.

PINGREE, HAZEN (1840–1901). Born in Maine, Hazen Stuart Pingree moved to Massachusetts at age 16 and began working in a shoe factory, learning the trade of a cobbler. In 1862, he joined the Union army and served throughout the Civil War. A prisoner of war at the notorious Andersonville facility in Confederate Georgia, he escaped and was present at the Appomattox Courthouse surrender of Robert E. Lee to **Ulysses S. Grant**. After the war, he moved to Detroit, Michigan, and started his own shoemaking company. In 1889, he ran for mayor of Detroit as a **Republican** on an anti-**corruption** platform. He won four terms and served 8 years, during which time he became known principally for challenging the privately owned utility companies that enjoyed monopolies in supplying the city with electricity and gas. He created cheaper municipal competitors in both industries, which pleased most townspeople greatly. During the national economic downturn resulting from the **Panic of 1893**, he started public works programs to relieve unemployment, increased public aid to the needy, and began planting potatoes on vacant public lands to provide another food source for the indigent. In 1896, he won the Michigan gubernatorial race as a Republican. He served two terms and 4 years, during which time he advocated several reforms that put him in the forefront of the Progressive movement, including a standard 8-hour workday, a state income tax, and direct election of U.S. senators. He died in London, England, following an African safari with Vice President **Theodore Roosevelt**.

PINKERTON DETECTIVE AGENCY. Founded in Chicago, Illinois, by Allan Pinkerton just before the Civil War, this organization grew from a small group of private investigators to a large private police force spread across the northern and western United States by the 1870s. The group's reputation rested at first on its protection of President Abraham Lincoln and Union interests in the war. (Pinkertons were not on the scene when John Wilkes Booth assassinated Lincoln.) In 1870, when Congress created the modern Department of Justice, but long before the Federal Bureau of Investigation was born, Congress hired the Pinkertons to do surveillance and provide law enforcement in times of emergency. Despite its ties to the federal government, it remained a private company, and various corporations hired the agency throughout the Gilded Age to infiltrate **trade unions**, to break strikes, to catch outlaws, and otherwise to intimidate opponents. Notably, it brought about the demise of the **Mollie Maguires** in 1877, it helped capture members of **Jesse James**'s gang, and it broke the **Homestead Strike** of 1892.

The Pinkertons pioneered the practice of collecting mug shots of criminals and of using all the latest technology available to fight crime. By the 1890s, the organization had begun investigating international crimes. It became such a powerful and controversial force, in fact, that some Americans feared it could potentially be used as a mercenary army for destructive purposes. Indeed, at one point it employed more men than did the entire United States military. Consequently, the state of Ohio outlawed it. It never developed as great a presence in the southern states as it did in the rest of the nation because of southern hostility resulting from the Civil War. After the turn of the century, it gradually ceased to be a major factor in American society, but its methods were largely adopted by the FBI. Its symbol of the all-watching eye gave us the popular term "private eye" to describe a private investigator.

PLESSY V. FERGUSON. Generally hailed as the low point in the history of American jurisprudence in terms of civil rights, the **U.S.**

Supreme Court case of *Plessy v. Ferguson* deliberated upon the constitutionality of a Louisiana state law called the Separate Car Act of 1890, which required racially segregated **railroad** cars. Homer Plessy, a New Orleans man of mixed racial ancestry but white in appearance, brought suit against the state in *Plessy v. State of Louisiana*, claiming the law was unconstitutional based on the Fourteenth Amendment and the Civil Rights Act of 1875. Noted Chicago **Republican Albion Tourgee** headed Plessy's legal team. When Judge John H. Ferguson of the New Orleans district court ruled against Plessy, Tourgee appealed the decision to higher courts. In 1896, the U.S. Supreme Court, led by Chief Justice Melville Fuller, ruled eight to one against Plessy and in favor of the state of Louisiana, holding that it was each state's right to make its own regulations about such issues; as long as the trains carrying segregated passengers did not cross state lines, and as long as each race was provided "equal" seating arrangements, the Louisiana law did not violate any federal statute. Justice **John Marshall Harlan**, the lone dissenter on the court, vehemently disagreed, saying essentially that civil rights was a more compelling cause for the court to defend than was the right of a state to be sovereign in its law making. Unlike previous civil rights cases brought during the Gilded Age, *Plessy v. Ferguson* established a precedent for the next generation heading into the 20th century. "Separate but equal" became ingrained in the court as constitutional until 1954. *See also* AFRICAN AMERICANS.

POLK, LEONIDAS (1837–1892). Not to be confused with his cousin of the same name who was called the "fighting Bishop" in the Civil War, this Leonidas Polk had a middle name of Lafayette. Born just above the South Carolina line in Anson County, North Carolina, he was the distant cousin of U.S. President James K. Polk (1844–1848). He grew up on a slaveholding farm and, upon his parents' deaths, inherited land and slaves. He served in the state legislature until the outbreak of the Civil War, when he enlisted to fight for the Confederacy. After the war, he founded the town of Polkton and in the early 1870s became a newspaperman and a **Granger**. An advocate of diversified farming, he led in the creation of the state Department of Agriculture in the late 1870s. In the early 1880s, he headed the state's Baptist Convention. By the late 1880s, he had emerged as a leader of the National **Farmers' Alli-**

ance, serving as its president from 1889 to 1891. Instrumental in creating the **People's Party**, he was the presumptive nominee of his fellow Populists for president of the United States in 1892. Unfortunately, he died unexpectedly from internal bleeding before he could run. The nomination subsequently went to **James B. Weaver**, who could not unite southern voters as Polk had. Whatever chance the Populists had of winning, therefore, died with Polk.

POMEROY, JESSE (1859–1932). Jesse Pomeroy, the notorious child monster of the Gilded Age, was born in Charlestown, Massachusetts, where he committed his first attacks on neighborhood playmates around age 10 or 11. Reared by a respectable mother who owned her own business, Pomeroy was a big boy with a large head, protruding ears, a wide mouth, and a whitish-colored left eye. Older boys routinely made fun of him. He complained of frequent headaches that made him take out his frustrations first on family pets and other animals, before he progressed to attacking people. After moving to South Boston in 1872, he was accused and found guilty of hanging a young boy by his wrists from the ceiling of an outhouse, stripping him half naked, and beating him mercilessly for his own sexual gratification; this was not the first but the last in a series of such offenses by this young predator. Ostensibly, he was reenacting a form of punishment that his father had meted out against him when he was a toddler.

Considered mentally ill and a menace to society, authorities placed Pomeroy in a nearby juvenile reform school. Paroled for good behavior after just 2 years, he immediately returned to a life of sadistic crime, murdering a young girl by cutting her throat and then mutilating her body before burying it in the basement of his mother's seamstress shop. Not until he had killed his next victim, however, was the girl's body discovered. In his final murderous act, he enticed a 4-year-old boy to the ocean side, where he cut his throat, stabbed him repeatedly, mutilated his genitalia, and hacked up his body. His trial took place swiftly on 9 and 10 December 1874. The jury pronounced the 14-year-old Pomeroy guilty of first degree murder and recommended the death penalty. The case drew national attention for the gruesomeness of the crimes and the moral question of whether such a young and mentally deranged criminal should hang. Eventually, the Commonwealth of Massachusetts decided to give him life in prison with no possibility of parole, with the first several years served in solitary confinement. As "the Boston boy fiend" disappeared from the public eye, he largely disappeared from public memory, although his frequent but unsuccessful escape attempts rescued him from oblivion repeatedly throughout the Gilded Age.

POPULISTS. *See* PEOPLE'S PARTY.

POWDERLY, TERENCE. *See* KNIGHTS OF LABOR.

PRESS, THE. Newspapers were the principal medium for disseminating information in the Gilded Age. Since no electronic media existed, newspapers had little competition in delivering the daily news. Competition within the print media was fierce, and even small towns frequently had more than one paper. America's largest cities, of course, usually generated the papers that set the industry standards, with New York leading the way. Occasionally, a paper in an out-of-the-way place, such as Springfield, Massachusetts, or Emporia, Kansas, would rise to the top by exhibiting excellent journalism. Although the newspaper business changed over the three decades of the Gilded Age, one constant standard of the industry was that editors openly showed partisanship, siding with the **Republican Party**, the **Democratic Party**, or a third party, and otherwise making their views known on most political topics. Not until Adolf Ochs took control of the *New York Times* in 1896 did this begin to change noticeably.

At the beginning of the Gilded Age, **Horace Greeley**'s *New York Tribune* stood among the foremost newspapers in America. Greeley's failed presidential bid in 1872 on the **Liberal Republican** ticket, however, put the paper in the hands of **Whitelaw Reid**, who would not be able to maintain the paper's popularity at the previous level (and who would lose as **Benjamin Harrison**'s regular Republican vice-presidential running mate in 1892). The *Tribune*'s biggest rival during the early Gilded Age was Charles A. Dana's *New York Sun*. Dana, a former editor of the *Tribune* himself, never permanently aligned with either major party, but rather supported individual presidential candidates. His philosophy of life likewise changed over time from extremely liberal to extremely conservative. He set high standards for journalistic integrity that others sought to imitate.

In the 1880s, two **foreign**-born editors/publishers, **Carl Schurz** and **Joseph Pulitzer**, both left Missouri to join the hunt for newspaper sales in New York. Each had enjoyed success in St. Louis, with Pulitzer building the *St. Louis Post-Dispatch* into a mid-American powerhouse. Schurz's *New York Evening Post* was successful, but Pulitzer's *New York World* ultimately became the leading paper in New York by the 1890s. In 1895, **William Randolph Hearst**, owner of the premier western U.S. paper the *San Francisco Examiner*, bought the *New York Journal* and began a circulation war with Pulitzer, which led to the infamous "yellow journalism" fad around the time of the **Spanish–American War**. Hearst temporarily dominated the New York press, until Adolf Ochs took over the *New York Times* and turned it into the nation's most successful and respected paper—a designation it held well beyond the Gilded Age.

Outside New York, Samuel Bowles Jr.'s *Springfield Republican* set the standard for journalistic excellence during the early Gilded Age, with its fair-minded approach to national politics despite its pro-Republican views. In the late Gilded Age, William Allen White's *Emporia* (Kansas) *Gazette* established its reputation by supporting **William McKinley** for the presidency in 1896, and continued it as a solid Republican organ for decades thereafter. In the Midwest, the most consistently important paper was probably Murat Halstead's *Cincinnati Commercial Gazette*. Halstead engaged in iconoclasm against various respected political leaders in both parties, which hurt his own political ambitions but propelled a book-writing career apart from journalism.

Down the Ohio River a few miles lay the most important newspaper of the upper South, Henry Watterson's *Louisville Courier-Journal*. Although formerly a Confederate soldier, Watterson distinguished himself after the war by his liberal views on Reconstruction and other issues of the Gilded Age. He served in Congress briefly as a Democrat, as well. Further South was **Henry Grady**'s *Atlanta Constitution*, which must be counted among the standard bearers for its promotion of the "New South" in the 1880s. To Grady, the New South meant an industrialized South, not a racially equal South. *See also* PERIODICALS.

PROGRESS AND POVERTY. Published in 1879 by author Henry George of San Francisco, *Progress and Poverty* became the best-selling economics book of all time. A treatise on contemporary American economic conditions, it stated that the growth of wealth in the Gilded Age, which came through industrialization, had not been evenly distributed to the working class. As economic progress occurred for some people, poverty increased proportionately for the rest. The root cause was private land ownership, which produced unearned income for the owners through rent to the non-owners. Abolish this system and allow all land to be communally owned, the book argued, and a massive redistribution of wealth to the working class would result. George did not advocate a revolutionary method of accomplishing this goal, however, but rather argued that a simple change in the nation's system of taxation would do the trick. Replace all existing taxes with a "single tax" on land, and soon landowners would find it disadvantageous to continue owning the land. They would then sell out to the community, and a utopian age would ensue.

The book, while radical in its proposed solution to the United States' economic problems, drew a worldwide audience immediately, launching George's career as a writer, lecturer, and hopeful politician. So great was the impact of the book that "single tax clubs" sprang up around the nation. Followers became known alternately as "single taxers" or "Georgists." New York City's contingent even drafted George as their mayoral candidate in 1886. The grip of **Tammany Hall** was too great, however, and George lost. Eleven years later, he ran again but died just before election day. Meanwhile, Georgists created an experimental single tax community in Fairhope, Alabama, in 1894, and soon added another in Arden, Delaware, in 1900. By 1897, however, George was dead, *Progress and Poverty* was an 18-year-old book, more pressing economic issues such as **free silver** had come to the fore, and millionaire capitalists/philanthropists had self-servingly reinforced the status quo, putting politicians in their pockets and filling the economics departments of America's major **colleges and universities** with conservative classical economists who opposed Georgism. *See also* LITERATURE.

PULITZER, JOSEPH (1847–1911). Born in Hungary to a Jewish father and a Roman Catholic mother, Joseph Pulitzer was a son of privilege, yet the old world held little attraction for him. In 1864, he immigrated to the United States seeking adventure and found it fighting in the Civil War. After the war, he moved west to St. Louis, Missouri, which had a large German-born population. He spoke little English at first but immersed himself in books at a local library and taught himself the language, ultimately becoming a gifted writer of English. In St. Louis, he impressed **Carl Schurz**, owner of the *Westliche Post* newspaper, and became a reporter in 1868. Within 4 years, he had bought the paper and had been elected to the Missouri legislature. In 1879, he bought out the rival *St. Louis Dispatch* and fused it with the *Post* to become the still-extant *St. Louis Post-Dispatch*. The paper proved so successful that within 3 years, Pulitzer had enough money to buy a major but financially struggling New York paper, the *New York World*, from the notorious **Jay Gould**.

Pulitzer quickly turned the *World's* fortunes around by changing its coverage from primarily hard news to more entertainment-based features, trying to reach the large but not-well-educated audience of **immigrants** and working class people. He hired **Nellie Bly** as an investigative reporter, focused on government **corruption** and business scandals, included stories of interest to **women**, added the first real **sports** section in an American paper, touted the first modern comic strip (the "Yellow Kid"), and employed elaborate illustrations. Even with this shift to the pop culture approach, he managed to turn the paper into the premier **Democratic Party** organ in the country. The paper can be credited for helping **Grover Cleveland** upset **James G. Blaine** in the presidential race of 1884. By the 1890s, the *World* had the largest circulation of any American paper, at over 600,000.

Despite such notable accomplishments, Pulitzer and the *World's* reputation became tarnished in the late 1890s, after Pulitzer had retired from actively running the paper because of poor health. His paper engaged in a sales war with rival **William Randolph Hearst** and Hearst's *New York Journal*, which resulted in both papers printing half-truths and outright falsehoods in order to make their stories more sensational. This "yellow journalism," as it was called, contributed directly to the unnecessary **Spanish–American War** in 1898. Pulitzer's reputation has largely been rejuvenated since his death by his endowment of Columbia University's school of journalism and the prize for journalistic excellence which still bears his name. *See also* PRESS, THE; STATUE OF LIBERTY.

PULLMAN STRIKE. Arguably the worst labor dispute in American history, the 1894 Pullman railroad workers' strike centered on the Chicago, Illinois, area but caused problems nationwide and had ramifications that lasted well beyond the Gilded Age. In 1867, George Pullman started his Pullman Palace Car Company, which built train cars that served as luxurious rolling hotels for cross-country travelers. In 1881, he began building his own utopian town just south of Chicago to house his workers. A model community in terms of working class living standards at the time, the town provided company housing with indoor plumbing and electricity, with the rent deducted automatically from each worker's paycheck. The trade-off for this seemingly comfortable lifestyle was absolute submission to the owner, his company, and his way of doing business. By the 1890s, some 4,000 workers and their families lived in Pullman's community, for a total population of about 12,000.

When the **Panic of 1893** hit, the railroad business suffered greatly, and Pullman cut wages sharply while leaving rent at its pre-depression level. Workers complained, and some even walked off the job on 11 May 1894, but Pullman refused to negotiate with them. **Eugene V. Debs**, head of the American Railway Union (ARU), then notified the company that beginning 26 June, ARU members would no longer work trains that had Pullman cars attached. An organization representing the railroad corporations, the General Managers Association, reacted by threatening that ARU members would be fired and replaced with scabs. The ARU and many thousands of non-members who supported the strike walked off the job at that point, realizing there was no way the railroads could find that many scabs. Moreover, the strikers began to attack Chicago-area trains that were still running, some of which carried the U.S. mail. This action put what had previously been a local problem under federal jurisdiction and prompted President **Grover Cleveland** and his Attorney General Richard Olney to get a federal injunction to stop the strike. The ARU ignored the injunction, however, and Cleveland ordered in thousands of federal troops. Beginning 3 July and lasting a week, rioting, arson, gunfights, and other acts of violence and vandalism claimed some 70 casualties and created millions of dollars of property damage. The strike ended with the arrest of Debs and his lieutenants on 10 July.

In the end, Debs went to prison for several months and came out the leader of the Socialist movement and party in America for the next quarter-century. The ARU was effectively destroyed, and most railroad workers went back to work on Pullman's parsimonious terms. Cleveland's strong-arm tactics incurred the wrath of Illinois Governor **John P. Altgeld**, causing a rift in the **Democratic Party** that contributed to a new **Republican** ascendancy for the next few years. Congress and the Cleveland administration conceded, however, to the creation of Labor Day as a national holiday. Pullman soon died—a multimillionaire despised by the working class. *See also* PEOPLE'S PARTY; TRADE UNIONS.

– R –

RAILROADS. From its inception in the 1820s, the railroad industry was destined to become America's first big business, giving rise to corporations that pooled both national and international capital. The first railroad chartered for use by the American public was the Baltimore and Ohio in 1828. It seems strangely fitting that the line's cornerstone was laid on 4 July by the last surviving signer of the Declaration of Independence, Charles Carroll. The fact that the nation's first national overland transportation system got its start in such a way is rich with symbolism.

The rail industry grew steadily before the Civil War, and the first **transcontinental railroad** was planned as early as 1852. Although it was delayed for a decade because of political disputes, construction on the first transcontinental line began in 1862. The Abraham Lincoln administration started the process of cooperation between the national government and two great trunk lines, the Union Pacific and the Central Pacific, to build what amounted to two separate lines starting from opposite sides of the country and meeting and merging in the middle to become one. Construction lasted 7 years but was completed in 1869, by which time the nationalist president Lincoln was no longer alive to see it.

It seems somewhat ironic but somehow appropriate that the transcontinental railroad was completed in the first year of the presidency of **Ulysses S. Grant**, whose administration would soon become notorious for scandals involving railroads and their builders and financiers. The infamous **Credit Mobilier scandal** showed that the national government was not merely in the business of facilitating the construction of railroads but had also taken on the position of the proverbial fox guarding the henhouse. With so much money to be made in this new national transportation network, how could the American people be sure that their elected officials in Washington—not to mention in their home states, districts, counties, and municipalities—could be trusted to administer laws concerning railroads honestly? Unfortunately, they could not be sure. Big business and government involvement with it bred cynicism, which would soon prove to be a national phenomenon.

A more immediate problem arose in this triangle between the railroads, the government, and the people, when railroad workers began striking for better pay, hours, working conditions, and benefits. There were eight railroad strikes in 1877, the year that marks the beginning of the psychological unification of the North and the South after the Civil War. The fact that in the first real year of sectional harmony the country should be torn by labor disputes involving its first national transportation network is, again, rife with symbolism. The question that loomed unanswered then and for the next few years was whether the national government had any duty and/or constitutional authority to intervene in such strikes. **Republican** President **Rutherford B. Hayes** mobilized troops during the most serious of these strikes (the **Great Railroad Strike of 1877**), which marked the beginning of a potential national policy; however, it did not guarantee that such action would be taken again. It could have just as easily been seen as a one-time emergency measure never to be repeated. These strikes of 1877 affected life in 12 states, shut down 22,000 miles of track, and caused the temporary unemployment of some one million men.

Certainly, strikes that shut down lines crossing state boundaries seemed to justify government intervention, but the complexities of constitutional law and the reluctance of all presidents during the late 1800s to test the limits of national government authority (and especially of presidential power) kept the issue unresolved until 1894. In that year, the great and devastating **Pullman Strike**, which shut down the transportation system upon which the U.S. Postal Service had come to depend for fast, efficient delivery of the mail, gave **Democratic** President **Grover Cleveland** and his Attorney General Richard Olney an opportunity to intervene. Even that action did not resolve the dispute over whether the national government had any business breaking up labor strikes. It would take several more years, quite a few more labor problems, and a reform-minded American public in the coming Progressive Era to settle this issue in the affirmative; the national government did indeed have a right and an obligation under the general welfare clause of the Constitution to intervene.

The problems that arose in 1877 between the railroad tycoons and their labor force amounted to little more than a hiccup for the railroad-building industry. Rather than construction slowing after 1877, it increased dramatically. The decade of the 1880s saw the biggest railroad-building boom in American history. Between 1877 and 1889, the industry standardized the width of tracks to 4 feet, 8 inches to allow any train to run on any tracks in the United States and Canada; track mileage doubled; and railroads became the world's leading revenue producer. Railroads fueled the steel industry and led to the development of time zones, as well. By the 1890s, there were four transcontinental lines, and railroad moguls such as **Cornelius Vanderbilt**, **Leland Stanford**, **Collis P. Huntington**, **James J. Hill**, and **Jay Gould** were among the richest men in the world. *See also* CORRUPTION; FLAGLER, HENRY M.; GRANGER CASES; TRADE UNIONS.

REED, THOMAS B. (1839–1902). Born in Portland, Maine, Thomas Brackett Reed attended Bowdoin **College**, studied law, taught school in California briefly, served in the U.S. Navy during the Civil War, practiced law in his hometown, and held a variety of offices in his home state government before being elected to Congress in 1876. A partisan Republican, he served in the U.S. House of Representatives from 1877 to 1899. His first notoriety there came in his first year when he was appointed to the commission investigating the controversial presidential election of 1876 and impressed observers with his sharp legal mind and his quick, sarcastic wit.

Appointed to the House Rules Committee in 1882, Reed studied the often dysfunctional parliamentary system that had grown by tradition over nearly a century and which allowed the minority party to thwart all legislation it disapproved. In 1889, he was elected Speaker of the House for the **Billion Dollar Congress**, where he proceeded to implement a new set of parliamentary procedures that came to be called the "Reed Rules." These new rules allowed the speaker to count all congressmen present, whether they answered the roll or not, thus securing a quorum with which to conduct business and vote on pending bills, regardless of the minority party's disapprobation. These rules ended the gridlock that had plagued the House throughout the first two decades of the Gilded Age. Reed and the GOP thus began the new tradition of the majority party ramming partisan legislation through the House with near-capricious power. In this way, several contested elections were decided in favor of the Republican candidates in 1890 alone, the racially charged **Federal Elections Bill** was passed (although it failed in the Senate), the controversial **McKinley** Tariff was passed, Civil War pensions were raised dramatically, and Congress spent the largest amount of money in American history to that point in time.

Reed's heavy-handed approach and no-nonsense but sharp-tongued personality garnered him the nickname "the Czar" and contributed to his party's ouster from majority status in 1891. The **Democrats** then seized the opportunity to retaliate. Within another 4 years, however, the Republicans were back in the majority, and Reed served two additional terms as speaker, from 1895 to 1899. His opposition to the **Spanish–American War** and the United States' fast-increasing imperialist tendencies led him to resign his seat in Congress. He served out his last years in a private law practice in New York. *See also* HARRISON, BENJAMIN; LANGSTON, JOHN MERCER; MORGAN, JOHN TYLER; TARIFFS.

REID, WHITELAW (1837–1912). Born in southwestern Ohio, Whitelaw Reid attended nearby Miami University, alma mater of his future presidential running mate, **Benjamin Harrison**. During the Civil War, he served as a war correspondent for the *Cincinnati Gazette* and as an aide to officers on the Union side. After the war, he served as librarian of the U.S. House of Representatives before being hired by **Horace Greeley** to write for the *New York Tribune* in 1868. He quickly distinguished himself as a hard news reporter and **foreign** war correspondent. He and Greeley were among the leaders of the **Liberal Republican** movement in 1872 to oust **Ulysses S. Grant** from the White House. Upon Greeley's untimely death in 1872 as he ran for president, Reid acquired financial and editorial control of the paper. After marrying California millionaire Darius Ogden Mills's daughter, he was set for life financially. Not until the 1888 election of Benjamin Harrison to the presidency did he enter politics. The new president appointed him Ambassador to France, a position he held to the end of the administration when the **Republican Party** put him on the ticket as Harrison's vice presidential running mate for 1892. The ticket lost the election, however, and Reid next endorsed fellow Ohioan **William McKinley** in 1896, hoping to obtain another diplomatic appointment. McKinley did not give him one, though, until 1898 when he put Reid on the Peace Commission for the **Spanish–American War**. In that position, Reid, in keeping with his pro-imperialist editorials, argued for long-term United States possession of the Philippines. He was later appointed by **Theodore Roosevelt** to serve as Ambassador to England, a position he held until his death.

RELIGION. The Gilded Age overlaps the second half of the English Victorian Era, and both were times of extreme religiosity. The Victorian Era is synonymous with the socio-political normalization of prudish, Protestant morality in English history, and the Gilded Age should be considered its equivalent in U.S. history. The fact that the Gilded Age is not primarily thought of in this way has a lot to do with this era's label. The emphasis often is placed on the **corruption** that characterized society and politics in this era, rather than on the "gilded" exterior that tried to cover it up. The gilding is often portrayed as a facade of financial opulence for some that obscured the dire poverty of others. Actually, however, the real gilding that covered this age was a thick layer of religion, particularly Protestant Christianity. It came in two forms, then as now: the politically liberal, earthly minded, improve-the-here-and-now **Social Gospel** variety, and the socially conservative, heavenly minded, salvation-of-the-soul-for-eternity variety. Between the two, religion permeated just about every aspect of American life. Blue laws were in effect in every state and were rarely challenged. Laws against cursing and swearing, gambling, pornography, birth control, and drinking were also pervasive. Presidents, congressmen, governors, and local elected officials were almost all unabashed Christians in their public lives, if sometimes hypocrites in their private lives. Yet few Americans complained about these outward displays of religion in the public square, and even fewer dared to do so on constitutional grounds. It was simply the norm; it was expected.

Religion played a conspicuous role in Gilded Age public policy, thanks partly to New York's **Anthony Comstock**, who became something of a morality czar, lobbying for and strictly enforcing obscenity laws dealing with the U.S. Postal Service. However, the presidents of the United States largely set the tone. Every one in this era had a Bible scripture read aloud at his inauguration, which had never been a tradition prior to this time and would cease to be a tradition after it. **Rutherford B. Hayes** was sworn in twice, once privately and once publicly, because the usual inauguration day of 4 March fell on a Sunday; he took the oath on Saturday night and again on Monday to avoid upsetting the norm. Because church members tended to vote as a bloc for one party over the other, President **Ulysses S. Grant** once declared with some veracity that the Methodist Church of the 1870s wielded more power than any other single organization in America. That was a bold statement considering that the **Grand Army of the Republic** at the time controlled nearly a million votes. Grant's **Republican Party** was indebted to both about equally for its electoral successes during the Gilded Age. The **Democratic Party**, by contrast, tended to attract non-mainstream religious elements, including Catholics, and those without any particular religious affiliation. It was, consequently, less prudish about moral vices than was the GOP. Those who enjoyed or profited from drinking, for instance, tended to be Democrats. More often than not, however, the Democrats were the minority party during the Gilded Age, which shows the popularity and persistence of the religious Republicans. Groups like the **American Protective Association**, which sought to keep Catholicism at bay, worked mainly through the GOP. The **People's Party**, although not as big as either major party, was as much an instrument of social uplift as political reform. It primarily tried to introduce the principles of Christian Socialism (i.e. level the playing field, spread the wealth, feed the poor, comfort the afflicted) into public policy. Despite its lack of electoral success, it helped pave the way for the Progressive movement at the beginning of the 20th century.

Evangelists like **D. L. Moody** attracted huge numbers to their crusades in the 1870s and continued to do so throughout the 1880s and 1890s. Most of the best-remembered songs from the Gilded Age came from evangelically minded hymn writers, such as Ira Sankey and Fannie Crosby, rather than from secular sources. Yet the wave of the future seemed to be with ministers like **Washington Gladden**, who preached the Social Gospel. Working through Christian organizations like the Young Men's Christian Association, the **American Red Cross**, and the Salvation Army, as well as through **periodicals** like the *Youth's Companion* and other educational venues, purveyors of the Social Gospel tried to make this world a better place to live rather than focusing on eternal salvation or damnation. They focused on civic responsibility rather than evangelism, and preached messages of hope and encouragement rather than repentance. Charles Sheldon's classic *In His Steps* (1897) made Jesus a role model for proper living rather than the savior of humankind by repeatedly asking in real-life situations "What would Jesus do?" Many Social Gospel authors tried to provide moral **education** to children. **Horatio Alger**'s inspirational dime novels could be considered examples. Francis Bellamy's 1892 poem "The Pledge of Allegiance," which did not contain the now-famous phrase "under God," was another example. Some Christian activists blurred the lines between evangelism and civic responsibility. **Frances Willard** and the **Women**'s Christian Temperance Union (WCTU), for instance, touted a cause that was akin to a holy crusade, yet it was as much aimed at producing a better society as at rescuing people from eternal damnation. Were it not for prohibitionists having their own political party for most of the Gilded Age, the WCTU would have probably been a tool of the GOP.

The largest Protestant denominations during the Gilded Age were the Methodists, Baptists, Presbyterians, Congregationalists, and Disciples of Christ. Most of them opposed strongly centralized governance. They tended to be local and autonomous, with a minimum of outside oversight. The Catholic Church was, then as now, larger than any of the individual Protestant churches, and it was, of course, centralized and hierarchical. Some small Protestant denominations that attracted a notable amount of attention included the Church of Jesus Christ of Latter Day Saints (Mormons); the **Church of Christ, Scientist**; and the Jehovah's Witnesses. Of the three, the Mormons' adherence to their doctrine of polygamy put them constantly at odds with the U.S. government, various state and territorial governments, and the vast majority of the American people. After repeatedly failing to get Congress to grant Utah statehood, and after an 1890 **U.S. Supreme Court** case ruled in favor of the disfranchisement of polygamists, the Mormons abandoned the doctrine. Utah then became a state in 1896. The Mormon requirement of compulsory tithing, meanwhile, guaranteed that the church would thrive financially. *See also* COXEY'S ARMY; ROCKEFELLER, JOHN D.; TURNER, BISHOP HENRY M.

REPUBLICAN PARTY. Also called the Grand Old Party, or GOP for short, the Republican Party held majority power in the United States for most of the Gilded Age. It won five presidential elections and lost two. It kept control of the Senate for all but 4 years, while dominating the House of Representatives for 18 years and being in the minority for the other 18. The party's greatest boon came from being installed into federal power during the Civil War. From then to the time of the **Spanish–American War**, its spokesmen portrayed it rightly as the party of Union, and arguably as the party of patriotism and loyalty, adherence to the Founding Fathers' original intent, and progress and forward thinking generally. With great effect its candidates rallied northern voters in federal elections by "waving the bloody shirt," which meant reminding them which party had bled and died to preserve the Union (Republican) and which had sponsored rebellion, secession, and traitorous activities (**Democratic**).

The main base of support for the party came from evangelically inclined Protestant Christians. Among the large denominations, Methodists were particularly prone to supporting the GOP, but Baptists, Presbyterians, Congregationalists, and Episcopalians tended to do so as well. Among the small denominations, Quakers were almost exclusively Republican. Ethnically, Americans of British and Scandinavian ancestry, along with **African Americans**, were the strongest supporters of the GOP, whereas those of German and French heritage were almost evenly divided. The only large **immigrant** group to oppose the party overwhelmingly was the Irish. The main issue that diverted these religious and ethnic groups into one party or the other was prohibition. A majority of Republicans favored it.

On other issues of ideology, the GOP's positions were not generally based on **religion** or ethnicity. The party stood for high taxes and **tariffs**; for increasing federal programs, spending, and regulation; for increasing civil rights for African Americans (but not necessarily other minorities); for the gold standard (mostly); and for an imperialistic **foreign** policy. In a party so large, of course, some members opposed each of these positions, and from one federal election to the next, a coalition had to be built within the ranks to keep the party unified. The coalition building proved successful more often than not.

The first presidential election of the Gilded Age (1872) saw the fragile coalition break down when **Liberal Republicans**, reacting to the **corruption** of **Ulysses S. Grant**'s first term, refused to support him for a second. The **Stalwarts** were bailed out, however, by the introduction of several hundred thousand black votes, which went to Grant. The coalition survived in 1876, but only because of the **Compromise of 1877**. It survived the split over civil service reform in 1880 but broke down again in 1884 when **James G. Blaine** lost the support of thousands of Catholics over a comment about "rum, Romanism, and rebellion." In 1888, the party was bailed out again, this time by an electoral college victory amid a popular vote defeat. In 1892, **Benjamin Harrison** lost the support of many poor voters because of the Populist revolt and the **McKinley** Tariff, and of some liberals because of his support of the **Federal Elections Bill**.

At the beginning of the Gilded Age, the most pressing issue for the GOP was Reconstruction. Although a majority within the party at first favored a radical policy aimed at achieving equal opportunity and treatment of blacks, by the mid-1870s, the racial reformers were in the minority. Civil service reform, the most divisive issue of the late 1870s and early 1880s, came to the fore in a tragic way with the assassination of Republican president **James A. Garfield** in 1880. Arguments over the tariff and pensions for Union veterans consumed the party's attention in the late 1880s and early 1890s, while combating the **free silver** issue and promoting a global imperialist foreign policy dominated the late 1890s. *See also* ARTHUR, CHESTER A.; BILLION DOLLAR CONGRESS; BUTLER, BENJAMIN F.; CHINESE EXCLUSION ACT; COLFAX, SCHUYLER, JR.; CONKLING, ROSCOE; HANNA, MARK; HAY, JOHN; HAYES, RUTHERFORD B.; LANGSTON, JOHN MERCER; MORTON, LEVI P.; MUGWUMPS; PENDLETON CIVIL SERVICE ACT; PEOPLE'S PARTY; REED, THOMAS B.; REID, WHITELAW; ROOSEVELT, THEODORE; SHERMAN, JOHN; STANFORD, LELAND; WHEELER, WILLIAM A.; WILSON, HENRY.

RIIS, JACOB. *See HOW THE OTHER HALF LIVES.*

"ROBBER BARONS." *See* CARNEGIE, ANDREW; DUKE, BUCK; FLAGLER, HENRY M.; FRICK, HENRY CLAY; GOULD, JAY; HILL, JAMES J.; HUNTINGTON, COLLIS P.; MORGAN, J. P.; PEOPLE'S PARTY; ROCKEFELLER, JOHN D.; STANFORD, LELAND; VANDERBILT, CORNELIUS.

ROCKEFELLER, JOHN D. (1839–1937). Born in western New York near Ithaca, John Davison Rockefeller moved with his family to Cleveland, Ohio, while a teenager. He began his career there, working as a clerk, a cashier, and a bookkeeper before starting his own accounting business. In 1862, he and a business partner ventured into the oil refining industry. Getting in on the ground floor of that new industry, he enjoyed great profits. Seeing a bright future in oil, he joined with his brother in 1866 to form William Rockefeller and Company. A year later, they added several partners, including **Henry M. Flagler**, and the making of a great corporation was in the works. In 1870, they incorporated their firm, naming it the Standard Oil Company of Ohio. Within 3 years, Standard Oil had swallowed up nearly all its competition in Cleveland, and John had emerged as the mastermind behind the juggernaut. He seized the opportunity in the **Panic of 1873** to buy struggling oil companies in Pennsylvania and New York.

Over the next decade, Rockefeller would prove a corporate genius, turning his corporation into a trust through horizontal integration. His primary method of accomplishing this was to secure special rates from **railroad** lines to ship his oil cheaper than the competition's. When his competitors could not keep pace, he would sometimes offer to buy them out at a fair price rather than simply let them go under. Other times he would basically take a controlling interest in their operations, acting as though he owned them. He also emphasized efficiency in operations, avoiding waste and keeping wages low. Consequently, he was numbered among the richest men in the world in the 1880s. Changes in Ohio state law forced him to move his trust to New Jersey in 1892. Thereafter, he managed to increase market share even more, until he controlled approximately 90 percent of the nation's oil supply.

In business, Rockefeller was ruthless to his competition, yet he firmly believed that God had blessed him with his fortune and expected him to be a good steward of it for the public good. His first major philanthropic project was the creation of the University of Chicago. Even so, he became the main target of reformers such as Henry Demarest Lloyd and Ida Tarbell, both of whom sought the destruction of his trust for what they believed was the common good. Diagnosed with a rare disease that caused him to lose all his hair, Rockefeller gave money for medical research. He retired in 1896 and thereafter spent the rest of his long life engaged in philanthropy, while leaving his son and grandsons to manage his business affairs. By the end of the Gilded Age, he was among the five richest men in the world.

ROCKY MOUNTAIN LOCUST SWARM. Striking the Great Plains and surrounding areas, from the Gulf of Mexico to Canada, the Rocky Mountain Locust Swarm, of the mid-1870s, is thought to have been the largest mass of zoological life in world history. Estimated to have extended for 1,800 miles north and south and more than 100 miles east and west, this swarm of 3.5 trillion grasshoppers (*Melanoplus spretus*), indigenous to the Rocky Mountains region, began flying west over the Great Plains in 1873 but returned in larger numbers for the next 3 years. At the worst points, the large, glossy-winged insects covered the sky in such a thick cloud as to block out all sunlight. They rained down upon unsuspecting homesteaders with a noisy thunder like a hailstorm, first destroying their crops, then consuming every other edible thing in their path. Many people reported that they ate everything from the bark off the trees to the wool off the sheep. Some 150,000 homesteaders were left utterly destitute as a result. The federal government was not known for its generosity in relieving such suffering during the Gilded Age, but this situation was so critical that the U.S. Army had to dispense tons of food to prevent widespread starvation. The government also allocated money for seeds for the farmers, lest they have no way to get back on their feet financially, and it allowed them to break the residency requirement of the Homestead Act of 1862 to find temporary employment elsewhere. By 1877, the swarms had simply disappeared, with rarely a sighting thereafter. Within 30 years, the species was apparently extinct. The last sighting of a live *Melanoplus spretus* was in 1902. No one knows for sure what happened to the species, but evidence suggests that farmers breaking new ground in their fields destroyed its egg-laying habitat.

ROOSEVELT, THEODORE (1858–1917). Generally remembered for his two-term presidency of the United States from 1901 to 1908, Theodore Roosevelt was also an important public figure during the Gilded Age. Born into a wealthy family of Dutch ancestry in New York City, "Teddy" matriculated at Harvard University in Massachusetts, where he earned a degree in history, then studied law at Columbia University in his home town. Elected to the New York State Assembly in 1881 as a **Republican**, he served 3 years, until the deaths of his wife and mother on the same day cast a pall upon his desire to be a public official. Grieving, he moved to the Dakota Territory to become a cattle rancher, where he lived the life of an actual **cowboy** for 2 years. After returning east in 1886, he remarried and resumed his life in politics. In 1889, President **Benjamin Harrison** appointed him to the U.S. Civil Service Commission, a position he held until 1895 when he became police commissioner of New York City. After serving at that post for only 2 years, he won appointment as Assistant Secretary of the Navy from President **William McKinley**, which afforded him the opportunity to push for a naval buildup and an imperialist **foreign** policy on the eve of the **Spanish–American War**. He resigned a year later so that he could raise a volunteer cavalry regiment nicknamed the Rough Riders to fight in the land war in Cuba.

Having been recognized as a war hero for his charge up San Juan Hill in Cuba in the summer of 1898, Colonel Roosevelt became a national celebrity because of the newspaper articles written by him or about him and his battlefield exploits. Later that year, he won the governorship of New York, and 2 years later was elected vice president of the United States as McKinley's second-term running mate. McKinley's assassination in 1901 elevated him to the presidency, an event that some historians say ended the Gilded Age and started the Progressive Era of American history.

Besides Roosevelt's political and military achievements, he was also notable for his many contributions as a professional historian. His first major book, *The Naval War of 1812* (1882), became the standard treatment of that topic for decades, showing his acumen for naval affairs, which qualified him for his post as Assistant Secretary of the Navy in McKinley's first term. His other great work of the Gilded Age was his four-volume *The Winning of the West* (1889–1896), which set forth the "frontier thesis" that his friend Frederick Jackson Turner expanded upon and made into a staple of American historiography for generations. Many of his other books did not match the greatness of these mentioned, but Roosevelt's contributions to the field were important and impressive enough to earn him the presidency of the American Historical Association later in life. *See also* LITERATURE; PENDLETON CIVIL SERVICE ACT; "SIGNIFICANCE OF THE FRONTIER IN AMERICAN HISTORY"; WOOD, LEONARD.

ROUGH RIDERS. *See* ROOSEVELT, THEODORE; SPANISH–AMERICAN WAR; WHEELER, "FIGHTIN' JOE"; WOOD, LEONARD.

"RUM, ROMANISM, AND REBELLION." *See* BLAINE, JAMES G.; REPUBLICAN PARTY.

– S –

SANBORN INCIDENT. *See* CORRUPTION; GRANT, ULYSSES S.

SCHURZ, CARL (1829–1906). Born in Prussia, Carl Schurz fled his homeland after participating in the Revolution that swept Europe in 1848. After some dangerous international adventures, Schurz ended up in the United States in 1852. He lived in several different places, including Pennsylvania; Wisconsin; Missouri; Washington, D.C.; and New York. As one of the original members of the **Republican Party**, he campaigned for Abraham Lincoln in 1860 and was rewarded with the ambassadorship to Spain upon his election. He resigned, however, to return and fight for the Union in the Civil War, where he rose to the rank of major general.

After the war, Schurz became a newspaperman and mouthpiece of the "radical" faction of his party during the Andrew Johnson years. After being elected to the U.S. Senate from Missouri in 1869, he quickly turned against President **Ulysses S. Grant** because of the **corruption** of his administration. He consequently headed up the **Liberal** faction that unsuccessfully opposed Grant's reelection in 1872. In 1877, President **Rutherford B. Hayes** appointed him Secretary of the Interior, a position which did not particularly fit his many talents but which he made the most of nonetheless. In the 1880s, he returned to newspaper editing and began writing books as well. He was perhaps most influential as the editor of the *New York Evening Post*. He became a **Mugwump** in 1884, supporting **Democrat Grover Cleveland** over fellow Republican **James G. Blaine**, again because of charges of corruption in his own party.

Principle was always more important than party to Schurz. He worked for civil service reform throughout the 1870s and early 1880s, and was only partly assuaged by the **Pendleton Civil Service Act** of 1883. He also stood among the vanguard of anti-imperialists. He opposed the annexation of Santo Domingo in the Grant administration and the decision by the **William McKinley** administration to go to war with Spain in 1898. He favored a progressive approach to race relations with **African Americans**, American **Indians**, and **foreign** peoples. Although he was often on the unpopular side of issues in his own generation, he has largely been vindicated by history as one of the real visionaries among Gilded Age Republicans. *See also* AMERICAN ANTI-IMPERIALIST LEAGUE; PRESS, THE; PULITZER, JOSEPH.

SEARS, ROEBUCK AND COMPANY. Founded by Richard W. Sears and Alvah C. Roebuck in Chicago, Illinois, in 1893, the midwestern corporation of Sears, Roebuck and Company built a retail merchandise empire through the mail-order method pioneered by Montgomery Ward. At a time when farmers often had very limited access to traditional general and department stores, Sears, a **railroad** depot worker in Minnesota, envisioned bringing the store to the farmer in the form of a catalogue, but doing so on a much larger scale than had Ward. After an early career as a watch salesman at train stations, Sears moved to Chicago in 1887 and placed an advertisement for a watchmaker in the *Chicago Daily News*, which Roebuck answered. Their partnership evolved into a corporate business within 6 years. By 1895, the Sears catalogue numbered more than 500 pages and boasted more than $750,000 in gross sales. Just as the company's growth began to explode, Roebuck left the partnership to pursue other business interests, although he continued to serve as a top-level manager over the watch and jewelry department. Sears then sold Roebuck's half of the partnership to Julius Rosenwald and his brother-in-law. Rosenwald, a clothier by vocation, added both a quality clothing line and his business acumen to the organization; he would go on in the 20th century to distinguish himself as a great philanthropist. Within another 5 years, the Sears catalogue offered a greater selection than even the largest city store, with its offerings of household appliances, furniture, firearms, toys, tools, **sporting** goods, groceries, jewelry, and clothing. By the end of the Gilded Age, "Sears and Roebuck," as it was commonly called, was a household name in the United States and the most successful business of its kind in American history, easily outselling the much older "Ward's."

SHERMAN, JOHN (1823–1900). Born in central Ohio, John Sherman, the younger brother of the famous Civil War general **William Tecumseh Sherman**, went into law and politics rather than the military. Elected to Congress in 1855 as an original **Republican**, he served three terms in the House of Representatives before being chosen to replace Salmon P. Chase in the Senate in 1861. He served there for 16 years, most notably on the Finance Committee, where he distinguished himself as one of the leading economic thinkers in the government. In 1873, he led in the passage of the Coinage Act (also called the Demonetization Act and the Crime of '73), which stopped the federal coinage of silver for 5 years. In 1875, he led in settling the greenbacks-versus-specie issue through passage of the Resumption Act, which required the government to replace paper money with gold, to the dismay of many working-class political leaders.

In 1877, President **Rutherford B. Hayes** tapped Sherman for U.S. Secretary of the Treasury. During his 4-year tenure in the Treasury Department, he carried out the policy he had written into law in the Resumption Act. He opposed the Bland-Allison Act of 1878, which reinstated federal coinage of silver on a limited basis, but 12 years later, while back in the Senate, he drafted the Sherman Silver Purchase Act of 1890, which increased the coinage of silver beyond the Bland-Allison Act, as a compromise with **free silver** advocates. He also wrote the Sherman Anti-Trust Act of 1890, which was supposed to break up and/or prevent certain kinds of monopolies—another measure, albeit a largely ineffective one, designed to appease Populists. By the time the presidential election of 1896 rolled around, the free silver issue and Populism had taken center stage. Sherman opposed both, becoming a staunch gold bug and **William McKinley** supporter. McKinley, not surprisingly, rewarded Sherman with the coveted post of secretary of state, a position he kept for only a year. The beginning of hostilities that led to the outbreak of the **Spanish–American War** took a toll on his health. He retired in 1898 and died less than 2 years later, in Washington, D.C. *See also* BILLION DOLLAR CONGRESS; HARRISON, BENJAMIN; PEOPLE'S PARTY.

SHERMAN, WILLIAM TECUMSEH (1820–1891). Born Tecumseh Sherman in central Ohio, this older brother of **John Sherman** was taken in by friends of the family who christened him in the Catholic faith as "William." Always called "Cump" by those who knew him well, he attended West Point Military Academy in New York, graduating in 1840. Although he first tried his hand at banking, teaching, and law, he ultimately rose to fame as the second most important Civil War general on the Union side. After the war, he continued behind only **Ulysses S. Grant** in rank, and upon Grant's presidential inauguration in 1869, he became Commanding General of the United States Army, a position he held until his retirement in 1883. He also served briefly as U.S. Secretary of War, but he had no desire to be a government bureaucrat. When admirers in the **Republican Party** tried to convince him to become a presidential candidate in 1884, he responded in a way that showed his honesty, his disdain for politics, and his brilliant way with words: "If drafted, I will not run; if nominated, I will not accept; if elected, I will not serve."

Meanwhile, Sherman's command of the Army put him on the front line of policymaking for dealing with the **Indian** tribes on the western frontier. His primary goals included making the frontier safe for white settlement and protecting the valuable **railroads**. He did not order the extermination of the tribes or the buffalo, but his top priorities clearly did not include humane treatment of the Indians or conservation of nature. In 1875, he published his memoirs, which were well-received by critics and laypeople alike, and which showed off his shrewd mind and clarity of thought. By the end of his life, he had resided and worked in every section of the United States, and had thus become about as ubiquitous as any individual American could be. Born in Ohio, he had lived everywhere from South Carolina to Kansas to California; he died in New York City, and his public funeral and burial occurred in St. Louis, Missouri. Although hailed as a great man and a war hero by his Gilded Age peers, Sherman's enduring legacy is his strategy of waging total war, which has been copied by some of the greatest military leaders in the world ever since.

SIERRA CLUB. Founded in San Francisco on 28 May 1892, this environmental conservation organization was the brainchild of John Muir, a Scottish **immigrant**. Muir came to the United States with his family in 1849 and settled in Wisconsin. After becoming interested in ecology in **college**, he devoted most of the rest of his life to protecting the beauty of the American western wilderness. Upon moving to California in 1868, he immediately discovered the incomparable Yosemite Valley region and became determined to save it from the commercial exploitation that had already begun. After publishing his first article on the subject in a New York paper in 1871, Muir found allies in the influential poet Ralph Waldo Emerson and the world-renowned geologist Louis Agassiz, among others. His Yosemite campaign lasted two full decades. When Congress finally acted, making Yosemite a national park on 30 September 1890, Muir was disappointed to learn that the law left his beloved Yosemite Valley under the control of the State of California. This led him to organize the Sierra Club, which still exists today, to educate the public about the need for wilderness preservation, to lobby Congress and the California legislature, to enlist more support among the general public, and to promote enjoyment of the great outdoors. The Sierra Club thus became the first of the modern environmentalist groups in the United States. Its greatest challenges initially lay in confronting hostile business interests and apathetic lawmakers and citizens. Quickly, however, another challenge arose in the person of Gifford Pinchot, who saw government's role as "conservation" rather than "preservation" of nature. Because he had the friendship and respect of future President **Theodore Roosevelt**, Pinchot's view of using natural resources wisely rather than preserving them untouched by human hands tended to gain ground by the end of the Gilded Age and beginning of the 20th century.

"SIGNIFICANCE OF THE FRONTIER IN AMERICAN HISTORY, THE." The provocative thesis "The Significance of the Frontier in American History" was written by a young historian from Wisconsin named Frederick Jackson Turner (1861–1932), who had only recently graduated from the Johns Hopkins University with his Ph.D. He delivered it as an essay at the American Historical Association's annual convention, which was held in Chicago, Illinois, at the **Columbian Exposition of 1893**. It fundamentally altered the way American history was conceptualized. Prior to its publication, historians tended to assume that American political institutions and social customs derived mainly from the traditions and habits of the Old World countries from which the people had emigrated. Turner's thesis focused instead on the role of the American environment, geography, topography, racial milieu, and similar factors in creating a civilization in the United States that was exceptional, if not altogether unique, in the world. Specifically, he argued (or later historians extrapolated) that the vast, open frontier that lay to the west of the original 13 states had provided a safety valve against overpopulation, had forced the American people to become the most innovative in the world in order to survive on the edges of civilization amid hostile **Indians**, and had allowed the nation to develop into a potential empire faster and easier than any other in history.

These ideas fit well into the **Social Darwinist** and laissez-faire capitalist thinking of the day, because they implied that the American frontier had produced the strongest, most intelligent race of people in the world. Taking his cue from the U.S. Census Bureau's report for 1890, Turner noted that the "frontier" no longer existed in the 1890s as it had in decades past and speculated that the lack of a frontier portended trouble for the future of the United States. American imperialists used Turner's thesis to argue for overseas expansion, claiming that the United States would need to begin looking beyond its own coastlines for a new frontier. Although it would be a stretch to say that Turner's thesis led directly to a change in American **foreign** policy, it did indirectly contribute to the United States' rise toward global imperialism at the end of the Gilded Age. *See also* ROOSEVELT, THEODORE.

SINGLE TAX. *See PROGRESS AND POVERTY.*

SINGLETON, BENJAMIN "PAP." *See* EXODUSTERS.

SITTING BULL (ca. 1831–1890). Born into the Hunkpapa band of Lakota Sioux **Indians** in the Dakota Territory (modern South Dakota), Sitting Bull became the most renowned Native American of the Gilded Age. His name in his native tongue was Tatanka (Sitting) Iyotake (Bull). After showing great valor on the battlefield in preliminary skirmishes against the U.S. Army in the 1860s, he was elevated to chief of his tribe around 1868. In that capacity, he served as a military, spiritual, and medical leader. He developed a strict policy against submitting to white rule, and particularly to surrendering his people's traditional land to the U.S. government. In 1876, when white men discovered gold on Lakota territory in the Black Hills, Sitting Bull refused to sell the sacred land to them or to the U.S. government. As whites poured into the area thereafter, he led his people westward and northward to avoid capture. Colonel George Custer and the Seventh Cavalry pursued and forced a showdown, however, which resulted in the annihilation of Custer's regiment at the **Battle of Little Big Horn**, although Sitting Bull played no direct role in the battle. The following year, Sitting Bull led his people into Canada, where they hoped to find refuge. The Canadian government did not welcome them, however, and less than 4 years later, Sitting Bull brought his starving band back to the United States and surrendered to federal authorities. After being held prisoner for the next 2 years at Fort Buford, he was released on the condition that he would stay within his tribe's assigned location, the Standing Rock reservation in the Dakota Territory.

In 1885, **Buffalo Bill** (William Cody) convinced authorities to allow Sitting Bull to leave the reservation to work in his "Wild West" show, in which he starred as the Indian chief—a role he played in real life without pay. After a few months of touring with Buffalo Bill, he returned to the reservation better educated about the white man's culture in the East. Realizing for the first time that his people stood no chance of defeating the white man, he nevertheless hoped for a miracle. In 1890, when the Ghost Dance movement swept through the West from tribe to tribe, Sitting Bull encouraged his people to join it. The dance ritual was supposed to give the Indians supernatural powers to be able to withstand the white man's bullets. It disturbed white authorities, who promptly ordered it stopped. When the Indians refused, General Nelson Miles had Sitting Bull arrested. The attempted arrest, unfortunately, resulted in the death of the great chief, who was shot in the head on 15 December at his cabin on the Standing Rock reservation. Two weeks later, this tragic episode was overshadowed by the infamous massacre of the Minneconjou Lakota of Chief Big Foot just a few miles away at **Wounded Knee**. Although Sitting Bull was already dead, his spirit of proud resistance was certainly present among his people, indirectly contributing to the tragedy. *See also* OAKLEY, ANNIE.

SLAUGHTERHOUSE CASES. The **U.S. Supreme Court** ruled on this set of legal suits in 1873. At issue was the "privileges and immunities clause" of the Fourteenth Amendment. The case involved the livestock processing industry in Louisiana. State law required that all slaughtering in the city of New Orleans be done in the Crescent City Live-Stock Landing and Slaughtering Company's facilities. This was in the interest of public health, because it confined the bloody and often unsanitary industry to a single location, and it allowed for easier government inspection and regulation. The restriction frustrated local butchers, however, who preferred the economy and convenience of preparing their meat fresh at their own facilities. It also gave a single corporation a government-sanctioned monopoly on the industry, which led to charges of kickbacks against the office-holders responsible for the deal. Since Reconstruction was at full stride at the time, the incident provided Louisiana **Democrats** and butchers a golden opportunity to accuse the **Republicans** (who controlled the state) of **corruption** and to tie them to the scandal-ridden **Ulysses S. Grant** administration in Washington, D.C.

Although the Fourteenth Amendment had been intended to protect the rights of black southerners, insightful lawyers in Louisiana realized that it could be interpreted in this case to be a protection of white butchers who were being denied the right to make an honest living by a corporation that enjoyed preferential treatment from the government. The U.S. Supreme Court, headed by Chief Justice Salmon Chase, ruled 5-4 in favor of the state and the monopoly, and did so by navigating the complicated legal maze that the amendment embodied. Yet, because the case presented a new way of looking at the Fourteenth Amendment, and because it was such a closely split decision, it amounted to an erosion of the Republicans' Reconstruction agenda. It led to further examinations of the meaning and intent of the Fourteenth Amendment, which would eventually result in that amendment's impotence in terms of its ability to protect the rights of **African Americans**. *See also* CIVIL RIGHTS CASES.

SMALLS, ROBERT (1839–1915). Born a slave in Beaufort, South Carolina, Robert Smalls had an unknown white father. He grew to be a ship pilot in the Charleston area, hauling cotton down the Pee Dee River. During the Civil War, he was compelled to serve as a pilot for the Confederacy. In 1862, however, he deliberately guided his ship, the *Planter*, into the Union navy's hands, for which he was hailed as a hero by the northern **press**. Thereafter, he became an abolitionist speaker and fundraiser until the war's end, when he joined the leadership of the Freedmen's Bureau in South Carolina. In 1868, he was elected as a **Republican** to the South Carolina legislature, a position he held until 1874, when he won a seat in the U.S. House of Representatives, where he served until 1878. In 1877, however, he was sentenced to 3 years in prison for accepting a bribe while in the legislature. After losing appeals in both the state and **U.S. Supreme Court**, he received a pardon from the governor in exchange for the **Rutherford B. Hayes** administration pardoning **Democratic** miscreants in South Carolina. He then lost three congressional races before winning again one last time in 1884. As South Carolina increasingly disfranchised blacks in the 1880s–1890s, Smalls spoke out against it, including through a speech given at the state's constitutional convention in 1895, but his advocacy was to no avail. Meanwhile, he received appointment as U.S. Customs Collector from the **Benjamin Harrison** administration, and from every subsequent Republican administration until his death. Like most **African Americans** of the Gilded Age, he lived without respect or acclaim in his own lifetime, and not until many decades later was fair regard for his accomplishments recovered.

SOCIAL DARWINISM. Although the ideology of Social Darwinism evolved over a matter of decades, the actual term "Social Darwinism" was not coined until 1879, and it was rarely used at the time. Popular usage of the term came from 20th century historians trying to describe the dominant philosophy employed to justify racism during the Gilded Age. This ideology had complex origins but arose mainly from the work of various scholars in England in the early and mid-19th century. Although the term derives from the foremost theorist of evolution, Charles Darwin, Darwin personally had very little to do with construction or propagation of this philosophy. One of the last really eclectic academicians, British scholar Herbert Spencer, who coined the term "survival of the fittest" to explain Darwin's "natural selection," had more to do with it. He studied the evolution of civilizations and societies and drew conclusions that other scholars, such as Francis Galton (the father of eugenics), built upon to show why the white race did, would, and probably should, dominate all others. These scientific theories, taken together with non-scientific racist ideas promulgated by French writer Arthur de Gobineau and American southern intellectuals like **John Tyler Morgan** and Hinton Rowan Helper, turned Social Darwinism into a pseudo-science that explained and justified white supremacy in the United States in the age of Jim Crow. Essentially, the ideology held that the white race was dominant because it was the "fittest" and thus the most "evolved." The other races—black, yellow, red, and brown—were less fit, were less evolved, and were thus automatically inferior to the white race. Consequently, the white race should, by nature, rule the world.

The main proponent of Social Darwinist ideology in the United States during the Gilded Age was Yale professor **William Graham Sumner**, but most of his fellow American scholars likewise spread the ideology in their publications and classroom lectures. By the 1890s, the ideology was thus institutionalized in American universities, the news media, and political circles, allowing a whole generation in the early 20th century to justify its racist views "scientifically." Imperialists made convenient use of Social Darwinism to justify territorial aggrandizement at the expense of dark-skinned islanders of the Pacific and Caribbean, although, paradoxically, many of the leading Social Darwinists argued strongly against imperialism. The Victorian age Christian reaction to Social Darwinism came to be known as the **Social Gospel**, an ideology that sometimes has been convoluted in popular perception with the "White Man's Burden" of Rudyard Kipling fame. *See also* AFRICAN AMERICANS; FOREIGN AFFAIRS; *THEORY OF THE LEISURE CLASS, THE.*

SOCIAL GOSPEL. A **religious**/political ideology that stressed Christian responsibility to *do* or *perform*, rather than to merely *preach* or *hear*, the Gospel, the Gilded Age Social Gospel grew out of the liberal Protestant theology of the antebellum period that produced the abolition movement, the early **women**'s rights movement, and the Transcendentalist and Universalist movements, among others. Although the term was not coined until the 20th century, the ideology had become a staple of the northern Congregationalist and Baptist Churches, and of others to a lesser degree, by the 1890s. Not exclusively an American phenomenon, the Social Gospel could be found throughout the English-speaking world at the time, indirectly spawning such charitable organizations as the Salvation Army, the **American Red Cross**, the Young Men's Christian Association, **Hull House**, and the Boy Scouts and Girl Scouts, among many others.

The ideology, explained broadly, held that church and state, as well as individuals, should labor to reform any and all dysfunctional elements and institutions within society. It thus blurred the lines of responsibility between government and the church, basically calling on the former to help carry out the work of feeding, clothing, sheltering, nursing, and educating the poor and needy. As such, it opposed the traditional American laissez-faire approach to governing and paved the way for the coming Progressive movement of the 20th century. Yet proponents of the Social Gospel did not seek to transfer responsibility for social welfare from the churches to the government; rather, they led by example through their own mission activities and hoped that political leaders would follow. Some of the most influential proponents included **Washington Gladden**, Josiah Strong, Lyman Abbott, Charles Sheldon, and Walter Rauschenbusch—ministers, authors, and educators all.

One important use of the Social Gospel was to counter the effects of **Social Darwinism** on imperialist **foreign** policy. Social Darwinism implied that if the poor, uneducated, "uncivilized" nations of the world were left to nature, they would become extinct. Christians, according to the Social Gospel, must not let that happen but rather must work diligently to uplift the people of those backward nations.

There was thus always a dynamic tension between Social Darwinism and the Social Gospel.

SOUSA, JOHN PHILIP (1854–1932). Born to Portuguese **immigrants** in Washington, D.C., John Philip Sousa was the son of a father who played in the U.S. Marine Corps band and who started his son in music studies at just 6 years of age. At 13, Sousa began playing in the marine band himself, and by age 25 he had become its director. In that capacity he composed his first notable piece, "Semper Fidelis" (1888), which is still widely played and recognizable to most Americans today. He played many instruments, including most horns and woodwinds, but he specialized in violin in his early years. In 1876, he played violin in the official U.S. **Centennial** Exposition band in Philadelphia, Pennsylvania. Over the course of his life, he wrote several operettas and miscellaneous musical pieces, but his lyricism never matched the greatness of his skill as a composer. His one memorable operetta, *El Capitan* (1896), ran on Broadway for several years. Ultimately, however, it was his marching band tunes that made him the most famous musician of the Gilded Age and earned him the title "the March King." His two most enduring pieces are "The *Washington Post*" (1889), which is, as the title indicates, a song he composed at the request of that newspaper, and "The Stars and Stripes Forever" (1896). He continued composing and performing for more than three decades in the 20th century, becoming one of America's first musical celebrities, but his golden decade for composition really ran from about 1888 to 1898.

SPANISH–AMERICAN WAR. Prior to 1898, the United States had not fought a **foreign** war since the Mexican War of 1848. During that half-century, its only major military conflict was the Civil War. It had cautiously avoided war with all potential foreign belligerents, although it came close on several occasions. The war that broke out in 1898 with Spain marked a departure from traditional American foreign policy in two ways. It was the first time the United States sent a military force overseas to wage war for reasons other than self-defense, and it was also the first time the United States waged war to acquire territory overseas. Historians generally see it, therefore, as the beginning of the era of American global imperialism. It can be seen, consequently, as a dividing point in American history—a time when all things domestic, so heavily emphasized during the Gilded Age, became secondary to foreign concerns and the United States' role in world affairs. In a sense, the war ended the Gilded Age.

The genesis of the war can be found partly in the Cuban revolution for independence from Spain, which began in 1895. Cuban **immigrants** lobbied the U.S. government and the American people for help, and for the most part American newspapers favored intervention. Two of New York's most prominent editors, **William Randolph Hearst** and **Joseph Pulitzer**, became leading "jingoes," as warmongers were called at the time. Presenting themselves as humanitarians with a mission to free the Cuban people from Spanish misrule (although they were actually more concerned with increasing their sales), they attempted to pressure the reluctant Presidents **Grover Cleveland** and **William McKinley** into intervening in the revolution. Cleveland resolutely refused. Exaggerated stories of Spanish "butcheries" and "concentration camps," however, aroused American sympathy to the point that, by the time McKinley became president, he could not so easily say no. The greatest impact of these jingoes came with the publication of the "De Lome Letter" on 9 February 1898, in which the Spanish ambassador to the United States disparaged McKinley's leadership abilities. All the while, jingoes within the U.S. military had been pining to try out their new and improved navy. Finally, McKinley sent the battleship U.S.S. *Maine* to Havana in early February to make a show of American power and support for Cuba. On 15 February, the ship mysteriously exploded, and American public opinion naturally assumed it had been bombed by the Spaniards. Diplomacy broke down rapidly thereafter, and by April the United States was ready for war. On 11 April, McKinley asked Congress to support a venture to liberate Cuba. Congress approved the request on 20 April. Five days later, it became official—the United States and Spain were at war.

The war itself was anticlimatic in the sense that it was over quickly, the United States won easily, and the loss of life and taxpayer money were minimal. It was, as Secretary of State **John Hay** said, "a splendid little war." With the focus having been on Cuba all along, the U.S. Navy under Commodore George Dewey caught the Spanish fleet in the Philippines, some 10,000 miles away, off guard and completely annihilated it in a single day, on 1 May. By June, the United States had landed ground troops on the island of Cuba. On 1 July, the American force, featuring **Theodore Roosevelt** and his Rough Riders, captured the Spanish strongholds of San Juan Hill and El Caney. Soon after, the Spanish fleet crumbled, Puerto Rico fell to the Americans, and Spain lost both the will a nd the ability to continue fighting. By 12 August, the war was over. The Treaty of Paris of 1898 ended the war officially on 10 December. The terms included the United States taking possession of Cuba, Puerto Rico, the Philippines, and Guam. This outcome made the United States one of the great world powers heading into the 20th century, and it effectively reduced Spain to a second-rate power. *See also* AMERICAN ANTI-IMPERIALIST LEAGUE; BUFFALO SOLDIERS; FISH, HAMILTON; WHEELER, "FIGHTIN' JOE"; WOOD, LEONARD.

SPORTS AND RECREATION. The Gilded Age was a time of major expansion in athletics and outdoor leisure activities. Largely this was because Americans had more disposable income and leisure time than ever before. The middle class had grown as industrialization, urbanization, and education increased, and this process, coupled with relative peace in both domestic and **foreign affairs**, meant that opportunity abounded for less work and more play, especially in the Northeast. Sports came in three basic varieties—amateur, collegiate, and professional—although the lines separating them were not well defined. There was a plethora of amateur sporting events and recreational activities during the Gilded Age—too many to list—but they ranged from hunting and shooting to fishing and rowing, from roller skating to running track, from billiards and board games to poker and marbles. In short, most of the games, races, tests of wit, and competitions of dexterity that exist today existed then, with the obvious exception of electronic and motor sports.

Few Gilded Age sports could truly be called professional in the modern sense, but among those considered professional for the time were **baseball**, boxing, and horseracing. Baseball became the first professional team sport when the Cincinnati Red Stockings fielded a slate of paid players in 1869. An extremely controversial issue, the paying of players divided Americans into purists who favored retaining amateurism and businessmen who sought to profit from the game.

Not until the 20th century would the conflict be resolved in favor of the profiteers. Boxing, also called pugilism and prizefighting, became a professional American sport after the official "Marquis of Queensberry" rules used in England were adopted in the United States. The first world heavyweight title bout in the United States took place in 1892 in New Orleans, Louisiana, when Gentleman Jim Corbett defeated John L. Sullivan. Professional horseracing, meanwhile, had been around a little longer in something resembling its modern form, but exactly what constitutes professional vis-á-vis amateur racing is debatable. In 1868, the American Stud Book, which catalogued thoroughbreds for the purpose of determining pedigree, was first published. The races that today form the Triple Crown—the Belmont Stakes (in New York City), the Preakness Stakes (in Baltimore, Maryland), and the Kentucky Derby (in Louisville)—were begun in 1866, 1873, and 1875, respectively. In 1894, the Jockey Club was formed in New York to regulate the horse breeding and racing industry.

Football, one of the most popular spectator sports in the United States today, had its origins in the Gilded Age as a **college and university** activity, although the game's early form resembled modern English rugby. Two New Jersey schools, Princeton and Rutgers, played the first intercollegiate game on 6 November 1869. In the 1870s and 1880s, football remained a regional game, played almost exclusively in the Northeast. Not surprisingly, the Ivy League, featuring Harvard, Yale, Cornell, and Columbia, among others, became the first collegiate athletic conference. In the early 1890s, the game spread rapidly, as the universities of Michigan, Notre Dame, Vanderbilt, North Carolina, Georgia Tech, **Stanford**, and California, among others, fielded teams. By the end of the decade, professional teams had begun to emerge, and the National Football League was created. Not until the 20th century, however, did professional football develop into something resembling its modern form.

Other outdoor sports, such as tennis and golf, caught on with the elite country club set in the Gilded Age. In 1881, the United States National Lawn Tennis Association was formed in Rhode Island, and in 1894 the United States Golf Association, which first hosted the U.S. Open a year later, was formed.

Among the indoor team sports of the Gilded Age, none was to become more important in American society over the long run than basketball. Before Dr. James A. Naismith invented the game at the Young Men's Christian Association in Springfield, Massachusetts, in 1891, there were no indoor team sports that could consistently attract and hold the attention of energetic and competitive young men. Basketball filled that void and had the added benefit that girls loved to play it, too. Volleyball was likewise invented in a Massachusetts YMCA, this time by William G. Morgan at Holyoke in 1895. It was not until the 20th century, however, that these indoor sports spread nationwide and advanced much beyond the amateur level. Meanwhile, bowling became such a widely popular activity that, in 1895, the American Bowling Congress was created in New York City to organize it into a professional sport.

Perhaps most notable of all was the bicycle-riding craze that swept the nation in the 1890s. Although primitive forms of the bicycle had been invented decades before, it was not until 1869 that the term "bicycle" was coined to describe the contraption, and even then some bikes had more than two wheels, making them really tricycles or quadracycles. Not until the early 1890s did bikes begin to take on uniform characteristics of their modern design. They became cheaper, safer, more comfortable, more reliable, and simpler to operate. One of the main reasons for the craze, however, was the fact that **women** wanted to ride, and men by and large did not try to prohibit them. Women's rights advocates such as **Elizabeth Cady Stanton**, **Susan B. Anthony**, **Frances Willard**, and **Nelly Bly** were all enthusiasts who found bicycling to be one of the most liberating things in their lives. Consequently, it is estimated that in 1897 alone, more than 2 million bikes were sold in the United States, and by the turn of the 20th century some 10 million bikes graced the city streets and dirt paths of America.

STALWARTS. When the **Republican Party** split in 1872 over whether to support President Grant for a second term or to replace him with **Horace Greeley**, the **Liberal Republican** candidate, those who remained faithful to Grant evolved into the Stalwart faction. By 1876, it was a defined entity headed by Senator **Roscoe Conkling** of New York. The Stalwarts supported Grant for a third term, they opposed North–South reconciliation, they generally practiced extreme partisanship, they favored continuing the customary patronage practice called the "spoils system," and they rejected civil service reform. Essentially, the Stalwarts were heirs of the old "Radical Republican" faction of the early Reconstruction years. Because they derived power from keeping the spoils system intact, they were conservatives. Yet the tradition they tried to preserve was **corrupt**, which gave their opponents within the party, the Half-Breeds, traction. Not until President **James Garfield** was assassinated in 1881 as a result of the spoils system, however, did the Half-Breeds gain the necessary impetus to reform the civil service. Thereafter, the Stalwarts dissipated, at least in name. *See also* ARTHUR, CHESTER A.; MORTON, LEVI P.

STANFORD, LELAND (1824–1893). Born near Albany, New York, Stanford moved to Wisconsin and opened a law office in 1848 before migrating to California in 1852. There he got involved in **railroad** building and politics, rising quickly to become both governor of the state and president of the Central Pacific Railroad in 1861. He had the honor of driving the golden spike that completed the **transcontinental railroad** in 1869. In the late 1880s, he also served as president of the Southern Pacific Railroad. Elected to the U.S. Senate in 1884, he epitomized the millionaires who tended to dominate that body during the Gilded Age. A philanthropist and a progressive thinker on most issues, he stood in the vanguard of humanitarian-minded reformers in the **Republican Party**. He supported efforts to improve **educational** opportunities for **African Americans**, for instance. His record in dealing with the Chinese and Indians in California, however, was mixed. Today he is best remembered for the university he built in 1890 in Palo Alto, California, that bears his name.

STANTON, ELIZABETH CADY (1815–1902). Born into a wealthy New York family, Elizabeth Cady Stanton married abolitionist Henry Stanton, by whom she bore seven children. She devoted her early years to fighting against slavery and for **women**'s rights. In 1848, she led in forming the famous Seneca Falls (New York) Conference which drew up a women's "Declaration of Sentiments," and in the 1850s she became a revolutionary and a pariah for wearing "bloomers" in public. In the Gilded Age, she and long-time friend **Susan B. Anthony** created the National Woman Suffrage Association (NWSA), which fought unsuccessfully for the right to vote based on the Fourteenth and Fifteenth Amendments to the U.S. Constitution. From 1880 to 1886, she led in writing the first three volumes of *History of Woman Suffrage*. In 1888, she helped found the International Council of Women, and in 1890 she was instrumental in getting the rival American Woman Suffrage Association to merge with the NWSA to form the National American Woman Suffrage Association (NAWSA), which would ultimately succeed in securing ratification of the Nineteenth Amendment some 30 years later. Stanton served as the first president of the NAWSA from 1890 to 1892. In the twilight of her life, she turned her attention to **religion**, writing a two-volume *Women's Bible* (1895–1898), which was a feminist version of the Christian Bible. Her final contribution to the long struggle for women's rights came in 1898 when she published her memoirs, *Eighty Years and More*. For all these and many more efforts and accomplishments, she was probably the single most influential women's rights advocate of the 19th century, and thus of the Gilded Age. *See also* LITERATURE.

STATUE OF LIBERTY. One of the most recognizable landmarks in the world, the Statue of Liberty, which stands in New York harbor today, was a product of the Gilded Age. In 1865, as the American Civil War was coming to an end, a French scholar, statesman, abolitionist, and admirer of the United States named Edouard Rene Lefevre de Laboulaye conceived the idea of building such a statue and presenting it to the American people as a gift. Discussing his plan with fellow Frenchmen and American **Republican** political leaders, it was agreed that the French people (not the government of Napoleon III) would fund the statue if the Americans would provide a site and build a pedestal for it.

Originally scheduled for completion in time for the 1876 U.S. **Centennial**, the project turned out to be more difficult than expected in terms of fundraising and bi-national coordination. The estimated cost of building the statue was more than two million francs, or $250,000, while the cost of building the stone base was about half that much. Meanwhile, the complexities of Reconstruction in the United States and the overthrow of the French government in Paris delayed the project. Moreover, the Americans essentially waited until the French had invested enough in their half of the project for the former to feel confident of its completion, before beginning in earnest to make arrangements to place the statue and to build its base. By then, several years had passed; thus, the actual completion date was 1886, fully a decade behind schedule.

Although Laboulaye supplied the general idea of a figure holding forth a light for the rest of the world, which was to represent American freedom from tyranny, the specific design and construction of the statue fell to French sculptor Frederic Auguste Bartholdi. He chose copper as the outer, visible material for the statue and decided that a 150-foot height with proportional features would be feasible. He worked with the structural engineer Alexander Gustave Eiffel (best remembered for the tower in Paris that bears his name), who headed the building of the unseen interior iron scaffolding upon which the copper plating would be fastened. They built the statue piecemeal in order to ship it overseas. By 1876, they had completed some pieces, which they displayed at the U.S. Centennial Exhibition in Philadelphia, Pennsylvania. This helped raise awareness and money in the United States. By 1884, the copper statue was complete, and it was then shipped to New York in 350 separate pieces.

Meanwhile, in the United States, fundraising for building the base fell primarily to **William M. Evarts**, a prominent New York lawyer and national Republican leader. The editor of the *New York World*, **Joseph Pulitzer**, ultimately drove the campaign for public donations through his paper beginning in 1883, after New York's **Democratic** Governor **Grover Cleveland** vetoed a bill to help fund the project. The task of designing the base, which would prove to be a great monument in its own right, went in 1877 to architect **Richard M. Hunt**, who chose granite for his material, built the base in the fashion that was then becoming popular for Civil War battlefield monuments, and decided the height should match that of the statue itself. Likewise in 1877, on the recommendation of Bartholdi and **William Tecumseh Sherman**, Congress named Fort Wood, a star-shaped military fortress on the 13-acre Bedloe's Island in New York harbor, home to the statue. Actual construction of the pedestal did not begin until 1884. After its completion in April 1886, the statue was assembled over the following 6 months.

On 28 October 1886, in a public ceremony watched by thousands, President Grover Cleveland (ironically) dedicated the statue. Thereafter, it served as a lighthouse for several years, as well as a tourist attraction. The famous poem by Emma Lazarus, "The New Colossus," which adorns the pedestal today, was penned in 1883 as part of the fundraising effort but was not put on display until 1903. *See also* MORTON, LEVI P.

STEVENSON, ADLAI (1835–1914). Born in Kentucky into a slave-holding and tobacco-growing family, Adlai Ewing Stevenson moved across the Ohio River to Illinois in 1852, where his family ran a sawmill. He kept his southern ties, however, attending **college** in the Bluegrass State. By the eve of the Civil War, he harbored southern states' rights political views. Admitted to the bar in Illinois, he practiced law and joined the **Democratic Party**. After working his way up in the party, he was elected to the U.S. House of Representatives in 1874, but he could not retain his seat for more than one term. In 1878, he won a second congressional race by fusing with the Greenback Party, but again he served only one term before being ousted. When **Grover Cleveland** won the presidency in 1884, Stevenson received the surprisingly powerful position of Assistant Postmaster General, which gave him the opportunity to fire **Republican** post office workers all over the country and replace them with Democrats. He earned the nickname "the Headsman" for slashing some 40,000 GOP postal workers' jobs. This pleased party bosses greatly but drew the ire of Senate Republicans, who in retaliation denied him confirmation to a federal judgeship. When Cleveland ran for president in 1892, the partisan Stevenson, who had both southern connections and Populist views on the **free silver** issue, was chosen as his running mate. The vice presidency proved to be the capstone of his career. Although his name was mentioned for the presidential nomination in 1896, he lost out to **William Jennings Bryan**. He supported Bryan, however, and in 1900 was chosen as Bryan's running mate in the futile campaign against the **William McKinley–Theodore Roosevelt** ticket. He also lost a race for governor of Illinois 8 years later. Thus, this one-term vice president became a forgotten man after the Gilded Age, although he left his name to his grandson, who would become the renowned Democratic governor of Illinois, a presidential candidate, and a key player in the Cuban missile crisis of the John F. Kennedy administration in 1962.

SUMNER, WILLIAM GRAHAM (1840–1910). Born in New Jersey and reared mostly in Hartford, Connecticut, William Graham Sumner graduated from Yale University before continuing his education abroad. Ordained an Episcopal minister in New Jersey in 1869, he served the church for 3 years before receiving an appointment as a professor of political and social sciences at Yale. From 1873 until well into the 20th century, he taught courses in what would later be called sociology, but his eclectic knowledge base included history, economics, anthropology, and political science. Consequently, he became one of the most influential academics in American history, and one of the two or three greatest of the Gilded Age. Among his equally influential students was Thorstein Veblen, whose *Theory of the Leisure Class* (1899) became a classic in sociology. Adhering to and furthering British Herbert Spencer's **Social Darwinism**, Sumner championed laissez-faire economic policies and opposed government help for the poor, making him quite conservative politically. He opposed Marxist ideology and was outspoken in his disagreement with socialist Utopianism as expressed in Edward Bellamy's *Looking Backward* (1888). He also believed in free trade and the gold standard, and wrote influential speeches and essays accordingly. A dispute with the administration of Yale over teaching methods and choices of assigned reading materials put him on the front line of the debate over academic freedom for professors, and he thus proved quite liberal on **educational** issues. Sumner dabbled in politics in the 1870s but decided that public life was not for him, and he mainly lived a quiet life as a scholar. In 1899, however, he came back into the public eye as the vice president of the **American Anti-Imperialist League**. In the last decade of his career, he enjoyed his greatest period of scholarly output. He wrote his most enduring books on sociology at the time, which introduced the concepts of "folkways" and "social mores" into the field. By the end of his life and career in the midst of the Progressive Era, he was standing on the unpopular side of every major issue he believed in except that of the gold standard. *See also* COLLEGES AND UNIVERSITIES.

SUPREME COURT OF THE UNITED STATES. *See* U.S. SUPREME COURT.

SWIFT, GUSTAVUS (1839–1903). Born Gustavus Franklin Swift on Cape Cod, Massachusetts, Swift came from a family of livestock raisers and butchers. With almost no **education** but plenty of common sense, he opened his own slaughterhouse and meat market near Boston in 1862. He soon migrated west and eventually settled in the boom town of Chicago, Illinois, in 1875, where he opened a meatpacking operation amid the huge **Union Stock Yards**. Within 3 years, his business had grown to the extent that he could afford to invest his profits in developing a practical refrigerated **railroad** car to carry meat beyond the confines of Chicago. By the 1880s, he had begun shipping meat all over the United States. His method was so successful, in fact, that the other large meatpacking companies copied it, and many small meat operations feared that Swift would drive them out of business. In 1886, these small competitors waged a campaign to convince the public that refrigerated meat was a health hazard, but they failed. By the early 1890s, Swift and Company had meatpacking plants spread from one end of the country to the other. Swift also pioneered environmentally friendly and commercially profitable ways to use previously discarded meat by-products, which all other meatpackers subsequently adopted. Finally, Swift was among the vanguard of Gilded Age capitalists to achieve and profit handsomely from vertical integration. By the turn of the 20th century, he controlled all major aspects of his meat enterprise, from raising the livestock to transporting them to his slaughterhouses, to owning refrigerator cars and the local butcher shops that sold the meat. *See also* ARMOUR, PHILIP.

– T –

TAMMANY HALL. From inauspicious beginnings as a Jeffersonian **Republican** club called the Tammany Society of New York in the 1780s, Tammany Hall emerged as the dominant political force in New York City throughout the Gilded Age. Beginning with the Andrew Jackson administration in the 1820s, the society became affiliated with the **Democratic Party**. In 1839, it made its headquarters in a building on 14th Street that it called "Tammany Hall." Eventually the society and the hall became synonymous in the popular perception, especially during the organization's apex from 1854 to 1934.

Tammany leaders built their power base by welcoming poor **immigrants** into New York as soon as they got off their ships at the dock and convincing them to vote Democratic. Largely uneducated, illiterate, and often Irish in nationality and Roman Catholic in **religion**, the immigrants saw Tammany as their ally in a harsh new land.

Tammany Hall fell into ignominy in the early Gilded Age under the rule of "Boss" **William Marcy Tweed**, who bilked New York City out of millions. Even after Tweed's fall in 1873, it continued to be the dominant political force in the city under bosses John Kelley and Richard Croker. For a time, its identity as a totally Democratic organization was lost, as candidates in New York became known more as pro-Tammany or anti-Tammany than as Democrats or Republicans. By the end of the Gilded Age and the beginning of the Progressive Era, Tammany Hall was under the control of progressive Republican Mayor Seth Low.

TARIFFS. A tariff is a tax placed on imported goods that is designed to increase their price and thereby encourage Americans to buy products made in the United States. During the Gilded Age, disagreements about which products should be protected from **foreign** competition and at what rate the foreign goods should be taxed were among the most important public issues. From election to election between 1883 and 1897, the overall tariff rate was the most consistently divisive issue. Debates in Congress and discussions of the issue in the **press** aroused about as much passion as could be found at the time, despite their lack of attractiveness to later generations. This was largely because tariffs served as the main source of national revenue during this pre-federal income tax era, and because low federal spending created a treasury surplus for some of these years.

Opinions on the subject were largely defined politically and geographically, as highly protective tariffs had their strongest support in the industrial sections of the North and among **Republicans**. Farmers, southerners, and **Democrats** tended to be for free trade, or at least for lower tariff rates, although there were some notable exceptions.

At the beginning of the Gilded Age, the Morrill Tariff, passed during the Civil War, was still in effect. It set the average rate at 38 percent. In 1883, the Republican-majority Congress hastily passed a new tariff at the close of the session as a compromise measure. Nicknamed the

Mongrel Tariff, it reduced the average rate by a mere 1.5 percent and pleased no one. In 1887, the Democratic-majority House of Representatives passed the lower Mills Tariff, but the Republican Senate revised it so much that House Democrats rejected it. Once the GOP took control of Congress and the presidency in 1888, it passed the **McKinley** Tariff of 1890, which raised rates on average to 50 percent. This, in combination with other divisive issues, resulted in a backlash against the GOP at the polls in the midterm elections of 1890. The Democrats passed the Wilson-Gorman Tariff in 1894, which lowered the rate to 42 percent. Voters repudiated the Democrats in 1896, however, and the GOP once again raised the rate back to 50 percent in the Dingley Tariff of 1897. There the issue stood for the next 12 years. With the advent of the Sixteenth (income tax) Amendment in 1913, the tariff ceased to be a major political issue. *See also* TRADE UNIONS.

TAYLORISM. Also known as "scientific management" or "systematic management," Taylorism takes its name from Frederick W. Taylor, a mechanical engineer from Philadelphia, Pennsylvania, who sought to make factory production more efficient. Studying plant operations at various steel companies and other factories in the 1880s and 1890s, Taylor saw much wasted time, labor, and money. He determined that a formal set of methods should be developed to make operations as cost effective as possible and which supposedly could be applied to virtually any manufacturing or assembly plant. He advocated specialized labor in a step-by-step process, stop-watch time studies to discover the optimal amount of time any particular task should take, incentives to workers to complete their tasks faster than minimum requirements, and careful supervision of workers by well-trained managers. He also recommended a hierarchical system of managers, rigorous inventory control, and the use of modern accounting techniques. The positive side of Taylorism was that it indeed increased efficiency and maximized profits for capitalists, but the negative side was that it reduced workers to automatons. Its effect on workers led to increased need and desire for unionization. By the beginning of the 20th century, Taylorism had become popular throughout the northeastern United States and would soon spread abroad. Certain aspects of Taylorism survive almost unchanged in some industries today, whereas many businesses and government operations have adapted selected parts of it to suit their needs. *See also* TRADE UNIONS.

TELLER AMENDMENT. Proposed by **Republican** senator **Henry M. Teller** of Colorado, the Teller Amendment was added to the congressional resolution calling for war with Spain on 19 April 1898. The amendment stipulated that the United States would not take possession of Cuba as a colony if and when American forces liberated the island from Spanish control. It passed narrowly in the Senate and overwhelmingly in the House of Representatives. It showed important forethought going into the **Spanish–American War**, which, unfortunately, was not matched with regard to the other Spanish colonial possessions that would be liberated in the war. The forethought resulted from the fact that there had been a great deal of discussion and disagreement about acquiring Cuba as an American territory for many years prior. The amendment proved too restrictive after the war and was superseded in 1901 by the Platt Amendment, which gave the United States more control over Cuban affairs. *See also* FOREIGN AFFAIRS.

TESLA, NIKOLA (1856–1943). Born in the Austro-Hungarian Empire in the region that is today Croatia, Nikola Tesla was an ethnic Serbian. Said to have been born at the stroke of midnight during a lightning storm, Tesla grew up a precocious child who had a fascination with electricity. He studied electrical engineering at universities in Budapest and Prague before taking a job with **Thomas Edison**'s French affiliate in Paris, the Continental Edison Company. Impressing everyone he met with his uncanny ability to couple a vivid imagination with practical engineering skill, he worked successfully on ways to improve the new invention of the telephone, among other things. In 1884, he immigrated to New York, where he went to work directly for Edison himself, improving several of Edison's patented designs for various inventions. The two soon had a serious disagreement over money, however, which resulted in their parting company and becoming bitter rivals for the rest of their lives.

In 1886, Tesla formed his own company and began focusing mainly on developing a workable form of long-distance electrical transmission called alternating current (AC), which he rightly believed would prove superior to Edison's direct current (DC). Fellow inventor and corporate mogul **George Westinghouse** was intrigued with Tesla's work and hired him. The Westinghouse-Tesla team then won the bid to provide the electricity for the **Columbian Exposition of 1893** in Chicago, Illinois, where it demonstrated indisputably to the world the superiority of AC over DC. Thereafter, the team earned the right to try the most financially and scientifically daring electrical experiment to date when it built the world's first hydroelectric power plant at Niagara Falls, in Buffalo, New York, which was switched on in 1895. In 1899, Tesla moved his laboratory to Colorado Springs, Colorado, where he conducted experiments that resulted in his being labeled a "mad scientist" for the rest of his life.

Besides his inventions pertaining to these fundamentals of our modern electrification systems, Tesla's second most important invention was probably radio, although he did not win the patent for it and received no credit for it in his own lifetime. His third most important invention was arguably the automotive spark plug, although his pioneering work with x-rays and radar also rank high on the list. In all, he managed to secure about 300 patents worldwide, although he never sought patents for countless scientific discoveries and electrical components, most of which lay within the realm that only electricians, engineers, and physicists understand today. Among these esoteric discoveries and devices are Tesla coils and turbines, rotating magnetic fields, and induction motors.

The split with Edison in the mid-1880s over money caused Tesla to rethink his priorities. Never again did he put his inventive mind to work for filthy lucre; instead, he would work for the pure love of scientific discovery. This would eventually lead to his living in poverty in his old age, rather than becoming the multimillionaire that he surely would have been had he so chosen. He never married, however, and he had no children to leave an inheritance to, although he certainly left a scientific legacy rivaled by few in history. Indeed, so great was the mind of this man who spoke five languages fluently, recited whole books from his photographic memory, considered **Mark Twain** his best friend, and kept company with **J. P. Morgan** and several of the most notable Gilded Age millionaires, that when he dared criticize Albert Einstein's relativity theories as metaphysical nonsense rather than physical science, no one refuted his argument.

Sadly, as he aged, Tesla became a victim of obsessive-compulsive disorder and often lapsed into episodes of mental derangement that observers considered lunacy or insanity.

THEORY OF THE LEISURE CLASS, THE. Subtitled *An Economic Study of Institutions*, this 1899 work was Thorstein Veblen's first monograph. It represented a convergence of the study of economics, sociology, and anthropology. It was a critique of the materialism and consumerism of Gilded Age America, as well as of the laissez-faire capitalist system that gave excess to a few at the expense of the many. Because it contained a fair amount of satire and was not overly dense in prose, it was one of the few academic books of the Gilded Age to enjoy commercial success.

Veblen was born and reared in Wisconsin by Norwegian **immigrant** parents who lived the American dream. He studied at four different **colleges and universities**, earned a Ph.D., and went on to teach at the University of Chicago in Illinois, where he wrote the book. As a student, his great influences were his Yale advisor **William Graham Sumner** and British scholars Charles Darwin and Herbert Spencer. Schooled thoroughly in **Social Darwinism** and neoclassical economics, he formulated his own opinions about the evolution of social institutions in the modern world, which differed significantly from those of his mentors. He observed what he called "conspicuous consumption" and "conspicuous waste" by the "leisure class" and noted that the poor and middle classes were always trying to rise in status to become wasteful consumers who lived lives of leisure themselves. In Gilded Age America, in other words, the measure of a person's success was his or her economic ability to avoid productive labor, to spend money lavishly, and to enjoy wasting resources without guilt. His ideas sounded somewhat Marxist on the surface, but his explanations and extrapolations were more complex than that; he did not identify himself as a Marxist or anything similar, nor did he encourage class warfare. His book served as one of the manifestos of Progressivism going into the 20th century.

TILDEN, SAMUEL J. (1814–1886). Born on the west side of the New York–Massachusetts border, Samuel Jones Tilden matriculated at Yale University in Connecticut and studied law at New York

University. Thereafter, he made a lucrative career as an attorney for **railroad** corporations. Active in the **Democratic Party** in the antebellum period, Tilden made his mark in New York politics after the Civil War. While heading the New York Democratic Party during Reconstruction, he waged a successful campaign to clean up the **corruption** of the **Tweed** Ring and reform **Tammany Hall**. This gave him name recognition and launched his great political aspirations. In 1874, he won the governorship of New York, and 2 years later, the national party nominated him for president of the United States. In the wake of the multiple scandals of the **Ulysses S. Grant** administration, his reputation as a reformer made him a serious contender. In keeping with tradition, however, he did not actively seek the position through public campaigning. The voters flocked to him nonetheless, and he received a 250,000 popular vote majority over the **Republican** candidate **Rutherford B. Hayes**. Unfortunately for Tilden and the Democrats, 20 electoral votes spread over four states were in dispute, and the dispute could only be solved through a bipartisan deal in which Tilden had no direct involvement. The resulting **Compromise of 1877** gave the election of 1876 to Hayes. Tilden graciously accepted the verdict and encouraged fellow Democrats to do the same. In so doing, he set an impressive standard for other candidates to follow in future disputed elections. He retired from public life thereafter and spent his final years living quietly in New York City.

TILLMAN, "PITCHFORK" BEN (1847–1918). Born in east-central South Carolina, Benjamin Ryan Tillman lost his left eye at age 17 while attempting to enlist in the Confederate army. The eye problem kept him out of the war, but he was always a Confederate at heart. After the war he began farming and cultivating an interest in politics. Garnering the nickname the "one-eyed plowboy," he joined the white supremacist "Red Shirts" and participated in the "Redemption" of South Carolina in 1876. A little more than a decade later, the **Democrat** Tillman led the state's **Farmers' Alliance** at the crucial point when the National Farmers' Alliance transformed into the main constituency of the nascent **People's Party**, effectively steering it clear of third-party politics by co-opting the Populist platform. Indeed, he agreed with so much of what the People's Party stood for initially, that he could rightly be called a "populist" (lowercase), if not a "Populist" with a capital *P*. Elected governor twice, he served from 1890 to 1894. In that position, he established the state agricultural **college** at Clemson, regulated the **railroads**, gave the state a monopoly on the sale of liquor, and argued for the disfranchisement of **African American** voters based on the model of the Mississippi Constitution of 1890. Thereafter, the state legislature sent him to the U.S. Senate for four terms, from 1894 to 1918. In that role, he championed **free silver**, made race-baiting speeches, argued against imperialist territorial aggrandizement after the **Spanish–American War**, and picked up his most illustrious nickname—"Pitchfork" Ben—after threatening to poke President **Grover Cleveland** in the ribs with his pitchfork if the latter did not change his position on bimetallism.

TOMBSTONE, ARIZONA. Perhaps the most famous of all the "wild West" frontier towns of the Gilded Age, Tombstone was located in the southeastern corner of the Arizona Territory, just north of the Mexican border, near present-day Tucson, on desert land that had traditionally belonged to the Apaches. Founded in 1879 as a silver-mining town, Tombstone's name implied the danger of living there, as **Indians** and outlaws alike menaced the area. **Geronimo** and his band frequented the town, as did reputed cattle-rustling, stagecoach-robbing **cowboy** gangs. Even so, the town grew rapidly, reaching a population of approximately 7,000 by the end of 1881. It hosted dozens of saloons, gambling houses, theaters, and brothels, giving it the reputation for vice and crime that since has been caricatured in many old movies and television shows as typical of the "wild West." Its most famous newspaper, the *Tombstone Epitaph*, was founded in 1880 and is primarily remembered not for its news coverage but its humorously catchy name. The event that immortalized the town was the **Gunfight at the O. K. Corral** in 1881, in which Wyatt Earp, his brothers, and Doc Holliday staged a shootout with the Clanton and McLaury gangs.

TOURGEE, ALBION (1838–1905). Born into an abolitionist family in Ohio, Albion Winegar Tourgee was descended from French ancestry. Growing up a Methodist on a farm, he attended school in both Ohio and Massachusetts, and later taught school in his home state. While attending **college** at the University of Rochester in New York, the Civil

War broke out. Active in the nascent **Republican Party** on campus, he enlisted as a private in the Union army, where he immediately saw combat at the first battle of Manassas in Virginia. After being severely wounded there, he was discharged only to reenlist with the rank of lieutenant. After being captured in Tennessee, he spent time in a Confederate prison before being exchanged and returning to service. After the war he became one of the many northern "carpetbaggers" to take up residence in the South. Settling in North Carolina, he quickly became a leading political figure in the state, one loved by blacks and reviled by local whites. He first edited a newspaper and championed the Radical Republican Reconstruction agenda. Next he served as a delegate to North Carolina's two constitutional conventions in 1868 and 1875, respectively. Mainly, however, he served as a state Superior Court judge from 1868 to 1874, where he sought to mete out "color blind" justice, as he termed it.

Tourgee's greatest claim to fame lay in his semi-autobiographical books on Reconstruction, *A Fool's Errand, by One of the Fools* (1879) and *Bricks without Straw* (1880), which showed the futility of trying to achieve racial equality in the South in light of the reality of the situation then present. Both were bestsellers, making him a national literary celebrity. Several other books he penned were not so commercially successful. An unfortunate magazine venture nearly ruined him financially, but he worked profitably as a newspaper columnist for most of the 1880s and 1890s, chiefly for the *Chicago Inter-Ocean*.

Tourgee never ceased to champion the rights of **African Americans**, even as Jim Crow laws began to take on a more national appeal in the 1890s. He attended the **Mohonk Conference on the Negro Question** in 1890, for example, where he was virtually the only defender of blacks among a mostly white, northern, **liberal** crowd. A lawyer as well as a journalist and author, Tourgee led the plaintiff's legal team in the infamous 1896 **U.S. Supreme Court** case *Plessy v. Ferguson*. In the same year, he tackled the **free silver** issue, which was so prevalent at the time, writing *The Battle of the Standards*, which argued the pro–gold standard viewpoint. For that, President-elect **William McKinley** appointed him as a consul to France, where he lived out the remainder of his days, dying in the land of his ancestry. *See also* LITERATURE.

TRADE UNIONS. Also known as "labor" unions, trade unions are organizations created by and for workers to facilitate collective negotiations with employers for better wages, hours, working conditions, benefits, and related causes. Although the first "National Labor Union" had been created in 1834, it proved mostly unsuccessful. Similarly, many local "craft" unions or "guilds," which organized workers within a particular specialty (such as carpentry or masonry), existed in early American history, but it was not until the Gilded Age that national unionization really blossomed in the United States. Such local trade unions could set standard rates to charge for their skilled labor, but they could hardly affect legislation or elevate the dignity of the working class in general. For that, nationwide unions, which were not craft specific, were needed.

The first important national union was the **Knights of Labor (KOL)**, founded in 1869. Within a decade, it came to boast more than 700,000 members. Its chief rival in organizing workers was the Federation of Organized Trades and Labor Unions, which became the American Federation of Labor (AFL) in 1886, headed by **Samuel Gompers**. Although the two groups did not always agree on every point and sometimes tried to undermine each other, they otherwise brought attention to the plight of workers that ultimately resulted in important reforms. Some of these reforms included the standardization of the 8-hour workday, the abolition of child labor and the **convict lease system**, a prohibition against importation of **foreign** contract laborers (indentured servants), the creation of Labor Day, the establishment of the Department of Labor, and the passage of high protective **tariffs**, although some of these were not achieved until the 20th century. There was some overlap in what these unions wanted and what the National **Grange**, the National **Farmers' Alliance**, the **People's Party**, and smaller third parties wanted, as well as some overlap in their membership, which helped accomplish their objectives. Later, Progressives in the 20th century did much more to help them.

Within these broad national organizations were many smaller trade unions. Virtually every industry in existence had its own union. Among them were the International Typographers Union, the United Mine Workers, the Amalgamated Meat Cutters, the Central Labor Union, the Brotherhood of Carpenters and Joiners, the Amalgamated

Association of Iron and Steel Workers, the International Molders and Foundry Workers, and the Coopers' International Union of North America. One important trade union was the powerful Western Federation of Miners (WFM), created in 1893 through the merging of several local craft guilds, including the Colorado and Idaho gold miners, the Montana lead miners, and the Nevada silver miners. Its genesis was the 1892 Couer d'Alene strike in Idaho in which the miners demanded $3.50 per day for every worker. Mine owners refused, and the state government supported them with troops to break the strike. Thereafter, the miners banded together across state lines, forming the WFM. In 1894, the WFM succeeded at getting its demands in the Cripple Creek strike in Colorado, thanks to sympathetic Populist Governor **"Bloody Bridles" Waite**, but a later strike in Idaho in 1899 provoked President **William McKinley** to send in federal troops.

Another important trade union was the American Railway Union (ARU), founded by **Eugene V. Debs** in Illinois in 1893, for organizing **railroad** workers. Although railroad workers had proven their ability to organize effective strikes prior to national unionization (as evidenced by the **Great Railroad Strike of 1877**), they staged their most notable strike of the Gilded Age—the **Pullman Strike**—under the banner of the ARU in 1894. It led to one of the most important **U.S. Supreme Court** cases of the Gilded Age, *in re Debs* (1895), in which the court ruled that the federal government had the constitutional authority to force the end of a labor strike when it was in the general welfare of the nation to do so.

While strikes were the most immediate and tangible problem that trade unions posed for Gilded Age society, there was a widespread suspicion and fear that unions were tied to **anarchism** and related radical Marxist ideologies. Many people thus saw them as un-American and wanted them outlawed or obliterated in the name of defending traditional Christian and capitalist values. This was especially true after the **Haymarket Incident** in Chicago, Illinois, in 1886, which made unionization and anarchism synonymous in the minds of millions of Americans. *See also* TAYLORISM.

TRANSCONTINENTAL RAILROAD, COMPLETION CEREMONY OF THE. Occurring barely 2 months into **Ulysses S. Grant**'s presidency, 10 May 1869 marked the symbolic beginning of the Gilded Age. On that day, the world's first transcontinental **railroad** was completed with the ceremonial driving of the last nail into the tracks at Promontory Point in the Utah Territory. **Leland Stanford**, on behalf of the Central Pacific line, and Thomas C. Durant, on behalf of the Union Pacific line, hammered the "golden" spike (it was actually and fittingly a *gilded* spike). Each line rolled a ceremonial locomotive (engine *No. 119* and the *Jupiter*) to the point of contact as well, where they kissed cowcatchers for the cameras. Throngs of railroad personnel, news reporters, and spectators surrounded the area to watch, and news of the event was broadcast from coast to coast instantly via telegraph. So momentous was the occasion that celebrations were staged from New York City to Chicago to San Francisco.

The two lines had begun construction from opposite directions—one in Sacramento, California, the other in Omaha, Nebraska—and had met near the middle, with the Central Pacific having laid 690 to the Union Pacific's 1,087 miles of track. Although construction began in 1862, the plans for tackling this enormous project date back to the California gold rush of 1849. The feat of engineering required was, for that day and time, comparable to that in history of the Chinese building the Great Wall or the Egyptians building the Great Pyramid. Unfortunately, the project required massive infusions of federal tax dollars, which inevitably created mismanagement, waste, and outright fraud, and in turn produced the worst case of **corruption** in the Grant administration—the **Credit Mobilier scandal**—which became the main source of inspiration for **Mark Twain**'s book that named this era the *Gilded Age*.

TREATY OF WASHINGTON. *See ALABAMA* CLAIMS DISPUTE; FISH, HAMILTON; FOREIGN AFFAIRS.

TURNER, BISHOP HENRY M. (1834–1915). Born a free black in the heart of South Carolina, Henry McNeal Turner largely educated himself by studying law books and the Bible. Shortly before the Civil War broke out, he received ordination into the ministry in the African Methodist Episcopal (AME) Church. During the war, he served as Chaplain of Negro Troops in the Union army. During the **Ulysses S. Grant** administration, he served as postmaster of Macon, Georgia, and as U.S. customs agent for the port of Savannah. Meanwhile, he pastored and published three different newspapers for black Christians simultaneously. After Reconstruction, he took the mantle of **Martin Delany** as the foremost black nationalist and proponent of his race's emigration out of the United States. Upon being elected vice president of the American Colonization Society and earning promotion to bishop in the AME Church in 1880, he came to hold a degree of influence in the black community that few others enjoyed. He used it to try to convince federal legislators to fund a colonization scheme, such as the Butler Emigration Bill of 1890. He made four exploratory trips to Africa to pick the most suitable location for a colony, establishing missions from Liberia to the Congo in the process. In the 1890s, he stood with **Ida B. Wells-Barnett** as an anti-lynching proponent. He did not see eye-to-eye with the dominant **African American** figure of his generation, **Booker T. Washington**, and because of his radical racial views, the white public never embraced him the way they did Washington. Although marginally famous during the Gilded Age, Turner did not get his due recognition as an African American leader until many years later. *See also* RELIGION.

TURNER, FREDERICK JACKSON. *See* "SIGNIFICANCE OF THE FRONTIER IN AMERICAN HISTORY, THE."

TWAIN, MARK (1835–1910). Born Samuel Langhorne Clemens, Mark Twain chose his pen name after spending much of his early life on or near the Mississippi River. Reared in the town of Hannibal, Missouri, Clemens apprenticed with a printer as a youth and also unsuccessfully tried his hand at writing newspaper articles. As an adult, he decided to live out his real dream—to be a riverboat pilot. While working on these boats, he met many interesting people who later served as models for some of his most memorable fictional characters. The Civil War forced him to leave the river and move west to Nevada, California, and temporarily Hawaii. He managed to find a niche as a newspaper reporter and public speaker in San Francisco, which eventually opened up doors for world travel. His first full-length book, *The Innocents Abroad* (1869), resulted from those travels and made him an instant literary star in America.

Soon thereafter, Twain moved to Hartford, Connecticut, and spent nearly three decades churning out well-received books. Among the most commercially successful was his co-authored *The Gilded Age* (1873), with Charles Dudley Warner. Among the most enduring, however, are *The Adventures of Tom Sawyer* (1876) and *The Adventures of Huckleberry Finn* (1884). The latter was hailed by literary critics at the time as the best work of its kind in American history and has stood the test of time in that regard, such that, still today, it is considered by many to be the "fountainhead of American **literature**." Common to all his writings are imaginative characters, inimitable wit and charm, and unusually illustrative language. He could turn a phrase as well as any writer anywhere at anytime. Although he made his living with humor—both written and oral—he did occasionally wax philosophical about **religion**, politics, and similarly serious subjects. He became something of a political satirist in his old age, and proved quite good at it. In the end, Twain became one of the few celebrities, not only of Gilded Age America, but of any nation at any time, who was larger than life and too complex for easy categorization. It would not be unreasonable to argue that he was the greatest writer in American history and, after Shakespeare, the second greatest writer in the history of the English language. *See also* HOWELLS, WILLIAM DEAN; TESLA, NIKOLA.

TWEED, WILLIAM MARCY (1823–1878). Born in New York City, William Marcy Tweed ascended through the ranks of local politics in the **Democratic Party** to become the most powerful, **corrupt**, and thus infamous leader in the history of **Tammany Hall**. Although he served in both the U.S. House of Representatives and the state senate in Albany, his greatest influence was always over city politics, patronage, and plunder. By 1869, "Boss Tweed" had assembled a political machine that came to be known as the "Tweed Ring." It was a team consisting of the mayor, the comptroller, the leading city councilman, and various judges and law enforcement personnel that helped him rob the taxpayers of New York City, mainly by rigging government contracts for construction projects. Tweed's modus operandi went far beyond dealing in mere graft; it included outright fraud. Typically, Tweed would arrange for contractors to overcharge the city for their services, often by many thousands of dollars per job, with the excess going straight into the pockets of the Tweed Ring. Tweed and his associates managed to swindle millions before being caught. How much he took cannot be ascertained, but estimates range from a minimum of $25 million up to possibly $200 million.

The *New York Times* first exposed the Tweed Ring. Although its editorials were damning, its cartoons by **Thomas Nast** lampooning Tweed actually had a greater effect on public opinion because of the illiteracy of the poor masses in New York at the time. **Samuel J. Tilden** made his first great claim to fame by prosecuting Tweed and securing a conviction in 1873. After serving only a year in prison on criminal charges, he walked free, only to be arrested again on civil charges, fined $6 million, and given bail of $3 million. In December 1875, he escaped from jail, fled to Cuba, and eventually tried to flee to Spain. After being caught by American and Spanish authorities, he was extradited to New York and sent back to jail, where he died less than 2 years later.

"TWISTING THE LION'S TAIL." *See* FOREIGN AFFAIRS.

– U –

UNION STOCK YARDS. Two competing livestock slaughtering operations used the name Union Stock Yards—one in Chicago, Illinois, and one in Omaha, Nebraska. The Chicago Union Stock Yard and Transit Company, commonly called "the Yards," opened in 1865 under the direction of Timothy Blackstone, who consolidated nine different companies' interests into one. The "Union" name represented a double entendre, referring to both the union of the nine companies and its support of the Union side in the Civil War. Starting as a more-than-300-acre swampy area on Chicago's south side, the Yards quickly developed into the world's largest slaughterhouse, covering 475 acres, employing some 25,000 workers, and producing about 80 percent of the nation's commercial meat supply by the turn of the 20th century. It also fostered economic development all around the Chicago area, helping turn the Windy City into America's second largest metropolis by the end of the Gilded Age. It would soon be immortalized infamously in Upton Sinclair's 1905 novel *The Jungle*, leading to Progressive Era reform of the meatpacking industry.

The Omaha Union Stockyards Company, by contrast, opened in 1883 as a western competitor to the Chicago concern. Many of the cattle that had been shipped to Chicago for slaughtering originated in the West, often in Texas. As **railroad** mileage crept across the vast western frontier in the 1870s and 1880s, Omaha offered a closer shipping point. With the expansion of **Gustavus Swift**'s and **Philip Armour**'s operations there, the Omaha Union Stockyards became the largest in the West and the third largest in the United States by 1900. Except for those living in the vicinity of Nebraska, however, people referring to the Union Stockyards typically mean the Chicago company.

UNIONS. *See* TRADE UNIONS.

U.S. SUPREME COURT. Prior to the Gilded Age, the number of justices serving on the highest court in the land had fluctuated from as few as 5 to as many as 10. Congress, however, in the Judiciary Act of 1869, set the number at 9, which it has remained ever since. Salmon P. Chase, a Lincoln appointee, served as Chief Justice until his death in 1873. Chase had the misfortune of being a progressive thinker presiding over a mostly conservative court, which often put him at odds with his fellow justices. He dissented from the majority, for example, in the **Slaughterhouse Cases** (1873) and in *Bradwell v. Illinois* (1873), each of which dealt with interpretations of the Fourteenth Amendment vis-á-vis either **African Americans** or **women**.

Upon Chase's death, President **Ulysses S. Grant** appointed the unlikely Morrison R. Waite as his replacement. Waite, who had never even argued a case before the court, but who also had never offended any high-ranking government officials, enjoyed the honor of being one of the few justices ever confirmed with a unanimous vote of the U.S. Senate. The Waite court, which sat from 1874 until his death in 1888, proved quite conservative on race and gender issues, as seen in the **Civil Rights Cases** (1883) and *Minor v. Happersett* (1875). It proved progressive in terms of government regulation of business, however, in the **Granger Cases** (1877).

Upon Waite's death, President **Grover Cleveland** appointed the previously obscure Melville W. Fuller as Chief Justice in 1888. Fuller, a very conservative judge, presided over the court from 1888 until his death in 1910. The Fuller court drew the ire of a sizeable percentage of the American public for its decision to strike down the income tax in 1895 in *Pollock v. Farmers' Loan and Trust Co.*, its refusal to break up the sugar trust in 1895 in *E. C. Knight Co. v. United States*, and its general philosophy of siding with big business over labor as seen in *in re Debs* (1895). These rulings fueled the Populist movement going into the presidential election of 1896 and indirectly began moving the **Democratic Party** to the political left. The public at large tended to approve of the Fuller court's conservatism on racial issues, however, in cases such as ***Plessy v. Ferguson*** (1896) and *Cumming v. Richmond County Board of Education* (1899).

The court was overloaded with cases and consequently overburdened with work throughout the Gilded Age. The only relief it got came with the 1887 congressional appointment of a permanent, full-time librarian to run the official Supreme Court Library, and with the end of its judges serving double duty as federal circuit judges, which came via the Judiciary Act of 1891 and created the first Federal Appeals Courts. Other changes included the court's reports, which had been published privately up to 1874, becoming public documents thereafter; the first woman (Belva Ann Lockwood) being admitted to the court's bar in 1879; and the court receiving original jurisdiction over certain types of cases that previously it could only hear on appeal through the Removal Act of 1875 and the Judiciary Act of 1887. *See also* HARLAN, JOHN MARSHALL; HAYMARKET INCIDENT; TOURGEE, ALBION; TRADE UNIONS.

U.S.S. *MAINE*. *See* FOREIGN AFFAIRS; MCKINLEY, WILLIAM; SPANISH–AMERICAN WAR.

– V –

VALPARAISO INCIDENT. Also called the "*Baltimore* Affair," the Valparaiso Incident occurred on 16 October 1891 at the port of Valparaiso, Chile. The background involved a civil war in Chile earlier in the year, which resulted in a change of government. The United States had sided with the losing faction, causing strained relations with the new government from the outset. Anti-American sentiment ran high in Chile as a result. When American sailors on shore leave from the U.S.S. *Baltimore* got into in a bar-room brawl with Chilean locals, 2 sailors ended up dead, 17 wounded, and more than 30 thrown in jail. The Chilean government justified the incident and the handling of it by claiming that the Americans were drunk and had started the brawl. A U.S. naval investigation concluded otherwise. In January 1892, U.S. Secretary of State **James G. Blaine** demanded reparations. When Chile refused, President **Benjamin Harrison** urged Congress to consider a declaration of war. Under this serious threat, Chile immediately backed down, issued an official apology, and paid the families of the victims some $75,000. The clamor for war subsided, but the United States had already started down the road toward global imperialism, and the jingoes would get a war before the decade was over. *See also* FOREIGN AFFAIRS; SPANISH–AMERICAN WAR.

VANDERBILT, CORNELIUS (1794–1877). Born and reared on a farm on Staten Island, New York, Cornelius Vanderbilt came from a Dutch family. He had little **education**, but he possessed insatiable ambition. He began his career as a ferryman in New York harbor, where he acquired the nickname "the Commodore." He then advanced to become a ship captain and owner, and ultimately emerged as the dominant figure in the New York shipping industry by the 1850s. In the 1860s, he and his son William Henry Vanderbilt began acquiring **railroads** and sowing the seeds for control of a northeastern transportation empire. By the mid-1870s, he controlled more miles of track than any other individual in the United States; his trunk line was the New York Central Railroad. Like all Gilded Age tycoons, he engaged in philanthropy, but he was not nearly as generous as some. Notably, he donated $1 million to start Vanderbilt University in Nashville, Tennessee. At the time, 1873, the South was still in the throes of Reconstruction, and it did not have a single university that could rival those of the Northeast. Vanderbilt sought to rectify that problem and in so doing set the pattern for his fellow millionaires to establish world-class universities. At the same time, when the **Panic of 1873** hit, Vanderbilt, unlike most of his transportation competitors, emerged unscathed. In the end, he left a large fortune and control of his business to William Henry Vanderbilt. Despite the Commodore's business acumen and philanthropy, he was not a well-liked man. He was ruthless to competitors, and his ability and willingness to create monopolies earned him few friends. *See also* COLLEGES AND UNIVERSITIES; GOULD, JAY; WOODHULL, VICTORIA.

VEBLEN, THORSTEIN. *See THEORY OF THE LEISURE CLASS, THE.*

VENEZUELAN BOUNDARY DISPUTE. An independent nation since 1830, Venezuela had suffered instability and turmoil from the beginning. Among its many troubles was a dispute over its eastern border with British Guiana, a newly established colony of England. Both nations claimed some 30,000 square miles of territory, which suddenly became an international concern when gold was discovered there in 1879. Unable to challenge mighty Great Britain on its own, Venezuela asked the **Grover Cleveland** administration to intervene based on the Monroe Doctrine. Thomas F. Bayard, secretary of state during Cleveland's first term, began diplomatic discussions with England over the issue, but they went nowhere. The issue lay dormant during the **Benjamin Harrison** administration, only to be resurrected in Cleveland's second term. New Secretary of State Richard Olney took a very strong stand on behalf of Venezuela, sending the British government a message demanding that it submit to U.S. arbitration over the dispute. The British rebuffed Olney, however, raising the ire of Cleveland, Congress, and the American people.

On 17 December 1895, Cleveland addressed Congress on the issue, essentially engaging in saber-rattling and twisting the lion's tail, which was odd considering his anti-imperialist stance on every other **foreign affairs** issue of his day. Feeling the pressure of a possible war with the United States, England then agreed to allow the United States to mediate. Ironically, after the American commission had thoroughly deliberated on the matter, it issued its ruling on 3 October 1899 that favored the British claims over those of the Venezuelans. The significance of this foreign issue is that it marked another step on the United States' path toward global imperialism, which came to fruition by the end of the Gilded Age.

***VIRGINIUS* AFFAIR.** *See* FISH, HAMILTON; FOREIGN AFFAIRS.

– W –

WAITE, "BLOODY BRIDLES" (1825–1901). Born in Chautauqua County in western New York, David Hanson Waite became a lawyer and moved to Wisconsin in the 1850s, then to Kansas in the 1870s, where he served as a **Republican** in each state's legislature. After moving to Leadville, Colorado, in 1879, he worked in the newspaper industry and became an officer in the local chapter of the **Knights of Labor**. As an avid supporter of the working man, he joined the **People's Party** and became a delegate to its formative conventions in St. Louis, Missouri, and Omaha, Nebraska, where he helped formulate the Omaha Platform. In 1892, he became the first and only People's Party governor ever elected. He quickly gained a reputation as a maverick, when, at an 1893 **free silver** convention in Denver, he proclaimed that he would make blood flow in the streets up to the horses' bridles before he would let the eastern money power and their accomplices abroad stop the free silver movement. He also advocated either the state of Colorado or the nation of Mexico coining silver dollars if the U.S. government refused to do so at an acceptable rate. Soon thereafter, he supported the Western Federation of Miners in their demand for $3 per diem for an 8-hour workday in the first Cripple Creek strike. In 1894, he supported **Eugene V. Debs** and the American Railway Union in the **Pullman Strike**. Perhaps his most controversial move, however, was his determination to rid Denver of its "wild West" image by forcing out the entrenched municipal politicians who controlled the gambling houses and saloons. To this end he called out the state militia against city law enforcement. To top off his radicalism, he supported **women**'s suffrage. He was not reelected. *See also* TRADE UNIONS.

WARD, MONTGOMERY. *See* SEARS, ROEBUCK AND COMPANY.

WARNER, CHARLES DUDLEY. *See* GILDED AGE, THE; LITERATURE; TWAIN, MARK.

WASHINGTON, BOOKER T. (1856–1915). Born a slave in rural Virginia, Booker Taliaferro Washington was the son of a white father and a black mother. As a teenager, he attended the Hampton

School for Negroes, where, under the tutelage of white educator Samuel Armstrong, he was trained to be a teacher. He inculcated the vocational approach to **education** for **African Americans** that Armstrong pioneered and took it with him to Tuskegee Institute in rural Alabama in 1881. He was appointed the first principal of the school at its inception, and he and Tuskegee became the brightest beacon of hope for oppressed blacks in the United States during the Gilded Age. Although Tuskegee was a teacher's **college**, Washington emphasized vocational education for non-teachers. Practical skills, such as those used in the construction industry, would provide more realistic opportunities for black self-improvement, he believed, than would traditional academic subject matter. At the time, the vast majority of blacks were locked into peonage as **sharecroppers**, so any skills young blacks could learn that would help them escape the cotton fields would be important and beneficial.

Washington became so adept at soliciting funds from rich white philanthropists, such as **Andrew Carnegie**, that he was able to build Tuskegee into something extraordinary, a much larger and more structurally impressive school than any other for blacks at the time. His success at hobnobbing with rich and powerful white men led him to become the heir of **Frederick Douglass** as the premier black leader in the 1890s and beyond. After he made his now famous "**Atlanta Compromise**" speech in 1895, in which he proclaimed the doctrine of "accommodationism" (as he called it) with racists, the white **press** anointed him as the supposed spokesman for all black Americans. Washington embraced his new role, much to the chagrin of other black leaders, who in time came to despise the "Wizard of Tuskegee" as a megalomaniac. By the time he died, he had solidified control over so many aspects of black society that the wizard label seems justified by history. Whether he did more good or harm through his placid, conciliatory, accommodationist approach to racial discrimination has been a controversial question that has divided scholars ever since.

WASHINGTON MONUMENT, COMPLETION OF THE. While the father of the United States of America was still living, some fellow Americans began calling for a great monument to honor him, to be placed in the nation's new capital, the District of Columbia. Following George Washington's death in 1799, Congress started the process but was met with various problems that prevented it from breaking ground on the project. In 1833, the Washington National Monument Society was organized, and for the next 43 years, private citizens laid the plans, raised the funds, and initiated the construction. Not until 1848 did the society lay the cornerstone of what was originally supposed to become a 600-foot-tall obelisk surrounded by marble columns in the style of the Roman pantheon. Hampered by political partisanship, disagreements about **religion**, and the Civil War, the society made little progress thereafter. **Mark Twain** commented in the 1860s that the 176-foot structure looked like a giant, unfinished smokestack. Some Americans considered it a national shame that it would not be completed in time for the 1876 U.S. **Centennial**. Immediately after the Centennial, therefore, Congress took over where the private society had left off. It appropriated $2 million, set up a joint commission to supervise the project, and assigned the work of completing the monument to the U.S. Army Corps of Engineers. Lt. Colonel Thomas L. Casey was put in charge.

How to go about completing a project that had been so poorly planned and executed thus far proved troubling to Casey. Upon inspection, he found that some of the masonry previously done in the blue gneiss stone did not meet acceptable engineering standards, so he removed 26 feet of it before proceeding. He also shored up the foundation, which he deemed incapable of supporting the weight of a 600-foot stone monument. Meanwhile, George Perkins Marsh, an American diplomat and Egyptologist, studied the plan for completion and argued that only the obelisk should be built and that it should be resized to be proportional to the famous ancient Egyptian obelisks, with a 10-to-1 ratio of height to base circumference. Since the base was already set at 55 feet, he determined, the height should be changed to 555 feet. All other features that had been proposed to adorn the monument should be discarded; the obelisk should stand alone. This plan prevailed, and the first new stone was added in 1880.

Lack of availability of quarried blue gneiss stone slowed the building thereafter, resulting in the monument not being completed on the outside until November 1884. In December, an aluminum capstone was added for the final touch. On 21 February 1885, a bitterly cold and snowy day, outgoing President **Chester A. Arthur** officially dedicated the Washington Monument—the tallest structure of its kind in the world at the time—in a ceremony more somber than festive. Thereafter, the interior of the structure remained to be finished. The stairway, elevator, windows, lighting, heating, and plumbing were all added over the next 3 years. Within another year, the monument was opened to the public, and the visitors poured in by the thousands, each climbing the 500-foot tower the old-fashioned way, taking the stairs.

"WAVING THE BLOODY SHIRT." *See* GRAND ARMY OF THE REPUBLIC; REPUBLICAN PARTY.

WEAVER, JAMES B. (1833–1912). Born in Dayton, Ohio, and brought up in rural Iowa, James Baird Weaver attended law school in Cincinnati before returning to Iowa to practice. In the 1850s, he became an outspoken abolitionist. At the outbreak of the Civil War, he enlisted as a private, but he rose to the rank of brigadier general by the war's end. Although he was initially a **Republican**, the **corruption** of the **Ulysses S. Grant** administration turned him into a member of the Greenback Party in the early 1870s. As such, he won a seat in the U.S. House of Representatives, first in 1878 and then for two terms starting in 1884. In between, he won his party's nomination for president of the United States in 1880. He barely made a dent in the popular vote, however, and won no electoral votes. In 1892, upon the death of **Leonidas Polk**, the **People's Party** turned to Weaver, the recent author of the Populist manifesto *A Call to Action* (1892), as their presidential nominee. He won Kansas, Colorado, Nevada, Idaho, and part of North Dakota and Oregon in the Electoral College, and garnered more than a million popular votes. Had his ardent stand for racial equality not alienated southern Populists, he might have made a more impressive showing. As it was, many southerners either remained loyal or made a return to the **Democratic Party**, giving the victory to **Grover Cleveland**. Weaver, along with the People's Party, soon faded into obscurity. His last public service came as mayor of the small town of Colfax, Iowa, after the turn of the 20th century.

WELLS-BARNETT, IDA B. (1862–1931). Born in northern Mississippi to a slave mother and an American **Indian** father, Ida Bell Wells grew to become one of the most determined advocates of racial justice in the late Gilded Age. She began as a newspaper reporter in Memphis, Tennessee, focusing on **African American** issues. There, she became one of the first muckrakers, exposing the problem of lynching in the South. In 1891, she published *Southern Horrors: Lynch Law in All Its Phases*, for which she was run out of Memphis and had her newspaper office vandalized. In 1895, she married Frederick Barnett and moved to his home in Chicago, Illinois, where she continued building a reputation as the nation's greatest anti-lynching crusader. In 1895, she published a second account called *A Red Record: Tabulated Statistics and Alleged Causes of Lynching in the United States*. These pioneering works served as the foundation for the National Association for the Advancement of Colored People's later campaign to stamp out lynching.

In addition to being remembered for her anti-lynching work, Wells-Barnett is also noted as one of the few blacks to challenge a Jim Crow laws successfully in a southern state court, having sued for the right to sit in the white section of a **railroad** car in Tennessee (although the Tennessee Supreme Court later overturned her victory). She also spoke out against the segregated school system in Memphis while teaching there, and lost her job as a result. She agreed with **Frederick Douglass**'s racial views, but she never embraced her contemporary **Booker T. Washington**, considering him too much of a compromiser with white racists. In the 20th century, she would go on to make several important contributions to African American and **women**'s history. *See also* PRESS, THE.

WESTERN UNION CORPORATION. *See* GOULD, JAY.

WESTINGHOUSE, GEORGE (1846–1914). Born in rural upstate New York near Albany, George Westinghouse became one of the most important inventors in American history. His first major invention, a pneumatic braking system for trains, came in 1868. Thereafter, he continued to work on various devices for the **railroads**, as well as delving into improving designs for steam ship turbines and beginning work on various applications for electric motors. In 1882, after his soon-to-be rival **Thomas Edison** switched on the world's first commercial electric lighting system in New York City using direct current

(DC), Westinghouse began trying to find a better power source for such large grids, leading him to experiment with alternating current (AC). Four years later, he turned on the first commercial AC system in Great Barrington, Massachusetts. He formed a corporation bearing his name to promote AC worldwide, spurring a feud with Edison, who clung tenaciously to DC until Westinghouse's success forced his capitulation in 1892. Meanwhile, the two titans of American invention got into a public tiff over the use of electricity for capital punishment. When the state of New York hired Edison to invent and perfect an "electric chair" in 1889, Westinghouse declaimed against the inhumanity of such a device. A year later, Westinghouse paid for the unsuccessful defense of the first man to be sentenced to die in the chair. The animosity between the two inventors was exacerbated by their mutually exclusive associations with fellow scientist and inventor **Nikola Tesla**, who had worked for Edison until Edison slighted him in a business deal. Tesla thereafter worked for or with Westinghouse to help him win the "war of the currents" against Edison.

Westinghouse enjoyed two other notable successes in the 1890s. One was his winning the contract to supply the electric power for the 1893 **Columbian Exposition** in Chicago, Illinois, in which he ironically used DC rather than AC out of necessity. The other was his contract to build the generators for the new hydroelectric power plant at Niagara Falls for supplying Buffalo, New York, with electricity. In his post–Gilded Age years, he was honored with the presidency of the American Society of Mechanical Engineers. Although his fame has never been as great or enduring as Edison's, his inventions and improvements to existing devices as a whole have been arguably just as important to humanity.

WHEELER, "FIGHTIN' JOE" (1836–1906). Born Joseph Wheeler in Augusta, Georgia, "Fightin' Joe" grew up mostly around his extended family in New England, but he identified himself as a southerner because his heart lay in the South. He graduated from the U.S. Military Academy at West Point, New York, in 1860, just in time to resign his new commission and join the Confederate army instead. He served with distinction and rose to the rank of major general. After the war, he moved to Alabama and began a career as a farmer and a lawyer. In 1880, he ran for the U.S. House of Representatives as a **Democrat**

and thought he had won, but his opponent successfully contested the results (although Wheeler held the seat for more than a year while the investigation dragged on). In 1882, therefore, Wheeler was forced to give up his seat, but his opponent died shortly thereafter, and Wheeler retook it for the remainder of the term. Although he did not run for reelection in 1882, he was thereafter reelected continuously from 1884 to 1900. When the **Spanish–American War** broke out in 1898, he asked for and received a commission as a major general in charge of volunteer troops. Specifically, he commanded the volunteer cavalry, which included **Theodore Roosevelt** and **Leonard Wood**'s Rough Riders. He thus played an important role in the war in Cuba, and he served on the peace commission that concluded the hostilities in Santiago. He then shipped off to fight in the Philippine Insurrection in 1899–1900. Thereafter, he retired, died in New York, and became one of the few former Confederates to be buried at Arlington National Cemetery in Virginia. *See also* FOREIGN AFFAIRS.

WHEELER, WILLIAM A. (1819–1887). Born near the Canadian border in New York, William Almon Wheeler had a hard childhood that forced him to become a self-made man. Poor and in bad health, he dropped out of college, yet managed to pass the bar and begin a law practice. Working his way up through various local government positions in Franklin County, he joined the Whig party and won election to the state Assembly in 1850. In 1858, after joining the nascent **Republican Party**, he won a seat in the state Senate and was chosen its president pro-tempore. Two years later, he was elected to the U.S. House of Representatives, where he served five terms over the next 17 years. During that time, he chaired the New York state constitutional convention.

Because of his experience and good reputation within the Empire State GOP, Wheeler could have enjoyed national fame and power. But his refusal to engage in partisan politics by cooperating with **Roscoe Conkling** and his **Stalwart** machine kept him down. He also kept himself down, lacking the ambition to be either a great leader or a famous one, and having either an actual illness or hypochondria (he frequently complained of being ill, and usually the sickness set in just as he was being called upon for a public appearance). Yet Wheeler's sterling integrity ultimately landed him on the ticket with **Rutherford**

B. Hayes in the presidential election of 1876. He had a spotless record, having utterly and completely spurned the opportunity to accept **Credit Mobilier** stock when so many of his colleagues were handsomely profiting from it. He had also, as head of a congressional delegation visiting Louisiana, proven himself to be a bipartisan and bisectional reconciler in dealing with Reconstruction issues in the mid-1870s. Even so, the Hayes-Wheeler ticket was an unlikely one, since neither man was well-known nationally, and neither had ever met the other before their respective nominations. In fact, Hayes had never even *heard* of Wheeler! They won the election only after the **Compromise of 1877**.

Since Hayes ran one of the most quiet, cautious, and reserved administrations in history, the widower Wheeler had little to do as vice president but to preside over the U.S. Senate and to sip lemonade at the White House with the president and first lady. Thus, his one term kept him in even greater obscurity than he had previously experienced. When his term expired, he ran for the Senate seat just vacated by Conkling, but he lost. He then retired quietly and became the most forgotten vice president of the Gilded Age and one of the most forgotten in all of American history.

WHISKEY RING. *See* CORRUPTION; GRANT, ULYSSES S.

"WILD BILL" HICKOK. *See* HICKOK, "WILD BILL."

WILLARD, FRANCES (1839–1898). Born Frances Elizabeth Caroline Willard in western New York state near Rochester, Willard migrated with her devout Methodist family of Puritan ancestry to southern Wisconsin early in life. Moving to Evanston, Illinois, as a teen, she was valedictorian of her high school class. Her love of learning and school launched her into a career as an educator, and she rose to the rank of dean at Northwestern University in Chicago, Illinois, before resigning to focus on what became her life's calling—prohibition. Alcohol abuse ran rampant in the United States after the Civil War, and by the 1870s it had become a major social problem that attracted the attention of reformers. In 1874, Willard helped found the Chicago **Women**'s Christian Temperance Union, which, thanks to her efforts, quickly spawned chapters around the country. In 1879, she became president of the national Women's Christian

Temperance Union (WCTU), a position she held for life. In 1883, she established an international WCTU, which generated much support in England. Touring and lecturing extensively around the world, she also published a magazine and authored books devoted to prohibition, women's rights, and socialism. In 1883, she helped create the Prohibition Party in the United States and 5 years later founded the National Council of Women. Never married, she devoted her life to her crusades, dying before her time from influenza while in New York City. Although she did not live to see the passage of either the Eighteenth or Nineteenth Amendments to the U.S. Constitution, she was as instrumental as any individual in bringing both to fruition. Posthumously she was chosen to be the first woman represented among the nation's greatest figures in Statuary Hall in the U.S. Capitol, a fact that testifies to the enormous impact she had on American history. *See also* COLLEGES AND UNIVERSITIES.

WILSON, HENRY (1812–1875). Born Jermiah Jones Colbath to a poor family in New Hampshire, Henry Wilson grew up as a farmer's apprentice, receiving almost no schooling in the process. Once grown and emancipated, he changed his name to Henry Wilson to disassociate himself from a family and upbringing of which he felt ashamed. After moving to Massachusetts, he learned the trade of a cobbler and built a successful shoe business near Boston. He educated himself and developed political opinions that turned him into an abolitionist, a Whig, a Free-Soiler, a Know-Nothing, and finally a **Republican**. Elected to the U.S. Senate, he served four terms, from 1855 to 1873, but he also led troops in the Union army during the Civil War. In 1868, his name was mentioned for the vice presidency, but he lost out to Schuyler Colfax. Four years later, he replaced Colfax on the ticket with **Ulysses S. Grant**. The timing was horrible, because the **Credit Mobilier scandal** had just come to light, and Wilson was implicated. He had indeed bought stock in the fraudulent company, but he had not kept it for long, so he was able to satisfy his inquisitors that he was guilty of no deliberate wrongdoing. Through touring and speaking on behalf of the Grant administration for the first 2 years of his term as vice president, he began to make a name for himself nationally with the intention of running for president in 1876. However, he suffered a stroke and paralysis and died midway through his term in November

1875. Although his political career left little in the way of a legacy, his great lasting contribution came in the fields of **literature** and history. He wrote the three-volume abolitionist treatise *History of the Rise and Fall of the Slave Power in America*, the last portion of which was published posthumously.

WOMEN. Because the Gilded Age represented the apex of Protestant Christian influence in American history, it was an era of extreme social conservatism. It is not surprising, therefore, that women's accepted role in society was very limited. The expectation was that girls would grow up to be wives, mothers, and homemakers, remaining in what people of that time called the "woman's sphere," or what historians have called the "cult of domesticity."

While perhaps 90 percent of women fit into this mold, the exceptions are notable. Carrying over what they had started in the antebellum era, women's rights crusaders such as **Elizabeth Cady Stanton**, **Susan B. Anthony**, Lucy Stone, Julia Ward Howe, Amelia Bloomer, Lucretia Mott, and the Grimke sisters, continued the struggle for equality under the law for both sexes. These leaders did not all agree on how to accomplish this goal, however, causing a fracture in the movement at the start of the Gilded Age that was not repaired until 1890. In 1869, Stanton and Anthony founded the National Woman Suffrage Association, which focused on federal legislation and/or constitutional amendments, while at the same time Stone and Howe created the American Woman Suffrage Association, which focused on grassroots campaigning at the local and state levels. The latter was successful in some places (mainly the West—Wyoming in 1869 became the first state to enfranchise women), whereas the former was not (the **U.S. Supreme Court** ruled in *Minor v. Happersett* in 1875 that the Fourteenth and Fifteenth Amendments did not apply to women). In 1890, the two groups repaired the rift and created the combined National American Woman Suffrage Association, which successfully pressed for the ratification of the Nineteenth Amendment to the U.S. Constitution in 1920.

Meanwhile, other female reformers focused mainly on solving other social problems. **Frances Willard**, for example, led the Women's Christian Temperance Union in a crusade to end alcohol abuse in the United States and founded the National Council of

Women, consequently becoming probably the single most influential woman of the Gilded Age. By contrast, **Ida B. Wells-Barnett**, an **African American**, spent her life trying to end lynching, which was generally considered a socially acceptable practice in the Gilded Age, making her seem out of step with the times, yet great in retrospect. **Helen Hunt Jackson** fought barely more successfully for American **Indian** rights. Jane Addams and Ellen Gates Starr, founders of Chicago's **Hull House**, pioneered in the settlement house movement and in what in modern parlance is called social work. Hull House also served as a gathering place for fellow female reformers, such as Florence Kelley, the great anti–child labor advocate and founder of the National Consumer's League, and Mary Kenney and Alzina Stevens, organizers respectively for the American Federation of Labor and the **Knights of Labor**. Clara Barton, meanwhile, founded the **American Red Cross**.

Many Gilded Age women distinguished themselves not as reformers or suffragists but as leaders within their chosen professions. Journalism and **literature** were the professions most open to women. **Nellie Bly**, for instance, pioneered in the journalistic art of muckraking while also becoming renowned as a world traveler, while Louisa May Alcott and Sarah Orne Jewett became successful novelists with *Little Women* (1868) and *A Country Doctor* (1884), respectively, among other works written by each. In the field of poetry, Emily Dickinson achieved great acclaim posthumously for her unconventional style, while Emma Lazarus is remembered only for her great poem, "The New Colossus" (1883), which adorns the **Statue of Liberty** in New York harbor. Frances "Fannie" Crosby, a blind poetess, distinguished herself as perhaps the greatest American hymn writer ever, penning some 9,000 hymns, including such mainstream Protestant Church classics as "Blessed Assurance," "To God Be the Glory," "Showers of Blessings," and "Praise Him, Praise Him."

A few women managed to succeed in other professions as well, despite a blow from the U.S. Supreme Court in the 1873 case *Bradwell v. Illinois*, which upheld a state's right to restrict women from certain professions, such as practicing law. Mary E. Lease is remembered primarily as the Kansas Populist who encouraged farmers to "raise less corn and more hell," but she was also a New York City lawyer and writer. Two English-born sisters, Elizabeth and

Emily Blackwell, along with German-born Elizabeth Zakrzewska, became three of the first women to earn medical degrees and practice medicine in the United States. Anna Howard Shaw, meanwhile, distinguished herself in two ways: in 1880, she was ordained the first female Methodist minister in the United States, and 6 years later, she graduated from Boston University as a medical doctor. Mary Baker Eddy of Boston founded the **Church of Christ, Scientist** in 1879. In the West, **Annie Oakley**, **Calamity Jane**, and Belle Starr all made names for themselves as shooting, riding, and show business specialists. Finally, Emma Goldman is an infamous character in history for her leadership as a labor organizer, feminist, birth control advocate, freethinker, and **anarchist**. She plotted with Alexander Berkman to murder **Henry Clay Frick** in the **Homestead Strike** in 1892, although she escaped prosecution for lack of evidence.

There was no shortage of clubs and sororal organizations for women to join during the Gilded Age. Hundreds existed at the local level, but a few came to prominence nationally and/or internationally. In addition to those already mentioned, a few of the most notable ones include the General Federation of Women's Clubs, founded in 1890; the National Association of Colored Women's Clubs, founded in 1896; the Association of Collegiate Alumnae (which became the American Association of University Women), founded in 1881; the United Daughters of the Confederacy, founded in 1894; and the Daughters of the American Revolution, founded in 1896. *See also* WOODHULL, VICTORIA.

WOMEN'S CHRISTIAN TEMPERANCE UNION. *See* WILLARD, FRANCES.

WOOD, LEONARD (1860–1927). Born in New Hampshire, Leonard Wood graduated from Harvard Medical School in Boston, Massachusetts, in 1884. He soon joined the army as a surgeon and was sent to Arizona at the height of the Apache war. There, in 1886, he helped track down **Geronimo** and force his surrender. Wood distinguished himself in the campaign and later received a Medal of Honor for trekking 100 miles through hostile **Indian** territory to carry army messages and orders. In 1893, while stationed at Fort McPherson in Atlanta, Wood attended the Georgia Institute of Technology, where he played on and coached the school's first football team. Two years later, he earned a position as official White House physician, first for **Grover Cleveland** and then for **William McKinley**. While in Washington, he met and formed a strong friendship with **Theodore Roosevelt**. When the **Spanish–American War** broke out, Wood (a colonel) and Roosevelt (a lieutenant colonel) jointly created the Rough Riders cavalry unit, which became instantly famous for its charge up San Juan Hill, among other exploits. In the midst of the war, Wood earned promotion to brigadier general. After the war, he was appointed military governor of Cuba from 1899 to 1902. He lived a full, active life thereafter in the early 20th century, engaging in military, political, and medical pursuits which ultimately made him more famous than his aforementioned Gilded Age activities. *See also* SPORTS AND RECREATION.

WOODHULL, VICTORIA (1838–1927). Born Victoria Claflin in central Ohio, Woodhull came from a family that some observers have described as gypsies. She married a distant cousin named Woodhull in New York at the age of 15. She had two children by her first husband, but came to favor divorce, "free love," and contraception to staying in an unhappy marriage and bearing unwanted children. This began her lifelong pursuit of **women**'s rights at a time when outspoken women were largely shunned by society. She and her sister "Tennessee" Claflin pioneered several areas of women's rights. They were first and foremost entrepreneurs, selling their services as fortune tellers, spiritualists, and medicine women/healers. In 1870, they opened the first female brokerage firm on Wall Street, with the help of their friend **Cornelius Vanderbilt**. At the same time, they started a weekly newspaper devoted to women's issues (including sex **education**) and radical political ideology (including communism). A year later Woodhull spoke on behalf of women's suffrage in front of the House Judiciary Committee, basing her argument on the Fourteenth Amendment. This engagement made her the most celebrated suffragette of the Gilded Age. In 1872, she stood as the Equal Rights Party's presidential nominee, although she received no electoral votes, and it is doubtful that she garnered more than a mere handful of popular votes. Meanwhile, in her newspaper, she broke the story of the scandalous affair between the New York City Reverend **Henry Ward**

Beecher and Elizabeth Tilton, which resulted in the most famous trial of its kind in the Gilded Age. In the same week, **Anthony Comstock** of the U.S. Postal Service had her arrested for distributing lewd material through the U.S. mail. In 1876, she divorced her second husband and moved to England, and then in 1883 remarried. She stayed in England off and on for the rest of her life, although she still ran for president of the United States in the 1880s and 1890s.

WOOLWORTH'S, F. W. What became the largest department store chain in the world in the early 20th century started off as a small business opened in 1879 by Franklin Winfield Woolworth of Watertown, New York. Woolworth began as a retail clerk in a local store, which, as was typical in the Gilded Age, kept merchandise behind the counter and did not allow customers to handle it until they had already paid for it. The store would, however, put sale items, rejects, and leftovers out for customer handling. Also typical was the fact that retailers did not have fixed prices but instead negotiated prices with customers. Woolworth thought it might be profitable to open a whole store that offered nothing but cheap merchandise at a fixed price and put it all out on display for customer inspection. With $300, he opened his first store in Utica, New York. Nothing was priced over 5 cents, but the store did not survive. A second store, opened soon after in Lancaster, Pennsylvania, did prove profitable. Woolworth changed his business plan to offer goods at no more than 10 cents, and thus was born what came to be known as the "five and dime" store—a retail model that was copied by many in the 20th century and which has evolved into the "dollar" store. By working with rivals rather than engaging in cutthroat competition, Woolworth was able to buy larger volumes of goods from wholesalers at cheaper prices, allowing both companies larger profit margins. By the end of the Gilded Age, Woolworth's consisted of about 100 stores in the United States and Canada.

WOUNDED KNEE MASSACRE. The Dakota Territory had been the traditional land of the nomadic Sioux (Lakota) **Indians** for generations prior to the Gilded Age. U.S. government policy, meanwhile, since the 1860s had been to round up all the nomadic tribes of the Great Plains and confine them to reservations. This policy led to frequent clashes between Native Americans and the U.S. cavalry. No clash was more tragic than the last great one in American Indian history, which occurred on the Pine Ridge reservation in the southwestern Dakota Territory, along Wounded Knee Creek. There, on 29 December 1890, some 350 Indians and 25 army personnel died in a bloody confrontation.

The genesis of the event traces back about 2 years, when a **religious** mystic named Wovoka of the Paiute tribe in Nevada introduced the ritual of the Ghost Dance, which he said would empower the Indians, drive out the white man, and lead to an idyllic era of peace and prosperity for his people. Giving renewed hope to a defeated and demoralized people, the dance caught on and spread like wildfire from tribe to tribe and reservation to reservation in 1890. By November, it had spread all the way to the Dakota area, where **Sitting Bull** and his Hunkpapa band of Sioux Indians sat captive on the Standing Rock reservation. The Ghost Dance appeared to white observers to be a war chant, and it scared them. Government officials and army officers thus sought to stop the Ghost Dance by arresting the Indian chiefs, such as Kicking Bear, Sitting Bull, and Big Foot, who were encouraging it.

One of these arrest attempts led to the death of Sitting Bull on 15 December. Two weeks later, Big Foot was arrested, and his band of Minneconjou Sioux (mainly composed of women and children) were rounded up and placed under guard of the heavily armed Seventh Cavalry. The soldiers then searched the Indians' tepees and personal belongings to seize any weapons they might be hiding. During this search and seizure, a deaf Indian named Black Coyote refused to give up his gun. In the ensuing scuffle, shots rang out, and pandemonium followed. The women and children fled, the warriors fought back as best they could, and the cavalry opened fire on all of them indiscriminately. More than 100 people died on the spot, while many others died later from wounds, exacerbated by exposure to the extreme cold in the snow-covered winter of the northern Great Plains.

– Y –

YELLOWSTONE NATIONAL PARK. The United States' and the world's first national park, Yellowstone, was created by Congress and

President **Ulysses S. Grant** on 1 March 1872. Comprising more than 2.2 million acres (3,472 square miles), the park is considerably larger than some of the eastern seaboard states. It is located mostly in the state of Wyoming today, although small portions of it also lie in Montana and Idaho. At an altitude of more than 7,000 feet above sea level, it sits astride the Continental Divide in the Rocky Mountains, with about two-thirds to the east and one-third to the west. It boasts features such as the 87,000-acre Yellowstone Lake, the Yellowstone and Snake Rivers, the 10,000-foot Mount Washburn, nearly 300 waterfalls, two canyons, one of the largest petrified forests in the world, the largest volcanic system in North America, and, of course, more than half of the world's geothermal formations (including the world's largest geyser, Old Faithful). With an ecologically important and impressive array of flora and fauna, including the world's largest herd of elk, the oldest naturally surviving herd of bison, the last undisturbed grizzly bear population, and some of the best trout fishing in North America, it is easy to see why Yellowstone was singled out for preservation in an era when humans otherwise exploited the western wilderness for commercial use.

Yellowstone's name, given to the area by indigenous American Indians and passed along to French explorers and fur traders in the colonial era, derives ostensibly from the yellow-colored rock cliffs along the Yellowstone River's northern headwaters. Although the earliest record of a Euro-American seeing the area dates to 1795, it was not until the late 1860s that white Americans began to explore the region well enough to understand what a unique and awe-inspiring place it was. Thereafter, the movement to turn it into a national park progressed with amazing speed. In 1871, Congress authorized Ferdinand Hayden, head of the U.S. Geological Survey, to explore, map, and document the area. With a team of experts, including a photographer and an artist, Hayden embarked. Upon returning, he delivered a 500-page report to Congress. Nathaniel Langford, an earlier explorer of the region, however, became the main lobbyist for turning Yellowstone into a national park. Within a year, his goal was accomplished, and Langford earned appointment as the park's first administrator, serving from 1872 to 1877.

Initially, Congress did not provide funding for the park, and encroachment into the area by poachers and other outlaws could not be stopped by either the administrator or the sole park ranger. Not until the U.S. army began patrolling it in the 1880s would this change. Meanwhile, the park was so remote that only a few hundred people visited it, until the early 1880s, when a **railroad** was built nearby in Montana. By the end of the Gilded Age, the park registered more than 5,000 tourists annually and had become the cornerstone of the U.S. national park system, which also included Yosemite in California and Mackinac Island in Michigan.

YOSEMITE NATIONAL PARK. *See* SIERRA CLUB.

Appendix A

Presidents and Their Administrations, 1869–1900

ULYSSES S. GRANT 1869–1877

Election Results:

Year	Candidate	Popular Votes	Electoral Votes
1868	Ulysses S. Grant	3,013,650	214
	Horatio Seymour	2,708,744	80
1872	Ulysses S. Grant	3,598,235	286
	Horace Greeley	2,834,761	69

Vice Presidents

Schuyler Colfax (1869–1873)
Henry Wilson (1873–1875)
Vacant (1875–1877)

Cabinet:

Secretary of State

Elihu B. Washburne (1869)
Hamilton Fish (1869–1877)

Secretary of Treasury

George S. Boutwell (1869–1873)
William Richardson (1873–1874)
Benjamin Bristow (1874–1876)
Lot M. Morrill (1876–1877)

Secretary of War

John A. Rawlins (1869)
William T. Sherman (1869)
William W. Belknap (1869–1876)
Alphonso Taft (1876)
James D. Cameron (1876–1877)

Attorney General

Ebenezer Hoar (1869–1870)
Amos T. Ackerman (1870–1871)
G. H. Williams (1871–1875)
Edwards Pierrepont (1875–1876)
Alphonso Taft (1876–1877)

Postmaster General

John A. Creswell (1869–1874)
James W. Marshall (1874)
Marshall Jewell (1874–1876)
James N. Tyner (1876–1877)

Secretary of Navy

Adolph E. Borie (1869)
George M. Robeson (1869–1877)

Secretary of Interior

Jacob D. Cox (1869–1870)
Columbus Delano (1870–1875)
Zachariah Chandler (1875–1877)

RUTHERFORD B. HAYES 1877–1881

Election Results:

Year	Candidate	Popular Votes	Electoral Votes
1876	Rutherford B. Hayes	4,034,311	185
	Samuel J. Tilden	4,288,546	184
	Peter Cooper	75,973	0

Vice President

William A. Wheeler (1877–1881)

Cabinet:

Secretary of State

William B. Evarts (1877–1881)

Secretary of Treasury

John Sherman (1877–1881)

Secretary of War

George W. McCrary (1877–1879)
Alex Ramsey (1879–1881)

Attorney General

Charles Devans (1877–1881)

Postmaster General

David M. Key (1877–1880)
Horace Maynard (1880–1881)

Secretary of Navy

Richard W. Thompson (1877–1880)
Nathan Goff Jr. (1881)

Secretary of Interior

Carl Schurz (1877–1881)

JAMES A. GARFIELD 1881 (DIED IN OFFICE)

Election Results:

Year	Candidate	Popular Votes	Electoral Votes
1880	James A. Garfield	4,446,158	214
	Winfield S. Hancock	4,444,260	155
	James B. Weaver	305,997	0

Vice President

Chester A. Arthur (1881)

Cabinet:

Secretary of State

James G. Blaine (1881)

Secretary of Treasury

William Windom (1881)

Secretary of War

Robert T. Lincoln (1881)

Attorney General

Wayne MacVeagh (1881)

Postmaster General

Thomas L. James (1881)

Secretary of Navy

William L. Hunt (1881)

Secretary of Interior

Samuel J. Kirkwood (1881)

CHESTER A. ARTHUR 1881–1885

Election Results:

Not elected; assumed office upon the death of James A. Garfield

Vice President

Vacant

Cabinet:

Secretary of State

F. T. Frelinghuysen (1881–1885)

Secretary of Treasury

Charles L. Folger (1881–1884)
Walter Q. Gresham (1884)
Hugh McCulloch (1884–1885)

Secretary of War

Robert T. Lincoln (1881–1885)

Attorney General

Benjamin H. Brewster (1881–1885)

Postmaster General

Timothy O. Howe (1881–1883)
Walter Q. Gresham (1883–1884)
Frank Hatton (1884–1885)

Secretary of Navy

William H. Hunt (1881–1882)
William E. Chandler (1882–1885)

Secretary of Interior

Samuel J. Kirkwood (1881–1882)
Henry M. Teller (1882–1885)

GROVER CLEVELAND 1881–1885

Election Results:

Year	Candidate	Popular Votes	Electoral Votes
1884	Grover Cleveland	4,874,621	219
	James G. Blaine	4,848,936	182
	Benjamin F. Butler	175,096	0
	John P. St. John	147,482	0

Vice President

Thomas A. Hendricks (1885)
Vacant (1885–1889)

Cabinet:

Secretary of State

Thomas F. Bayard (1885–1889)

Secretary of Treasury

Daniel Manning (1885–1887)
Charles S. Fairchild (1887–1889)

Secretary of War

William C. Endicott (1885–1889)

Attorney General

Augustus H. Garland (1885–1889)

Postmaster General

William F. Vilas (1885–1888)
Don M. Dickinson (1888–1889)

Secretary of Navy

William C. Whitney (1885–1889)

Secretary of Interior

Lucius Q. C. Lamar (1885–1888)
William F. Vilas (1888–1889)

Secretary of Agriculture

Norman J. Colman (1889)

BENJAMIN HARRISON 1889–1893

Election Results:

Year	Candidate	Popular Votes	Electoral Votes
1888	Benjamin Harrison	5,447,129	233
	Grover Cleveland	5,537,857	168

Vice President

Levi P. Morton (1889–1893)

Cabinet:

Secretary of State

James G. Blaine (1889–1892)
John W. Foster (1892–1893)

Secretary of Treasury

William Windom (1889–1891)
Charles Foster (1891–1893)

Secretary of War

Redfield Proctor (1889–1891)
Stephen B. Elkins (1891–1893)

Postmaster General

John Wanamaker (1889–1893)

Secretary of Navy

Benjamin F. Tracy (1889–1893)

Secretary of Interior

John W. Noble (1889–1893)

Secretary of Agriculture

Jeremiah M. Rusk (1889–1893)

GROVER CLEVELAND 1893–1897

Election Results:

Year	Candidate	Popular Votes	Electoral Votes
1892	Grover Cleveland	5,555,426	277
	Benjamin Harrison	5,182,600	145
	James B. Weaver	1,029,846	22

Vice President

Adlai E. Stevenson (1893–1897)

Cabinet:

Secretary of State

Walter Q. Gresham (1893–1895)
Richard Olney (1895–1897)

Secretary of Treasury

John G. Carlisle (1893–1897)

Secretary of War

Daniel S. Lamont (1893–1897)

Attorney General

Richard Olney (1893–1895)
James Harmon (1895–1897)

Postmaster General

Wilson S. Bissell (1893–1895)
William L. Wilson (1895–1897)

Secretary of Navy

Hilary A. Herbert (1893–1897)

Secretary of Interior

Hoke Smith (1893–1896)
David R. Francis (1896–1897)

Secretary of Agriculture

Julius S. Morton (1893–1897)

WILLIAM MCKINLEY 1897–1901

Election Results:

Year	Candidate	Popular Votes	Electoral Votes
1896	William McKinley	7,102,246	271
	William Jennings Bryan	6,492,559	176
1900	William McKinley	7,218,039	292
	William Jennings Bryan	6,358,345	155
	John G. Woolley	209,004	0
	Eugene V. Debs	86,935	0

Vice President

Garrett Hobart (1897–1899)
Vacant (1899–1901)
Theodore Roosevelt (1901)

Cabinet:

Secretary of State

John Sherman (1897–1898)
William R. Day (1898)
John Hay (1898–1901)

Secretary of Treasury

Lyman J. Gage (1897–1901)

Secretary of War

Russell A. Alger (1897–1899)
Elihu Root (1899–1901)

Attorney General

Joseph McKenna (1897–1898)
John W. Griggs (1898–1901)
Philander C. Knox (1901)

Postmaster General

James A. Gary (1897–1898)
Charles E. Smith (1898–1901)

Secretary of Navy

John D. Long (1897–1901)

Secretary of Interior

Cornelius N. Bliss (1897–1899)
Ethan A. Hitchcock (1899–1901)

Secretary of Agriculture

James Wilson (1897–1901)

Appendix B

Constitutional Amendment
Fifteenth Amendment

Passed by Congress 26 February 1869. Ratified 2 February 1870.

Section 1. The right of citizens of the United States to vote shall not be denied or abridged by the United States or by any State on account of race, color, or previous condition of servitude.

Section 2. The Congress shall have power to enforce this article by appropriate legislation.

Select Bibliography

Contents

INTRODUCTION

An exhaustive bibliography on the Gilded Age would require a separate volume. This "select" bibliography merely contains some of the most seminal books and articles on the Gilded Age, with emphasis on the more recent and easily accessible ones. Older works are sometimes omitted with the understanding that, once readers consult the newer ones on this list, the bibliographies therein will point, should they have need of them, to older sources. Some entries are included not so much for their importance in the historiography of the Gilded Age as for the fact that they are in the author's personal library, and hence he has an intimate familiarity with them. By necessity this list omits hundreds of worthy books, some of which are hot off the press and have not been reviewed by the author, some of which are not readily accessible to the general public because of being shelved in special collections libraries or because of being self-published or locally published, and some of which are too erudite (or obfuscated) for all but a few scholars to understand. It also omits hundreds of worthy journal articles, because preference is given to books when possible. Although there is no up-to-date "thorough" or "complete" bibliography of the Gilded Age currently available, Vincent P. DeSantis did give us one in 1971 that contains virtually every publication of any merit up to that time.

Students and casual readers would do well to begin exploring the Gilded Age by reading a few surveys of the period. Every American history textbook, of course, contains a section on this era, some of which are better than others. More recent publications often are not as thorough as older ones because of the need to save space to make room for each passing decade of the 20th and 21st centuries. The best textbook treatment is arguably found in Samuel Eliot Morison's *The Growth of the American Republic* (1980) or its abridged version, *A Concise History of the American Republic* (1983), both of which were revised with the help of equally venerable historians Henry Steele Commager and William Leuchtenberg. Beyond textbooks, several good specialized surveys of the period are widely available. The best in terms of comprehensive coverage and readability is arguably Sean Cashman's *America in the Gilded Age* (1984). Just as comprehensive but more dense and scholarly is Mark Summers's *The Gilded Age: or, the Hazard of New Functions* (2004). A good social history for non-specialists is Joel Schrock's *The Gilded Age* (1997).

Although the era is not noted for strong presidential leadership, books on the Gilded Age's seven presidents of the United States dominate the literature of the period. Three important presidential series are widely available. "The American Presidency" series, published by the University Press of Kansas, contains a scholarly but succinct volume on each president except Ulysses S. Grant. Times Books of New York commissioned venerable historian Arthur M. Schlesinger to edit a collection called "The American Presidents," which has a volume on each president. The American Political Biography Press in Connecticut, meanwhile, has collected some of the most scholarly and most thorough accounts of the presidents (which were first published by others separately over several decades and became standards) and has reprinted them. It also has a volume on each president. Every individual book in any of these series is recommendable.

Political topics generally are the bread and butter of any era of history, and the Gilded Age is no exception. Two of the best broad national treatments are Wayne Morgan's *From Hayes to McKinley* (1969) and Morton Keller's *Affairs of State* (1977). Many others are more specialized, such as Vann Woodward's *Origins of the New South* (1951) and Edward Ayers's *The Promise of the New South* (1992), which obviously deal with the South and its politics vis-á-vis black–white racial issues. The Populist movement and the People's Party provide much fodder for historical inquiry. John Hicks wrote the first seminal study in this sub-field, *The Populist Revolt* (1931), but Lawrence Goodwin made an important revisionist assessment in *Democratic Promise* (1976), while Robert McMath gave us one of the most readable syntheses in *American Populism* (1992). Currently, Connie Lester is doing some of the most impressive work in the field.

Despite the chronological overlap, Reconstruction constitutes a large, separate field of study from the Gilded Age. It also has been one of the most hotly debated subjects in American history. The historiography has undergone massive, dramatic revisions over the past century. This bibliography, therefore, will in no way do justice to the topic. The earliest histories of this divisive topic came from the pro-southern perspective, thanks to William Dunning and his students at Columbia University. Although early attempts at revision came from black authors such as W. E. B. Du Bois and John R. Lynch, their interpretation did not become mainstream until white writers in the 1940s and 1950s began to reevaluate Reconstruction. The current standard monograph on it is Eric Foner's *Reconstruction: America's Unfinished Revolution* (1988). A good textbook treatment is Claudine Ferrill's *Reconstruction* (2003), but an important primary source collection is Greenhaven Press's *Opposing Viewpoints on Reconstruction*. A volume in the Scarecrow Press encyclopedic series edited by Jon Woronoff entitled *Historical Dictionary of the Civil War and Reconstruction* (2004), written by William L. Richter, makes a valuable contribution to the field, particularly because of its chronology section.

Undoubtedly, race is the most profoundly revised subject area in American history, as evidenced by the fact that "Negro" history was once a standard label, but now, not only is that no longer the case, but the very word "Negro" has no place in the modern English lexicon. The most readable, broad survey of that topic is John Hope Franklin's *From Slavery to Freedom*, which is available in eight editions spread over a half-century. "Jim Crow" is a sub-field of African American history that has particular relevance to the Gilded Age. The standard work on it is Vann Woodward's *The Strange Career of Jim Crow*, which likewise has been revised and reprinted for a half-century. Rayford Logan's book, which is commonly known by its subtitle "*The Nadir*," is also a classic dealing with the same issue. Fitzhugh Brundage is considered the pre-eminent specialist on the subject of lynching, while Nell Irvin Painter gives us the standard treatment on the Exodusters. William Leckie does the same for the Buffalo Soldiers, and Louis Harlan likewise for Booker T. Washington. A scholarly explanation of how the American people as a whole came to accept racial discrimination as normal and necessary during the Gilded Age can be found in Thomas Adams Upchurch's book *Legislating Racism* (2004).

Other racial and ethnic groups have likewise benefited from revisionism in the historical profession over the past century. The most enthralling account of American Indian history is Dee Brown's revolutionary *Bury My Heart at Wounded Knee* (1970), which portrayed the Native American rather than the Anglo-American perspective. Robert Utley's books, meanwhile, tend to be scholarly, balanced, and easy to read. Andrew Gyory's *Closing the Gate* is a solid piece of work on the Chinese, while multiculturalism and the American melting pot are tackled notably by Leonard Dinnerstein and Roger Daniels.

Another subject area in American history that has benefited from revisionist history is women/gender. Unfortunately, there is a serious paucity of books dealing specifically with women's issues in the Gilded Age. Partly this is because so few women lived and worked in the public eye during this era. Those who were public figures have been written about extensively, but rarely have all of them been brought together in a comprehensive volume. Ruth Borden's *Women and Temperance* would make a good starting point for exploring the topic.

Unlike the aforementioned topics, American diplomatic and military history has not undergone so much revisionism in the decades since the Gilded Age. Mainly this is because the anti-imperialist point of view has mostly prevailed. Exceptions include the writings of contemporary imperialists such as Alfred Thayer Mahan and Theodore Roosevelt, and a few modern scholars like Ernest May and James A. Field. The first generation of historians to analyze the causes and consequences of the expansionist foreign policy, the Progressives, sided with the anti-imperialists, generally blaming greedy capitalists and demagogic politicians for the unnecessary Spanish–American War and its aftereffects. Charles and Mary Beard's work is exemplary in this regard. The writings of Samuel Flagg Bemis, Julius Pratt, William Appleman Williams, and Walter LeFeber in succeeding decades continued the trend. A majority of the American people themselves, however, largely do not follow the predominantly anti-nationalist, pro-globalist leanings of scholars, considering that viewpoint unpatriotic.

Business history seems to be the field that in the popular imagination is most nearly synonymous with the Gilded Age. As with foreign affairs, there have been two opposing schools of thought on the American capitalist system and big business from the beginning. Contemporary writers and later historians alike have debated whether the corporate tycoons of the era were "captains of industry" or "robber barons." The millionaire industrialists themselves were among those who tried to shape public perception of their role in society as the former. Andrew Carnegie, for example, was ostensibly the first to use that term to describe himself in his *Gospel of Wealth*. The Populists and soon-to-be Progressives were among the first writers to see them as the latter, with William Peffer of Kansas supposedly coining the term. Henry Demarest Lloyd's *Wealth Against Commonwealth* (1894) was the first to take them to task, specifically targeting John D. Rockefeller and the Standard Oil Company. His work would soon be followed by Ida Tarbell's muckraking *History of Standard Oil*. The biggest boost to this anti–big business point of view came in the middle of the Great Depression in the 1930s with Matthew Josephson's *The Robber Barons*, which dominated American thinking on the topic despite the work of revisionists such as Allan Nevins. Not until Alfred D. Chandler Jr. became the scholar of note in the field in the 1970s, however, did the perception change to something approaching balanced. His *The*

Visible Hand (1977) is perhaps the best work on the subject to date. For a brief analysis of the topic, Glenn Porter's *The Rise of Big Business* (1973) is a good starting point. Despite such balanced accounts, the prevailing view in academia still tends to be more negative than positive in analyzing the Rockefeller, Vanderbilt, and Carnegie types of Gilded Age fame.

Should the reader of this volume want to follow the Gilded Age into the next era of American history—the Progressive Era—a solid treatment and excellent beginning point is Scarecrow Press's *The Historical Dictionary of the Progressive Era* (2009) by Catherine Cocks, Peter Holloran, and Alan Lessof.

The following bibliography is arranged alphabetically within broad, and hopefully self-explanatory, categories. Many entries could easily fit into more than one category, but to avoid redundancy, each has been included in only the category that in the author's estimation best reflects its contents.

SURVEYS AND ESSAY COLLECTIONS

Calhoun, Charles W., ed. *The Gilded Age: Essays on the Origins of Modern America.* Wilmington, Del.: SR Books, 1996.

Cashman, Sean Dennis. *America in the Gilded Age: From the Death of Lincoln to the Rise of Theodore Roosevelt.* New York: New York University Press, 1984.

DeSantis, Vincent. *The Shaping of Modern America: 1877–1920.* 2nd ed. Wheeling, Ill.: Forum Press, 1989.

Edwards, Rebecca. *New Spirits: Americans in the Gilded Age, 1865–1905.* New York: Oxford University Press, 2006.

Espejo, Roman, ed. *The Age of Reform and Industrialization, 1896–1920.* Farmington Hills, Mich.: Greenhaven Press, 2003.

Garraty, John A. *The New Commonwealth, 1877–1890.* New York: Harper & Row, 1968.

Garraty, John A., ed. *The Transformation of American Society, 1870–1890.* New ed. Columbia: University of South Carolina Press, 1969.

Ginger, Ray. *Age of Excess: The United States from 1877 to 1914.* New York: Macmillan, 1965.

Gould, Lewis L. *America in the Progressive Era, 1890–1914.* Harlow, UK: Longman, 2001.

Hoogenboom, Ari, and Olive Hoogenboom, eds. *The Gilded Age*. Englewood Cliffs, N.J.: Prentice-Hall, 1967.

Morgan, H. Wayne, ed. *The Gilded Age*. Rev. ed. Syracuse, N.Y.: Syracuse University Press, 1970.

Painter, Nell Irwin. *Standing at Armageddon: The United States, 1877–1919*. New York: Norton, 1987.

Shrock, Joel. *The Gilded Age*. Westport, Conn.: Greenwood Press, 2004.

Summers, Mark Wahlgren. *The Gilded Age: Or, the Hazard of New Functions*. Upper Saddle River, N.J.: Prentice Hall, 1997.

Weinstein, Allen, ed. *Origins of Modern America, 1860–1900*. New York: Random House, 1970.

Wiebe, Robert H. *The Search for Order, 1877–1920*. New York: Hill and Wang, 1967.

PRESIDENTS OF THE UNITED STATES

Ackerman, Kenneth D. *Dark Horse: The Surprise Election and Political Murder of President James A. Garfield*. New York: Carroll & Graf, 2003.

Barnard, Harry. *Rutherford B. Hayes and His America*. Rev. ed. Newtown, Conn.: American Political Biography Press, 1994.

Bunting, Josiah. *Ulysses S. Grant*. New York: Times Books, 2004.

Calhoun, Charles W. *Benjamin Harrison*. New York: Times Books, 2005.

Chessman, G. Wallace. *Theodore Roosevelt and the Politics of Power*. Prospect Heights, Ill.: Waveland Press, 1969.

Davison, Kenneth E. *The Presidency of Rutherford B. Hayes*. Westport, Conn.: Greenwood Press, 1972.

Doenecke, Justus D. *The Presidencies of James A. Garfield and Chester A. Arthur*. Lawrence: University Press of Kansas, 1981.

Gould, Lewis L. *The Presidency of William McKinley*. Lawrence: University of Kansas Press, 1981.

Graff, Henry F. *Grover Cleveland*. New York: Times Books, 2002.

Hesseltine, William Best. *Ulysses S. Grant: Politician*. Phoenix, Ariz.: Simon Publications, 2001.

Hoogenboom, Ari. *The Presidency of Rutherford B. Hayes*. Lawrence: University Press of Kansas, 1988.

Karabell, Zachary. *Chester Alan Arthur*. New York: Times Books, 2004.

Leech, Margaret. *In the Days of McKinley*. Rev. ed. Newtown, Conn.: American Political Biography Press, 1999.

McFeeley, William S. *Ulysses S. Grant*. Rev. ed. New York: W. W. Norton, 2002.

Merrill, Horace S. *Bourbon Leader: Grover Cleveland and the Democratic Party*. Boston: Little, Brown and Company, 1957.

Morgan, H. Wayne. *William McKinley and His America*. Rev. ed. Kent, Ohio: Kent State University Press, 2004.

Nevins, Allan. *Grover Cleveland: A Study in Courage*. Rev. ed. 2 vols. Newtown, Conn.: American Political Biography Press, 2002.

Philips, Kevin. *William McKinley*. New York: Times Books, 2003.

Reeves, Thomas C. *Gentleman Boss: The Life of Chester Alan Arthur*. Rev. ed. Newtown, Conn.: American Political Biography Press, 1991.

Rutkow, Ira. *James A. Garfield*. New York: Times Books, 2006.

Sievers, Harry J. *Benjamin Harrison: Hoosier Statesman, Hoosier President*. Rev. ed. 2 vols. Newtown, Conn.: American Political Biography Press, 1997.

Smith, Jean Edward. *Grant*. New York: Simon & Schuster, 2002.

Socolofsky, Homer E., and Allan B. Spetter. *The Presidency of Benjamin Harrison*. Lawrence: University Press of Kansas, 1987.

Taylor, John M. *Garfield of Ohio: The Available Man*. Rev. ed. Newtown, Conn.: American Political Biography Press, 2005.

Trefousse, Hans. *Rutherford B. Hayes*. New York: Times Books, 2002.

Tugwell, Rexford G. *Grover Cleveland*. New York: Macmillan, 1968.

Welch, Richard E., Jr. *The Presidencies of Grover Cleveland*. Lawrence: University Press of Kansas, 1988.

GOVERNMENT, LAW, AND NATIONAL POLITICS

Abrams, Richard M., ed. *The Issues of the Populist and Progressive Eras, 1892–1912*. Columbia: University of South Carolina Press, 1969.

Argersinger, Peter H. *Populism and Politics: William Alfred Peffer and the People's Party*. Lexington: University Press of Kentucky, 1974.

Barrows, Chester L. *William M. Evarts: Lawyer, Diplomat, Statesman*. Chapel Hill: University of North Carolina Press, 1941.

Bensel, Richard Franklin. *Yankee Leviathan: The Origins of Central State Authority in America, 1859–1877*. New York: Cambridge University Press, 1995.

Beth, Loren P. *John Marshall Harlan: The Last Whig Justice*. Lexington: University Press of Kentucky, 1992.

Beth, Loren P. *The Development of the American Constitution, 1877–1917*. New York: Harper Torchbooks, 1971.

Bicha, Karel Denis. "Jerry Simpson: Populist without Principle." *Journal of American History* 54 (1967): 291–306.

Blum, Edward J. *Reforging the White Republic: Race, Religion, and American Nationalism, 1865–1898*. Baton Rouge: Louisiana State University Press, 2005.

Clancy, Herbert J. *The Presidential Election of 1880*. Chicago: Loyola University Press, 1958.

Clanton, Gene. *Congressional Populism and the Crisis of the 1890s*. Lawrence: University Press of Kansas, 1998.

Clanton, Gene. *Populism: The Human Preference in America, 1890–1900*. Boston: Twayne Publishers, 1991.

Colletta, Paolo E. *William Jennings Bryan: Political Evangelist, 1860–1908*. Lincoln: University of Nebraska Press, 1964.

Cooper, William J., Jr. *Jefferson Davis, American*. New York: Random House, 2000.

Cross, Coy F. *Justin Smith Morrill: Father of the Land-Grant Colleges*. East Lansing: Michigan State University Press, 1999.

Davis, William C. *Jefferson Davis: The Man and His Hour*. New York: HarperCollins, 1991.

Dearing, Mary P. *Veterans in Politics: The Story of the G. A. R*. Baton Rouge: Louisiana State University Press, 1952.

DeSantis, Vincent P. *Republicans Face the Southern Question: The New Departure Years, 1877–1897*. Baltimore, Md: Johns Hopkins University Press, 1959.

Dobson, John M. *Politics in the Gilded Age: A New Perspective on Reform*. New York: Praeger Publishers, 1972.

Durden, Robert F. *The Climax of Populism: The Election of 1896*. Lexington: University of Kentucky Press, 1965.

Eaton, Clement. *Jefferson Davis*. New York: Free Press, 1977.

Fink, Leon. *Workingmen's Democracy: The Knights of Labor and American Politics*. Urbana: University of Illinois Press, 1983.

Foner, Eric. *Reconstruction: America's Unfinished Revolution, 1863–1877*. New York: Harper & Row, 1988.

Foster, Gaines M. *Moral Reconstruction: Christian Lobbyists and the Federal Legislation of Morality, 1865–1920*. Chapel Hill: University of North Carolina Press, 2002.

Fredman, Lionel E. *The Australian Ballot: The Story of an American Reform*. East Lansing: Michigan State University Press, 1968.

Ginger, Ray. *Altgeld's America: The Lincoln Ideal Versus Changing Realities, 1892–1905*. New York: Funk and Wagnall's, 1958.

Ginger, Ray. *The Bending Cross: A Biography of Eugene Victor Debs*. New Brunswick, N.J.: Rutgers University Press, 1949.

Glad, Paul W. *McKinley, Bryan and the People*. Philadelphia: J. B. Lippincott, 1964.

Glad, Paul W. *The Trumpet Soundeth: William Jennings Bryan and His Democracy, 1896–1912*. Lincoln: University of Nebraska Press, 1960.

Glass, Mary Ellen. *Silver and Politics in Nevada: 1892–1902*. Reno: University of Nevada Press, 1969.

Goldman, Robert M. *"A Free Ballot and a Fair Count": The Department of Justice and the Enforcement of Voting Rights in the South, 1877–1893*. New York: Fordham University Press, 2001.

Goodwyn, Lawrence. *Democratic Promise: The Populist Moment in America*. New York: Oxford University Press, 1976.

Hicks, John D. *The Populist Revolt: A History of the Farmers' Alliance and the People's Party*. Minneapolis: University of Minnesota Press, 1931.

Hirshson, Stanley P. *Farewell to the Bloody Shirt: Northern Republicans & the Southern Negro, 1877–1893*. Bloomington: Indiana University Press, 1962.

Hollingsworth, J. Rogers. *The Whirligig of Politics: The Democracy of Cleveland and Bryan*. Rev. ed. Chicago: University of Chicago Press, 1969.

Hoogenboom, Ari. *Outlawing the Spoils: A History of the Civil Service Reform Movement*. Urbana: University of Illinois Press, 1961.

Howe, M. A. De Wolfe. *Justice Holmes: The Proving Years, 1870–1882*. Cambridge, Mass.: Harvard University Press, 1963.

James, Scott C. *Presidents, Parties, and the State: A Party System Perspective on Democratic Regulatory Choice, 1884–1936*. New York: Cambridge University Press, 2000.

Jones, Marnie. *Holy Toledo: Religion and Politics in the Life of "Golden Rule" Jones*. Lexington: University Press of Kentucky, 1998.

Jones, Stanley L. *The Presidential Election of 1896*. Madison: University of Wisconsin Press, 1964.

Jordan, David M. *Roscoe Conkling of New York: Voice in the Senate*. Ithaca, N.Y.: Cornell University Press, 1971.

Josephson, Matthew. *The Politicos, 1865–1896*. New York: Harcourt, Brace and Company, 1938.

Kaczorowski, Robert J. *The Politics of Judicial Interpretation: The Federal Courts, Department of Justice and Civil Rights, 1866–1876*. Dobbs Ferry, N.Y.: Oceana Publications, 1985.

Kantrowitz, Stephen. *Ben Tillman and the Reconstruction of White Supremacy*. Chapel Hill: University of North Carolina Press, 2000.

Kehl, James A. *Boss Rule in the Gilded Age: Matt Quay of Pennsylvania*. Pittsburgh, Pa.: University of Pittsburgh Press, 1981.

Keller, Morton. *Affairs of State: Public Life in Late Nineteenth Century America*. Cambridge, Mass: Belknap Press, 1977.

Keller, Morton. *The Art and Politics of Thomas Nast*. New York: Oxford University Press, 1968.

Knoles, George H. *The Presidential Campaign and Election of 1892*. Palo Alto, Calif: Stanford University Press, 1942.

Koenig, Louis W. *Bryan: A Political Biography of William Jennings Bryan*. New York: G. P. Putnam's Sons, 1971.

Lofgren, Charles A. *The Plessy Case: A Legal-Historical Interpretation*. New York: Oxford University Press, 1987.

Magrath, C. Peter. *Morrison R. Waite: The Triumph of Character*. New York: Macmillan, 1963.

Marcus, Robert D. *Grand Old Party: Political Structure in the Gilded Age, 1880–1896*. New York: Oxford University Press, 1971.

McKinney, Gordon. *Zeb Vance: North Carolina's Civil War Governor and Gilded Age Political Leader*. Chapel Hill: University of North Carolina Press, 2003.

McMath, Robert C. *American Populism: A Social History, 1877–1898*. New York: Hill and Wang, 1992.

McMurray, Donald L. *Coxey's Army: A Study in the Industrial Army Movement of 1894*. Seattle: University of Washington Press, 1968.

Morgan, H. Wayne. *From Hayes to McKinley: National Party Politics, 1877–1896*. Syracuse, N.Y.: Syracuse University Press, 1969.

Morgan, H. Wayne. *William McKinley and His America*. Syracuse, N.Y.: Syracuse University Press, 1963.

Nash, Howard, Jr. *Stormy Petrel: The Life and Times of Gen. Benjamin F. Butler, 1818–1893*. Rutherford, N.J.: Fairleigh Dickinson University Press, 1969.

Nevins, Allan. *Hamilton Fish: The Inner History of the Grant Administration*. New York: Dodd, Mead, 1936.

Paul, Arnold M. *Conservative Crisis and the Rule of Law: Attitudes of Bar and Bench, 1887–1895*. Ithaca, N.Y.: Cornell University Press, 1960.

Perman, Michael. *Struggle for Mastery: Disfranchisement in the South, 1888–1908*. Chapel Hill: University of North Carolina Press, 2001.

Polakoff, Keith I. *The Politics of Inertia: The Election of 1876 and the End of Reconstruction*. Baton Rouge: Louisiana State University Press, 1973.

Pollack, Norman, ed. *The Populist Mind*. New York: Macmillan, 1967.

Ridge, Martin. *Ignatius Donnelly: The Portrait of a Politician*. Chicago: University of Chicago Press, 1962.

Rothman, David J. *Politics and Power: The United States Senate, 1869–1901*. Cambridge, Mass.: Harvard University Press, 1966.

Schwartz, Bernard. *A Basic History of the United States Supreme Court*. Huntington, N.Y.: Robert L. Krieger Publishing Company, 1979.

Seip, Terry L. *The South Returns to Congress: Men, Economic Measures, and Intersectional Relationships, 1868–1879*. Baton Rouge: Louisiana State University Press, 1983.

Silbey, Joel H. *The American Political Nation, 1838–1893*. Palo Alto, Calif.: Stanford University Press, 1991.

Stern, Clarence A. *Republican Heyday: Republicanism through the McKinley Years*. Ann Arbor, Mich.: Edwards Brothers, 1962.

Strode, Hudson. *Jefferson Davis: Tragic Hero*. New York: Harcourt, Brace & World, 1964.

Summers, Mark W. *The Press Gang: Newspapers and Politics, 1865–1877*. Chapel Hill: University of North Carolina Press, 1994.

Teaford, John C. *The Unheralded Triumph: City Government in America, 1870–1900*. Baltimore, Md.: Johns Hopkins University Press, 1984.

Thompson, Margaret Susan. *The "Spider Web": Congress and Lobbying in the Age of Grant*. Ithaca, N.Y.: Cornell University Press, 1985.

Trefousse, Hans L. *Carl Schurz: A Biography*. Knoxville: University of Tennessee Press, 1982.

Upchurch, Thomas Adams. *Legislating Racism: The Billion Dollar Congress and the Birth of Jim Crow*. Lexington: University Press of Kentucky, 2004.

Van Deusen, Glyndon G. *Horace Greeley: Nineteenth-Century Crusader*. Philadelphia: University of Pennsylvania Press, 1953.

Viorst, Milton. *Fall from Grace: The Republican Party and the Puritan Ethic*. New York: New American Radio, 1968.

Wang, Xu. *The Trial of Democracy: Black Suffrage and Northern Republicans, 1860–1910*. New York: Oxford University Press, 1998.

Welch, Richard E., Jr. *George Frisbie Hoar and the Half-Breed Republicans*. Cambridge, Mass.: Harvard University Press, 1971.

West, Richard S. *Satire on Stone: The Political Cartoons of Joseph Keppler*. Urbana: University of Illinois Press, 1988.

White, Leonard D. *The Republican Era: A Study in Administrative History, 1869–1901*. New York: Free Press, 1958.

Wiecek, William M. *The Lost World of Classical Legal Thought: Law and Ideology in America, 1886–1937*. New York: Oxford University Press, 1908.

Williams, R. Hal. *Years of Decision: American Politics in the 1890s*. New York: John Wiley and Sons, 1978.

Woodward, C. Vann. *Reunion and Reaction: The Compromise of 1877 and the End of Reconstruction*. New York: Oxford University Press, 1991.

DIPLOMACY, FOREIGN AFFAIRS, AND THE MILITARY

Abrahamson, James L. *America Arms for a New Century: The Making of a Great Military Power*. New York: Free Press, 1981.

Allen, Helena G. *Sanford Ballard Dole: Hawaii's Only President, 1844–1926*. Spokane, Wash.: Arthur H. Clark, 1988.

Armstrong, William M. *E. L. Godkin and American Foreign Policy, 1865–1900*. New York: Bookman Associates, 1957.

Beisner, Robert L. *Twelve Against Empire: The Anti-Imperialists, 1898–1900*. New York: McGraw-Hill, 1968.

Bradford, Richard. *The Virginius Affair*. Boulder: Colorado Association University Press, 1980.

Budnick, Richard. *Stolen Kingdom: An American Conspiracy*. Honolulu, Hawaii: Aloha Press, 1992.

Campbell, Charles S. *The Transformation of American Foreign Relations, 1865–1900*. New York: Harper and Row, 1976.

Challener, Richard D. *Admirals, Generals, and American Foreign Policy, 1898–1914*. Princeton, N.J.: Princeton University Press, 1973.

Conroy, Hilary. *The Japanese Frontier in Hawaii, 1868–1898*. Berkeley: University of California Press, 1953.

Cosmas, Graham A. *An Army for Empire: The United States Army in the Spanish–American War*. Columbia: University of Missouri Press, 1971.

Damon, Ethel M. *Sanford Ballard Dole and His Hawaii*. Palo Alto, Calif.: Pacific Books, 1957.

Devine, Michael J. *John W. Foster: Politics and Diplomacy in the Imperial Era, 1873–1917*. Athens: Ohio University Press, 1981.

Dulles, Foster R. *Prelude to World Power: American Diplomatic History, 1860–1900*. New York: Macmillan, 1965.

Dulles, Foster R. *The Imperial Years: The History of America's Brief Moment of Imperial Fervor*. New York: Crowell, 1956.

Faulkner, Harold U. *Politics, Reform and Expansion, 1890–1900*. New York: Harper & Row, 1959.

Foner, Philip. *The Spanish–Cuban–American War and the Birth of American Imperialism, 1895–1902*. New York: Monthly Review Press, 1972.

Gould, Lewis L. *The Spanish–American War and President McKinley*. Lawrence: University Press of Kansas, 1982.

Graebner, Norman A. *Foundations of American Foreign Policy: A Realist Appraisal from Franklin to McKinley*. Wilmington, Del.: Scholarly Resources, 1985.

Healy, David. *U. S. Expansionism: The Expansionist Urge in the 1890s*. Madison: University of Wisconsin Press, 1970.

Hobsbawm, Eric. *The Age of Empire, 1875–1914*. New York: Vintage Books, 1987.

Lasch, Christopher. "The Anti-Imperialists, the Philippines, and the Inequality of Man." *Journal of Southern History* 24 (August 1954): 319–31.

LeFeber, Walter. *The New Empire: An Interpretation of American Expansion, 1860–1898*. Ithaca, N.Y.: Cornell University Press, 1998.

Love, Eric T. L. *Race over Empire: Racism & U. S. Imperialism, 1865–1900*. Chapel Hill: University of North Carolina Press, 2004.

May, Ernest R. *Imperial Democracy: The Emergence of America as a Great Power*. Chicago: Imprint Publications, 1991.

McWilliams, Tennant S. *The New South Faces the World: Foreign Affairs and the Southern Sense of Self, 1877–1950*. Baton Rouge: Louisiana State University Press, 1988.

Miller, Stuart Creighton. *Benevolent Assimilation: The American Conquest of the Philippines, 1899–1903*. New Haven, Conn.: Yale University Press, 1982.

Osborne, Thomas J. *"Empire Can Wait": American Opposition to Hawaiian Annexation, 1893–1898*. Kent, Ohio: Kent State University Press, 1981.

Perez, Louis A., Jr. *Cuba Between Empires, 1878–1902*. Pittsburgh, Pa.: University of Pittsburgh Press, 1983.

Perez, Louis A., Jr. *The War of 1898: The United States and Cuba in History and Historiography*. Chapel Hill: University of North Carolina Press, 1998.

Perkins, Dexter. *The Monroe Doctrine, 1867–1907*. Baltimore, Md.: Johns Hopkins University Press, 1937.

Plesur, Milton. *America's Outward Thrust: Approaches to Foreign Affairs, 1865–1900*. DeKalb: Northern Illinois University Press, 1971.

Pletcher, David M. *The Awkward Years: Foreign Policy under Garfield and Arthur*. Columbia: University of Missouri Press, 1962.

Pratt, Julius. *Expansionists of 1898: The Acquisition of Hawaii and the Spanish Islands*. Gloucester, Mass.: Peter Smith, 1959.

Puleston, William D. *Mahan: The Life and Work of Captain Alfred Thayer Mahan*. New Haven, Conn.: Yale University Press, 1939.

Russ, William A. *The Hawaiian Republic and Its Struggle to Win Annexation: 1894–1898*. Selinsgrove, Pa.: Susquehanna University Press, reprint 1992.

Russ, William A. *The Hawaiian Revolution, 1893–94*. Selinsgrove, Pa.: Susquehanna University Press, 1959.

Stevens, Sylvester. *American Expansion in Hawaii, 1842–1898*. Harrisburg, Pa.: Archives Publishing Company, 1945.

Tansill, Charles C. *The Foreign Policy of Thomas F. Bayard, 1855–1897*. New York: Fordham University Press, 1940.

Tompkins, E. Berkeley. *Anti-Imperialism in the United States: The Great Debates, 1890–1920*. Philadelphia: University of Pennsylvania Press, 1970.

Trask, David F. *The War with Spain in 1898*. New York: Macmillan, 1981.

Turk, Richard W. *The Ambiguous Relationship: Theodore Roosevelt and Alfred Thayer Mahan*. New York: Greenwood Press, 1987.

Welch, Richard E. *Response to Imperialism: The United States in the Philippine–American War, 1899–1902*. Chapel Hill: University of North Carolina Press, 1979.

Young, Marilyn B. *The Rhetoric of Empire: American China Policy, 1895–1901*. Cambridge, Mass.: Harvard University Press, 1968.

Younger, Edward. *John A. Kasson: Politics and Diplomacy from Lincoln to McKinley*. Iowa City: State Historical Society of Iowa, 1955.

BUSINESS, ECONOMICS, FINANCE, AND INDUSTRY

Alberts, Robert C. *The Good Provider: H. J. Heinz and his 57 Varieties*. Boston: Houghton Mifflin, 1973.

Allen, Frederick L. *The Great Pierpont Morgan*. New York: Harper & Brothers, 1949.

Anderson, Avis A. *A & P: The Story of the Great Atlantic and Pacific Tea Company*. Charleston, S.C.: Arcadia, 2002.

Andrews, Wayne. *The Vanderbilt Legend*. New York: Harcourt, Brace, 1941.

Browder, Clifford. *The Money Game in Old New York: Daniel Drew and His Times*. Lexington: University Press of Kentucky, 1986.

Carosso, Vincent P. *The Morgans: Private International Bankers, 1854–1913*. Cambridge, Mass.: Harvard University Press, 1987.

D'Antonio, Michael. *Hershey: Milton S. Hershey's Extraordinary Life of Wealth, Empire, and Utopian Dreams*. New York: Simon and Schuster, 2007.

Decker, Leslie E. *Railroads, Lands, and Politics: The Taxation of Railroad Land Grants, 1864–1897*. Providence, R.I.: Brown University Press, 1964.

Dudley, William, ed. *The Industrial Revolution: Opposing Viewpoints*. San Diego, Calif.: Greenhaven Press, 1998.

Durden, Robert F. *Bold Entrepreneur: A Life of James B. Duke*. Durham, N.C.: Carolina Academic Press, 2003.

Eggert, Gerald G. *Railroad Labor Disputes: The Beginnings of Federal Strike Policy*. Ann Arbor: University of Michigan Press, 1967.

Fine, Sidney. *Laissez-Faire and the General Welfare State: A Study of Conflict in American Thought, 1865–1901*. Ann Arbor: University of Michigan Press, 1956.

Friedel, Robert, and Paul Israel. *Edison's Electric Light: Biography of an Invention*. New Brunswick, N.J.: Rutgers University Press, 1986.

Friedman, Milton, and A. J. Schwartz. *A Monetary History of the United States, 1867–1920*. New ed. Princeton, N.J.: Princeton University Press, 1971.

Garraty, John A. *Labor and Capital in the Gilded Age: Testimony Taken by the Senate Committee upon the Relations between Labor and Capital—1883*. Boston: Little, Brown, 1968.

Grodinsky, Julius. *Jay Gould: His Business Career, 1867–1892*. Philadelphia: University of Pennsylvania Press, 1957.

Hacker, Louis M. *The World of Andrew Carnegie, 1865–1901.* Philadelphia: J. B. Lippincott, 1968.

Hawke, David F. *John D.: The Founding Father of the Rockefellers.* New York: Harper & Row, 1980.

Hays, Samuel P. *The Response to Industrialism, 1885–1914.* Chicago: University of Chicago Press, 1957.

Hobsbawm, Eric. *The Age of Capital, 1848–1873.* New York: Vintage Books, 1987.

Hoffman, Charles. "The Depression of the Nineties." *Journal of Economic History* 16 (1956): 137–64.

Josephson, Matthew. *The Robber Barons: The Great American Capitalists, 1861–1901.* New York: Harcourt, Brace, 1938.

Kirkland, Edward C. *Business in the Gilded Age: The Conservatives' Balance Sheet.* Madison: University of Wisconsin Press, 1952.

Kirkland, Edward C. *Dream and Thought in the Business Community, 1860–1900.* Ithaca, N.Y.: Cornell University Press, 1956.

Kirkland, Edward C. *Industry Comes of Age: Business, Labor and Public Policy, 1860–1897.* New York: Quadrangle, 1967.

Klein, Maury. *The Life and Legend of Jay Gould.* Baltimore, Md.: Johns Hopkins University Press, 1986.

Kolko, Gabriel. *Railroads and Regulation, 1877–1916.* Princeton, N.J.: Princeton University Press, 1965.

Lewis, Oscar. *The Big Four: The Story of Huntington, Stanford, Hopkins, and Crocker, and the Building of the Central Pacific.* New York: Alfred A. Knopf, 1938.

Lewtin, William. *Law and Economic Policy in America: The Evolution of the Sherman Anti-Trust Law.* New ed. Chicago: University of Chicago Press, 1981.

Lindsay, Almont. *The Pullman Strike.* Chicago: University of Chicago Press, 1942.

Livesay, Harold C. *Andrew Carnegie and the Rise of Big Business.* 2nd ed. New York: Longman, 2000.

Miller, George H. *Railroads and the Granger Laws.* Madison: University of Wisconsin Press, 1971.

Nevins, Allan. *Study in Power: John D. Rockefeller, Industrialist and Philanthropist.* New York: Charles Scribner's Sons, 1953.

Nugent, Walter T. K. *Money and American Society, 1865–1880.* New York: Free Press, 1968.

Palmer, Bruce. *"Man Over Money": The Southern Populist Critique of American Capitalism.* Chapel Hill: University of North Carolina Press, 1980.

Patterson, Jerry E. *The Vanderbilts.* New York: Harry N. Abrams, 1989.

Pendergrast, Mark. *For God, Country, and Coca-Cola: The Definitive History of the Great American Soft Drink and the Company that Makes It*. New York: Charles Scribner's Sons, 1993.

Porter, Glenn. *The Rise of Big Business, 1860–1920*. 2nd ed. Wheeling, Ill.: Harlan Davidson, 1992.

Ritter, Gretchen. *Goldbugs and Greenbacks: The Antimonopoly Tradition and the Politics of Finance, 1865–1896*. New ed. Cambridge, UK: Cambridge University Press, 1999.

Rodgers, Daniel T. *The Work Ethic in Industrial America, 1850–1920*. Chicago: University of Chicago Press, 1974.

Sanger, Martha Frick Symington. *Henry Clay Frick*. New York: Abbeville Press, 1998.

Schivelbusch, Wolfgang. *Disenchanted Night: The Industrialization of Light in the Nineteenth Century*. Berkeley: University of California Press, 1988.

Shulman, Seth. *The Telephone Gambit: Chasing Alexander Graham Bell's Secret*. New York: W. W. Norton, 2008.

Skaggs, Jimmy M. *The Cattle-Trailing Industry: Between Supply and Demand, 1866–1890*. Norman: University of Oklahoma Press, 1973.

Stern, Clarence A. *Golden Republicanism: The Crusade for Hard Money*. Ann Arbor, Mich.: Edwards Brothers, 1964.

Stover, J. F. *Railroads of the South, 1865–1900: A Study in Finance and Control*. Chapel Hill: University of North Carolina Press, 1955.

Summers, Mark W. *The Era of Good Stealings*. New York: Oxford University Press, 1993.

Trachtenberg, Alan. *The Incorporation of America: Culture and Society in the Gilded Age*. New York: Hill and Wang, 1982.

Unger, Irwin. *The Greenback Era: A Social and Political History of American Finance, 1865–1879*. Princeton, N.J.: Princeton University Press, 1964.

Wall, Joseph F. *Andrew Carnegie*. New York: Oxford University Press, 1970.

Weberg, F. B. *The Background of the Panic of 1893*. Washington, D.C.: Catholic University of America, 1929.

Weil, Gordon L. *Sears, Roebuck, U. S. A.: The Great American Catalog Store and How It Grew*. New York: Stein and Day, 1977.

Weinstein, Allen. *Prelude to Populism: Origins of the Silver Issue, 1867–1878*. New Haven, Conn.: Yale University Press, 1970.

White, Gerald T. *The United States and the Problem of Recovery after 1893*. Tuscaloosa: University of Alabama Press, 1982.

Williamson, Harold F., and Arnold R. Daum. *The American Petroleum Industry: The Age of Illumination, 1859–1899*. Evanston, Ill.: Northwestern University Press, 1959.

Wolff, Leon. *Lockout–The Story of the Homestead Strike of 1892: A Study of Violence, Unionism, and the Carnegie Steel Empire*. London: Longmans, Green, 1965.

Woodman, Harold D. *King Cotton and His Retainers: Financing and Marketing the Cotton Crop of the South, 1800–1925*. Lexington: University of Kentucky Press, 1968.

CULTURE, EDUCATION, LITERATURE, RELIGION, SOCIETY, AND WOMEN

Abell, Aaron. *The Urban Impact of American Protestantism, 1865–1900*. Hamden, Conn.: Archon Books, 1962.

Adams, Bluford. *E Pluribus Barnum: The Great Showman and the Making of U.S. Popular Culture*. Minneapolis: University of Minnesota Press, 1997.

Adams, Richard P. "Southern Literature in the 1890's." *Mississippi Quarterly* 21 (1968): 277–281.

Allen, Robert C. *Horrible Prettiness: Burlesque and American Culture*. Chapel Hill: University of North Carolina Press, 1991.

Applegate, Debbie. *The Most Famous Man in America: The Biography of Henry Ward Beecher*. New York: Doubleday, 2006.

Avrich, Paul. *The Haymarket Tragedy*. Princeton, N.J.: Princeton University Press, 1984.

Baker, Paul R. *Richard Morris Hunt*. Cambridge, Mass.: MIT Press, 1980.

Barker, Charles A. *Henry George*. New York: Oxford University Press, 1955.

Barnes, William D. "Oliver H. Kelley and the Genesis of the Grange: A Reappraisal." *Agricultural History* 41 (1967): 229–42.

Beals, Carleton. *The Great Revolt and Its Leaders: The History of Popular American Uprisings in the 1890's*. London: Abelard-Schuman, 1968.

Beasley, Norman. *The Cross and the Crown: A History of Christian Science*. New York: Duell, Sloan, and Pearce, 1952.

Bederman, Gail. *Manliness and Civilization: A Cultural History of Gender and Race in the United States, 1880–1917*. Chicago: University of Chicago Press, 1995.

Beer, Thomas. *The Mauve Decade: American Life at the End of the Nineteenth Century*. New York: Carroll & Graf, 1997.

Benfrey, Christopher. *The Double Life of Stephen Crane: A Biography*. New York: Knopf, 1992.

Berton, Pierre. *The Klondike Fever*. New York: Knopf, 1958.

Bierley, Paul E. *John Philip Sousa: American Phenomenon*. Upper Saddle River, N.J.: Prentice Hall, 1973.

Boller, Paul F. *American Thought in Transition: The Impact of Evolutionary Naturalism, 1865–1900.* New ed. Lanham, Md.: University Press of America, 1981.

Borden, Ruth. *Women and Temperance: The Quest for Power and Liberty, 1873–1900.* Philadelphia: Temple University Press, 1981.

Brian, Denis. *Pulitzer: A Life.* New York: John Wiley & Sons, 2001.

Broehl, Wayne G., Jr. *The Molly Maguires.* Cambridge, Mass.: Harvard University Press, 1964.

Broun, Heywood, and Margaret Leech. *Anthony Comstock: Roundsman of the Lord.* New York: Literary Guild of America, 1927.

Brown, Joshua. *Beyond the Lines: Pictorial Reporting, Everyday Life, and the Crisis of Gilded Age America.* Berkeley: University of California Press, 2002.

Bruce, R. V. *1877: Year of Violence.* Indianapolis, Ind.: Bobbs-Merrill, 1959.

Bryan, John M. *Biltmore Estate: The Most Distinguished Private Place.* New York: Rizzoli International Publications, 1994.

Budd, Louis D. *Mark Twain: Social Philosopher.* New ed. Columbia: University of Missouri Press, 2001.

Buder, Stanley. *Pullman: An Experiment in Industrial Order and Community Planning, 1880–1930.* New York: Oxford University Press, 1967.

Carter, Paul A. *The Spiritual Crisis of the Gilded Age.* DeKalb, Ill.: Northern Illinois University Press, 1971.

Cikovsky, Nicolai, and Franklin Kelly. *Winslow Homer.* New Haven, Conn.: Yale University Press, 1995.

Cohen, Michael P. *The History of the Sierra Club, 1892–1970.* New York: Random House, 1988.

Creech, Joe. *Righteous Indignation: Religion and the Populist Revolution.* Urbana: University of Illinois Press, 2006.

Cross, Robert D. *The Church and the City, 1865–1910.* Indianapolis, Ind.: Bobbs-Merrill, 1967.

Davies, Margery W. *Women's Place Is at the Typewriter: Office Workers, 1870–1930.* Philadelphia: Temple University Press, 1982.

Dick, William M. *Labor and Socialism in America: The Gompers Era.* Port Washington, N.Y.: Kennikat Press, 1972.

Dorn, Jacob H. *Washington Gladden: Prophet of the Social Gospel.* Columbus: Ohio State University Press, 1967.

Dupree, A. Hunter, ed. *Science and the Emergence of Modern America, 1865–1916.* Chicago: Rand McNally, 1963.

Eckley, Wilton. *The American Circus.* Boston: Twayne, 1984.

Falzone, Vincent J. *Terence V. Powderly: Middle Class Reformer.* Washington, D.C.: University Press of America, 1978.

Findlay, James F., Jr. *Dwight L. Moody: American Evangelist, 1837–1899.* Chicago: University of Chicago Press, 1969.

Fite, Gilbert. *The Farmer's Frontier: 1865–1900.* New York: Holt Rinehart & Winston, 1966.

Fones-Wolf, Ken. *Trade Union Gospel: Christianity and Labor in Industrial Philadelphia, 1865–1915.* Philadelphia: Temple University Press, 1989.

Forman, John, and Robbe P. Stimson. *The Vanderbilts and the Gilded Age: Architectural Aspirations, 1879–1901.* Boston: St. Martin's, 1991.

French, Bryant Morey. *Mark Twain and "The Gilded Age": The Book that Named an Era.* Dallas, Tex.: Southern Methodist University Press, 1965.

Gilbo, Patrick F. *The American Red Cross: The First Century.* New York: HarperCollins, 1981.

Gimble, Francis. *Fashions in the Gilded Age.* 2 vols. San Francisco, Calif.: Lavolta Press, 2004.

Goldberg, Michael L. *An Army of Women: Gender and Politics in Gilded Age Kansas.* New ed. Baltimore, Md.: Johns Hopkins University Press, 2000.

Gould, Joseph E. *The Chautauqua Movement: An Episode in the Continuing American Revolution.* Albany: State University of New York Press, 1961.

Griffith, Elisabeth. *In Her Own Right: The Life of Elizabeth Cady Stanton.* New York: Oxford University Press, 1984.

Gundry, Stanley. *Love Them In: The Life and Theology of D. L. Moody.* Chicago: Moody Publishers, 1999.

Hall, Lee. *Olmsted's America: An "Unpractical Man" and His Vision of Civilization.* Boston: Little, Brown, 1995.

Harlow, Alvin F. *Joel Chandler Harris, Uncle Remus, Plantation Storyteller.* New York: Julian Messner, 1952.

Hawkins, Hugh. "Charles W. Eliot, University Reform and Religious Faith in America, 1869–1909." *Journal of American History* 51 (1964): 191–213.

Hayter, Earl W. *The Troubled Farmer, 1850–1900: Rural Adjustment to Industrialism.* DeKalb: University of Northern Illinois, 1968.

Hilkey, Judy A. *Character Is Capital: Success Manuals and Manhood in Gilded Age America.* Chapel Hill: University of North Carolina Press, 1997.

Hill, Hamlin L., ed. *Mark Twain: The Gilded Age and Later Novels.* New York: The Library of America, 2002.

Hofstadter, Richard. *Social Darwinism in American Thought.* Rev. ed. New York: George Brazillier, 1955.

Homberger, Eric. *Mrs. Astor's New York: Money and Power in the Gilded Age.* New Haven, Conn.: Yale University Press, 2002.

Horowitz, Helen H. *Culture and the City: Cultural Philanthropy in Chicago from the 1880s to 1917.* Chicago: University of Chicago Press, 1976.

Kaplan, Justin. *Mr. Clemens and Mark Twain*. New York: Simon & Schuster, 2003.

Kasson, John F. *Amusing the Million: Coney Island at the Turn of the Century*. New York: Hill and Wang, 1978.

Kaufman, Stuart B. *Samuel Gompers and the Origins of the American Federation of Labor, 1848–1896*. Westport, Conn.: Greenwood Press, 1973.

Kroeger, Brooke. *Nellie Bly: Davedevil, Reporter, Feminist*. New York: Crown: 1994.

Levine, Susan. *Labor's True Woman: Carpet Weavers, Industrialization, and Labor Reform in the Gilded Age*. Philadelphia: Temple University Press, 1984.

Livesay, Harold. *Samuel Gompers and Organized Labor in America*. Boston: Little, Brown and Company, 1978.

Lockwood, Jeffrey A. *Locust: The Devastating Rise and Mysterious Disappearance of the Insect that Shaped the American Frontier*. New ed. New York: Basic Books, 2005.

Mandelbaum, Seymour J. *Boss Tweed's New York*. New York: John Wiley, 1965.

Martin, Jay. *Harvests of Change: American Literature, 1865–1914*. Upper Saddle River, N.J.: Prentice Hall, 2000.

McCallum, Henry D., and Frances T. McCallum. *The Wire that Fenced the West*. Norman: University of Oklahoma Press, 1965.

McConnell, Stuart. *Glorious Contentment: The Grand Army of the Republic, 1865–1900*. Chapel Hill: University of North Carolina Press, 1992.

Messer, Pamela Lynn. *Biltmore Estate: Frederick Law Olmsted's Landscape Masterpiece*. Asheville, N.C.: WorldCom Press, 1993.

Moldow, Gloria. *Women Doctors in Gilded Age Washington: Race, Gender, and Professionalization*. Urbana: University of Illinois Press, 1987.

Monaghan, Jay. *The Great Rascal: The Life and Adventures of Ned Buntline*. Boston: Little, Brown, 1952.

Monkkonen, Eric H. *Police in Urban America, 1860–1920*. Cambridge, UK: Cambridge University Press, 1981.

Mott, Frank W. *A History of American Magazines, Volume IV: 1885–1905*. Cambridge, Mass.: Belknap Press, 1957.

Nordin, D. Sven. *Rich Harvest: A History of the Grange, 1967–1900*. Jackson: University Press of Mississippi, 1974.

Proctor, Ben. *William Randolph Hearst: The Early Years, 1863–1910*. New York: Oxford University Press, 1998.

Pryor, Elizabeth B. *Clara Barton: Professional Angel*. Philadelphia: University of Pennsylvania Press, 1988.

Rader, Benjamin G. *The Academic Mind and Reform: The Influence of Richard T. Ely in American Life*. Lexington: University of Kentucky Press, 1966.

Rehak, David. *Did Lizzie Borden Axe for It?* Wilmington, Ohio: Just My Best, 2005.

Rice, Otis K. *The Hatfields and the McCoys.* Lexington: University of Kentucky Press, 1982.

Roberts, Gary L. *Doc Holliday: The Life and Legend.* Hoboken, N.J.: John Wiley & Sons, 2006.

Roper, Laura Wood. *FLO: A Biography of Frederick Law Olmsted.* Baltimore, Md.: Johns Hopkins University Press, 1973.

Rosa, Joseph G., and Robin May. *Buffalo Bill and His Wild West.* Lawrence: University Press of Kansas, 1989.

Rosenberg, Charles E. *The Trial of the Assassin Guiteau: Psychiatry and Law in the Gilded Age.* Chicago: University of Chicago Press, 1968.

Rybczynski, Witold. *A Clearing in the Distance: Frederick Law Olmsted and America in the Nineteenth Century.* New York: Scribner, 1999.

Scharnhorst, Gary, and Jack Bales. *The Lost Life of Horatio Alger, Jr.* Bloomington: Indiana University Press, 1992.

Schechter, Harold. *Fiend: The Shocking True Story of America's Youngest Serial Killer.* New York: Pocket Books, 2000.

Schlereth, Thomas J. *Victorian America: Transformations in Everyday Life, 1876–1915.* New York: HarperCollins, 1991.

Seymour, Harold. *Baseball: The Early Years.* New York: Oxford University Press, 1960.

Sheehan, Donald. *This Was Publishing: A Chronicle of the Book Trade in the Gilded Age.* Bloomington: Indiana University Press, 1952.

Smith, Timothy B. *This Great Battlefield of Shiloh: History, Memory, and the Establishment of a Civil War National Military Park.* Knoxville: University of Tennessee Press, 2004.

Sproat, John G. *"The Best Men": Liberal Reformers in the Gilded Age.* New York: Oxford University Press, 1968.

Stein, Susan R., ed. *The Architecture of Richard Morris Hunt.* Chicago: University of Chicago Press, 1986.

Stross, Randall E. *The Wizard of Menlo Park: How Thomas Alva Edison Invented the Modern World.* New York: Crown, 1997.

Sutherland, Daniel E. *The Expansion of Everyday Life, 1860–1876.* New York: Harper & Row, 1989.

Taft, Philip A. *The A. F. of L. In the Time of Gompers.* New York: Harper & Brothers, 1957.

Thomas, John L. *Alternative America: Henry George, Edward Bellamy, Henry Demarest Lloyd and the Adversary Tradition.* Cambridge, Mass.: Belknap Press, 1983.

Utley, Robert M. *Billy the Kid.* Lincoln: University of Nebraska Press, 1989.

Walker, Robert H. *Everyday Life in the Age of Enterprise, 1865–1900*. New York: Putnam, 2000.

Wilkes, Stephen. *Ellis Island: Ghosts of Freedom*. New York: W. W. Norton, 2006.

Woods, Thomas A. *Knights of the Plow: Oliver H. Kelley and the Origins of the Grange in Republican Ideology*. Ames: Iowa State University Press, 1991.

Ziff, Larzer. *The American 1890's: Life and Times of a Lost Generation*. Lincoln: University of Nebraska Press, 1979.

AFRICAN AMERICANS

Anderson, James D. *The Education of Blacks in the South, 1865–1935*. Chapel Hill: University of North Carolina Press, 1988.

Anderson, Eric. *Race and Politics in North Carolina, 1872–1901: The Black Second*. Baton Rouge: Louisiana State University Press, 1981.

Angell, Stephen W. *Bishop Henry McNeal Turner and African-American Religion in the South*. Knoxville: University of Tennessee Press, 1992.

Blassingame, John W. *Black New Orleans, 1860–1880*. Chicago: University of Chicago Press, 1973.

Bromberg, Alan B. "John Mercer Langston: Black Congressman from the Old Dominion." *Virginia Cavalcade* 30 (1980): 60–67.

Brundage, W. Fitzhugh, ed. *Under Sentence of Death: Lynching in the South*. Chapel Hill: University of North Carolina Press, 1997.

Cheek, William F. "A Negro Runs for Congress: John Mercer Langston and the Virginia Campaign of 1888." *Journal of Negro History* 52 (1967): 14–34.

Edwards, Linda McMurray. *To Keep the Waters Troubled: The Life of Ida B. Wells*. New York: Oxford University Press, 1998.

Fischel, Leslie H. "The Negro in Northern Politics, 1870–1900." *Mississippi Valley Historical Review* 42 (December 1955): 466–89.

Franklin, John Hope, and Alfred A. Moss Jr. *From Slavery to Freedom: A History of African Americans*. 8th ed. Boston: McGraw-Hill, 2000.

Frederickson, George M. *The Black Image in the White Mind: The Debate on Afro-American Character and Destiny, 1817–1914*. New York: Harper & Row, 1971.

Gaither, Gerald H. *Blacks and the Populist Revolt: Ballots and Bigotry in the New South*. Tuscaloosa: University of Alabama Press, 1977.

Gatewood, Willard. *Black Americans and the White Man's Burden, 1898–1903*. Urbana: University of Illinois Press, 1975.

Harlan, Louis R. *Booker T. Washington, Volume I: The Making of a Black Leader, 1856–1901*. New York: Oxford University Press, 1975.

Leckie, William H., and Shirley A. Leckie. *The Buffalo Soldiers: A Narrative of the Negro Cavalry in the West*. Rev. ed. Norman: University of Oklahoma Press, 2007.

Logan, Rayford W. *The Betrayal of the Negro: From Rutherford B. Hayes to Woodrow Wilson*. London: Collier-Macmillan, 1965.

Logan, Rayford W. *The Negro in American Life and Thought: The Nadir, 1877–1901*. New York: Dial Press, 1954.

Marszalek, John F. *A Black Congressman in the Age of Jim Crow: South Carolina's George Washington Murray*. Gainesville: University Press of Florida, 2006.

McFeely, William S. *Yankee Stepfather: General O. O. Howard and the Freedmen*. New Haven, Conn.: Yale University Press, 1968.

McPherson, James M. *The Abolitionist Legacy: From Reconstruction to the NAACP*. Princeton, N.J.: Princeton University Press, 1975.

Meier, August. *Negro Thought in America, 1880–1915: Racial Ideologies in the Age of Booker T. Washington*. Ann Arbor: University of Michigan Press, 1988.

Mjagkij, Nina, ed. *Portraits of African American Life since 1865*. Wilmington, Del.: SR Books, 2003.

Packard, Jerrold M. *American Nightmare: The History of Jim Crow*. New York: St. Martin's, 2002.

Painter, Nell Irwin. *Exodusters: Black Migration to Kansas after Reconstruction*. New York: Alfred A. Knopf, 1977.

Oshinsky, David M. *Worse than Slavery: Parchman Farm and the Ordeal of Jim Crow Justice*. New York: Free Press, 1997.

Rabinowitz, Howard N. *Race Relations in the Urban South, 1865–1890*. New York: Oxford University Press, 1978.

Redkey, Edwin S. *Black Exodus: Black Nationalist and Back-to-Africa Movements, 1890–1910*. New Haven, Conn.: Yale University Press, 1969.

Rice, Lawrence D. *The Negro in Texas, 1874–1900*. Baton Rouge: Louisiana State University Press, 1971.

Schecter, Patricia Ann. *Ida B. Wells-Barnett and American Reform, 1880–1930*. Chapel Hill: University of North Carolina Press, 2001.

Sinkler, George. *The Racial Attitudes of American Presidents: From Abraham Lincoln to Theodore Roosevelt*. Garden City, N.Y.: Doubleday, 1971.

Smith, John David, ed. *When Did Southern Segregation Begin?* Boston: Bedford/St. Martin's, 2002.

Upchurch, Thomas Adams. "Senator John Tyler Morgan and the Genesis of Jim Crow Ideology, 1889–1891." *Alabama Review* 57 (2004): 110–31.

Upchurch, Thomas Adams. "The Butler Emigration Bill of 1890 and the Path Not Taken in Southern Race Relations." *Southern Studies* 9 (1998): 37–68.

Uya, Okon Edet. *From Slavery to Public Service: Robert Smalls, 1839–1913*. New York: Oxford University Press, 1971.

Wharton, Vernon L. *The Negro in Mississippi: 1865–1890*. New York: Harper & Row, 1947.

Williamson, Joel, ed. *The Origins of Segregation*. Boston: Heath, 1968.

Woodward, C. Vann. *The Strange Career of Jim Crow*. 3rd ed. New York: Oxford University Press, 1974.

Wynes, Charles E., ed. *The Negro in the South since 1865: Selected Essays in American Negro History*. Tuscaloosa: University of Alabama Press, 1965.

AMERICAN INDIANS

Brown, Dee. *Bury My Heart at Wounded Knee: An Indian History of the American West*. New York: Henry Holt and Company, 1970.

Carlson, Leonard A. *Indians, Bureaucrats, and Land: The Dawes Act and the Decline of Indian Farming*. Westport, Conn.: Greenwood Press, 1981.

Dippie, Brian W. *The Vanishing American: White Attitudes and U. S. Indian Policy*. Lawrence: University Press of Kansas, 1982.

Faulk, Odie B. *The Geronimo Campaign*. New York: Oxford University Press, 1960.

Fritz, Henry E. *The Movement for Indian Assimilation, 1860–1890*. Philadelphia: University of Pennsylvania Press, 1963.

Grinnell, George B. *The Fighting Cheyennes*. Norman: University of Oklahoma Press, 1956.

Hoxie, Frederick W. *A Final Promise: The Campaign to Assimilate the Indians, 1880–1920*. Lincoln: University of Nebraska Press, 1984.

Josephy, Alvin M. *The Nez Perce Indians and the Opening of the Northwest*. New Haven, Conn.: Yale University Press, 1965.

Priest, Loring B. *Uncle Sam's Stepchildren: The Reformation of United States Indian Policy, 1865–1887*. New Brunswick, N.J.: Rutgers University Press, 1942.

Rolle, Andrew F. *Helen Hunt Jackson, A Century of Dishonor: The Early Crusade for Indian Reform*. Gloucester, Mass.: Peter Smith, 1978.

Spicer, Edward H. *A Short History of the Indians of the United States*. Malabar, Fla.: Krieger Publishing Company, 1983.

Utley, Robert M. *Custer and the Great Controversy: The Origin and Development of a Legend*. Lincoln: University of Nebraska Press, 1998.

Utley, Robert M. *Frontier Regulars: The United States Army and the Indians, 1866–1891*. New York: Macmillan, 1973.

Utley, Robert M. *The Last Days of the Sioux Nation.* 2nd ed. New Haven, Conn.: Yale University Press, 2004.

Wooster, Robert. *The Military and U.S. Indian Policy, 1865–1903.* New Haven, Conn.: Yale University Press, 1988.

IMMIGRATION

Crapol, Edward. *America for Americans: Economic Nationalism and Anglophobia in the Late Nineteenth Century.* Westport, Conn.: Greenwood Press, 1973.

Daniels, Roger. *Not Like Us: Immigrants and Minorities in America, 1890–1924.* Chicago: Ivan R. Dee, 1997.

Daniels, Roger, and Otis L. Graham, eds. *Debating American Immigration, 1882–Present.* Lanham, Md.: Rowman and Littlefield, 2001.

Gyory, Andrew. *Closing the Gate: Race, Politics, and the Chinese Exclusion Act.* Chapel Hill: University of North Carolina Press, 1998.

Handlin, Oscar. *The Uprooted: The Epic Story of the Great Migrations that Made the American People.* New York: Grosset & Dunlap, 1951.

Kessner, Thomas. *The Golden Door: Italian and Jewish Immigrant Mobility in New York City, 1880–1915.* New York: Oxford University Press, 1977.

Kraut, Alan M. *The Huddled Masses: The Immigrant in American Society, 1880–1921.* Arlington Heights, Ill.: Harlan-Davidson, 1982.

Peffer, George Anthony. *If They Don't Bring Their Women Here: Chinese Female Immigration Before Exclusion.* Urbana: University of Illinois Press, 1999.

Saxton, Alexander. *The Indispensable Enemy: Labor and the Anti-Chinese Movement in California.* Berkeley: University of California Press, 1975.

LOCAL AND REGIONAL TOPICS

Alston, Lee J., and Joseph P. Ferrie. *Southern Paternalism and the American Welfare State: Economics, Politics, and Institutions in the South, 1865–1965.* Cambridge, UK: Cambridge University Press, 1999.

Argersinger, Peter H. *The Limits of Agrarian Radicalism: Western Populism and American Politics.* Lawrence: University Press of Kansas, 1995.

Ayers, Edward. *The Promise of the New South: Life after Reconstruction.* New York: Oxford University Press, 1992.

Barnes, Kenneth C. *Who Killed John Clayton? Political Violence and the Emergence of the New South, 1861–1893.* Durham, N.C.: Duke University Press, 1998.

Barr, Alwyn. *Reconstruction to Reform: Texas Politics, 1876–1906*. Austin: University of Texas Press, 1971.

Benson, Lee. Merchants, *Farmers, and Railroads: Railroad Regulation and New York Politics, 1850–1887*. Cambridge, Mass: Harvard University Press, 1955.

Blodgett, Geoffrey. *The Gentle Reformers: Massachusetts Democrats in the Cleveland Era*. Cambridge, Mass.: Harvard University Press, 1966.

Bond, Bradley G. *Political Culture in the Nineteenth-Century South: Mississippi, 1830–1900*. Baton Rouge: Louisiana State University Press, 1995.

Butler, Anne M. *Daughters of Joy, Sisters of Misery: Prostitutes in the American West, 1865–90*. Urbana: University of Illinois Press, 1985.

Callow, Alexander B., Jr. *The Tweed Ring*. Westport, Conn.: Greenwood Press, 1981.

Campbell, Ballard C. *Representative Democracy: Public Policy and Midwestern Legislatures in the Late Nineteenth Century*. Cambridge, Mass.: Harvard University Press, 1980.

Chessman, G. Wallace. *Governor Theodore Roosevelt: The Albany Apprenticeship, 1898–1900*. Cambridge, Mass.: Harvard University Press, 1965.

Cooper, William J., Jr. *The Conservative Regime: South Carolina, 1877–1890*. Baltimore, Md.: Johns Hopkins University Press, 1968.

Corbin, David A. *Life, Work, and Rebellion in the Coal Fields: The Southern West Virginia Miners, 1880–1922*. Urbana: University of Illinois Press, 1981.

Cresswell, Stephen. *Multi-Party Politics in Mississippi, 1877–1902*. Jackson: University Press of Mississippi, 1995.

Davis, Harold E. *Henry Grady's New South: Atlanta, a Brave and Beautiful City*. Tuscaloosa: University of Alabama Press, 1990.

Dorset, Phyllis F. *The New Eldorado: The Story of Colorado's Gold and Silver Rushes*. New York: Macmillan, 1970.

Doster, James F. *Railroads in Alabama Politics, 1875–1914*. Tuscaloosa: University of Alabama Press, 1951.

Eller, Ronald D. *Miners, Millhands, and Mountaineers: Industrialization of the Appalachian South, 1880–1930*. Knoxville: University of Tennessee Press, 1982.

Evans, Frank B. *Pennsylvania Politics, 1872–1877: A Study in Political Leadership*. Harrisburg: Pennsylvania Historical Society, 1966.

Foster, Gaines M. *Ghosts of the Confederacy: Defeat, the Lost Cause, and the Emergence of the New South, 1865 to 1913*. New York: Oxford University Press, 1987.

Gilbert, James. *Perfect Cities: Chicago's Utopias of 1893*. Chicago: University of Chicago Press, 1991.

Going, Allen J. *Bourbon Democracy in Alabama: 1874–1890*. Tuscaloosa: University of Alabama Press, 1951.

Gould, Lewis L. *Wyoming: A Political History, 1869–1896*. New Haven, Conn.: Yale University Press, 1968.

Hackney, Sheldon. *Populism to Progressivism in Alabama*. Princeton, N.J.: Princeton University Press, 1969.

Hahn, Steven. *The Roots of Southern Populism: Yeoman Farmers and the Transformation of the Georgia Upcountry, 1850–1890*. New York: Oxford University Press, 1985.

Hair, William I. *Bourbonism and Agrarian Protest: Louisiana Politics, 1877–1900*. Baton Rouge: Louisiana State University Press, 1969.

Hart, Roger L. *Redeemers, Bourbons and Populists: Tennessee, 1870–1896*. Baton Rouge: Louisiana State University Press, 1975.

Holli, Melvin G. *Reform in Detroit: Hazen S. Pingree and Urban Politics*. New York: Oxford University Press, 1969.

Hyman, Michael R. *The Anti-Redeemers: Hill-Country Political Dissenters in the Lower South from Redemption to Populism*. Baton Rouge: Louisiana State University Press, 1990.

Jackson, Joy J. *New Orleans in the Gilded Age: Politics and Urban Progress, 1880–1896*. Baton Rouge: Louisiana State University Press, 1969.

Jacobs, Wilbur R. *On Turner's Trail: 100 Years of Writing Western History*. Lawrence: University of Kansas Press, 1994.

Jenson, Richard. *The Winning of the Midwest: Social and Political Conflict, 1888–1896*. Chicago: University of Chicago Press, 1971.

Jordan, Philip D. *Ohio Comes of Age, 1870–1900*. Columbus: Ohio Historical Society, 1943.

Kleppner, Paul. *The Cross of Culture: A Social Analysis of Midwestern Politics, 1850–1900*. New York: Free Press, 1970.

Kousser, J. Morgan. *The Shaping of Southern Politics: Suffrage Restriction and the Establishment of the One-Party South*. New Haven, Conn: Yale University Press, 1974.

Lamar, Howard F. *Dakota Territory, 1861–1889: A Study of Frontier Politics*. New ed. New Haven, Conn.: Yale University Press, 1966.

Larson, Robert W. *Populism in the Mountain West*. Albuquerque: University of New Mexico Press, 1986.

Lester, Connie L. *Up from the Mudsills of Hell: The Farmers' Alliance, Populism, and Progressive Agriculture in Tennessee, 1870–1915*. Athens: University of Georgia Press, 2006.

Love, Robertus, and Michael Fellman. *The Rise and Fall of Jesse James*. Lincoln: University of Nebraska Press, 1990.

Luebke, Frederick C. *Immigrants and Politics: The Germans of Nebraska, 1880–1900*. Lincoln: University of Nebraska Press, 1969.

McKinney, Gordon. *Southern Mountain Republicans, 1865–1900*. Chapel Hill: University of North Carolina Press, 1978.

McLaurin, Melton A. *The Knights of Labor in the South*. Westport, Conn.: Greenwood Press, 1978.

Metz, Leon C. *John Wesley Hardin: Dark Angel of Texas*. New ed. Norman: University of Oklahoma Press, 1998.

Miner, Craig. *West of Wichita: Settling the High Plains of Kansas, 1865–1890*. Lawrence: University Press of Kansas, 1986.

Moger, Allen W. *Virginia, Bourbonism to Byrd: 1870–1925*. Charlottesville: University Press of Virginia, 1968.

Morris, John R. *Davis A. Waite: The Ideology of a Western Populist*. Washington, D.C.: University Press of America, 1982.

Nugent, Walter T. K. *The Tolerant Populists: Kansas Populism and Nativism*. Chicago: University of Chicago Press, 1963.

Oestreicher, Richard J. *Solidarity and Fragmentation: Working People and Class Consciousness in Detroit, 1875–1900*. Urbana: University of Illinois Press, 1986.

Ostler, Jeffrey. *Prairie Populism: The Fate of Agrarian Radicalism in Kansas, Nebraska, and Iowa, 1880–1892*. Lawrence: University of Kansas Press, 1993.

Perman, Michael. *Road to Redemption: Southern Politics, 1869–1879*. Chapel Hill: University of North Carolina Press, 1984.

Pierce, Bessie L. *A History of Chicago, Volume III: The Rise of a Modern City, 1871–1893*. Chicago: University of Chicago Press, 2007.

Saloutos, Theodore. *Farmer Movements in the South, 1865–1933*. Berkeley: University of California Press, 1960.

Shaw, Barton C. *The Wool Hat Boys: Georgia's Populist Party*. Baton Rouge: Louisiana State University Press, 1984.

Spratt, John S. *The Road to Spindletop: Economic Change in Texas, 1875–1901*. Dallas: University of Texas Press, 1955.

Syrett, Harold C. *The City of Brooklyn, 1865–1898: A Political History*. New York: Columbia University Press, 1944.

Thelen, David P. *The New Citizenship: Origins of Progressivism in Wisconsin, 1893–1900*. Columbia: University of Missouri Press, 1972.

Upchurch, Thomas Adams. "Why Populism Failed in Mississippi." *Journal of Mississippi History* 65 (2003): 249–76.

Warner, Sam B., Jr. *Streetcar Suburbs: The Process of Growth in Boston, 1870–1900*. 2nd ed. Cambridge, Mass.: Harvard University Press, 2004.

Wayne, Michael. *The Reshaping of Plantation Society: The Natchez District, 1860–1880*. Baton Rouge: Louisiana State University Press, 1983.

Williams, R. Hal. *The Democratic Party and California Politics, 1880–1896*. Palo Alto, Calif.: Stanford University Press, 1973.

Winther, Oscar O. *The Transportation Frontier: Trans-Mississippi West, 1865–1890*. New York: Holt, Rinhart and Winston, 1964.

Woodward, C. Vann. *Origins of the New South*. Baton Rouge: Louisiana State University Press, 1951.

AUTOBIOGRAPHIES, MEMOIRS, PERSONAL PAPERS COLLECTIONS, AND CONTEMPORARY WRITINGS

Adams, Henry. *The Education of Henry Adams*. New York: Oxford University Press, 1999.

Armstrong, William M., ed. *The Gilded Age Letters of E. L. Godkin*. Albany: State University of New York Press, 1974.

Bancroft, George, ed. *Speeches, Correspondence, and Political Papers of Carl Schurz*. 6 vols. New York: G. P. Putnam's Sons, 1913.

Barnum, P. T. *The Life of P. T. Barnum, Written by Himself*. Urbana: University of Illinois Press, 2000.

Blaine, James G. *Political Discussions: Legislative, Diplomatic, and Popular: 1856–1886*. Norwich, Conn.: Henry Bill, 1887.

Blaine, James G. *Twenty Years in Congress*. Norwich, Conn.: Henry Bill, 1884.

Bryan, William Jennings. *The Memoirs of William Jennings Bryan*. Philadelphia: United Publishers of America, 1925.

Bryce, James. *The American Commonwealth*. Chicago: Charles H. Sergel, 1891.

Catt, Carrie C., and Nettie R. Shuler. *Woman Suffrage and Politics: The Inner Story of the Suffrage Movement*. Seattle: University of Washington Press, 1970.

Contosta, David N., and Jessica R. Hawthorne, eds. *Rise to World Power: Selected Letters of Whitelaw Reid, 1895–1912*. Philadelphia: American Philosophical Society, 1986.

Dunne, Finley Peter. *Mr. Dooley in Peace and War*. Boston: Small, Maynard, and Company, 1899.

Foner, Philip, ed. *The Life and Writings of Frederick Douglass*, Vols. IV and V. New York: International Publishers, 1964, 1975.

Grant, Ulysses S. *The Personal Memoirs of Ulysses S. Grant*, Vol. II.. Northridge, Calif.: Aegypan Press, 2006.

Harlan, Louis R., ed. *The Booker T. Washington Papers*. Urbana: University of Illinois Press, 1974.

Hinsdale, Burke A., ed. *The Works of James Abram Garfield*. 2 vols. Boston: James R. Osgood and Company, 1883.

Hoar, George Frisbie. *Autobiography of Seventy Years*. New York: Charles Scribner's Sons, 1903.

Langston, John Mercer. *From the Virginia Plantation to the National Capitol*. New York: Johnson Reprint Corporation, 1968.

McKinley, William. *The Speeches and Addresses of William McKinley, from March 1, 1897 to May 30, 1900*. New York: Doubleday and McClure, 1900.

Nevins, Allan, ed. *Hamilton Fish: The Inner History of the Grant Administration*. 2 vols. New York: Frederick Unger, 1936.

Nevins, Allan, ed. *The Letters of Grover Cleveland, 1850–1908*. Boston: Houghton Mifflin, 1933.

Ogden, Rollo, ed. *Life and Letters of Edward Lawrence Godkin*. 2 vols. New York: Macmillan, 1907.

Sandhurst, Philip, et al. *The Great Centennial Exhibition Critically Illustrated and Described*. Philadelphia: P. W. Ziegler, 1876.

Schurz, Carl. *The Reminiscences of Carl Schurz*. London: J. Murray, 1909.

Seager, Robert, II, and Doris D. Maguire, eds. *Letters and Papers of Alfred Thayer Mahan*. 2 vols. Annapolis, Md.: Naval Institute Press, 1975.

Tindall, George B., ed. *A Populist Reader: Selections from the Works of American Populist Leaders*. Rev. ed. Boston: Peter Smith, 1976.

Volwiler, Albert T., ed. *The Correspondence between Benjamin Harrison and James G. Blaine, 1882–1893*. Philadelphia: American Philosophical Society, 1940.

Williams, Charles Richard, ed. *Diary and Letters of Rutherford Burchard Hayes, 19th President of the United States*. 5 vols. Columbus: Ohio Archaeological and Historical Society, 1922–1926.

PRIMARY SOURCE DOCUMENT COLLECTIONS

Commager, Henry Steele, ed. *Documents of American History*. 7th ed. New York: Appleton-Century-Crofts, 1963.

Escott, Paul D., et al., eds. *Major Problems in the History of the American South, Volume II: The New South*. Boston: Houghton Mifflin, 1999.

Ginger, Ray, ed. *The Nationalizing of American Life, 1877–1900*. New York: Free Press, 1965.

Greenwood, Janette T., ed. *The Gilded Age: A History in Documents*. New York: Oxford University Press, 2003.

Holt, Thomas C., and Elsa Barkley Brown, eds. *Major Problems in African-American History, Volume II: From Freedom to "Freedom Now," 1865–1990s*. Boston: Houghton Mifflin, 2000.

Norton, Mary B., ed. *Major Problems in American Women's History*. Lexington, Mass.: D. C. Heath, 1989.

Steinfeld, Melvin. *Cracks in the Melting Pot: Racism and Discrimination in American History*. Beverley Hills, Calif.: Glencoe Press, 1970.

Tindall, George B., ed. *A Populist Reader: Selections from the Works of American Populist Leaders*. New York: Harper & Row, 1966.

REFERENCE WORKS

Boyer, Paul S., ed. *The Oxford Companion to United States History*. New York: Oxford University Press, 2001.

Cocks, Catherine, et al. *The Historical Dictionary of the Progressive Era*. Lanham, Md.: Scarecrow Press, 2009.

Hall, Kermit L., ed. *The Oxford Companion to the Supreme Court of the United States*. 2nd ed. New York: Oxford University Press, 2005.

Lowery, Charles D., and John F. Marszalek, eds. *The Greenwood Encyclopedia of African American Civil Rights: From Emancipation to the Twenty-First Century*. Rev. ed. Westport, Conn.: Greenwood Press, 2003.

Morison, Samuel Eliot, et al., eds. *A Concise History of the American Republic*. 2nd ed. New York: Oxford University Press, 1983.

BIBLIOGRAPHIES

Adam, Anthony J., and Gerald H. Gaither. *Black Populism in the United States: An Annotated Bibliography*. Westport, Conn.: Praeger, 2004.

DeSantis, Vincent. *The Gilded Age, 1877–1896*. Northbrook, Ill.: AHM Publishing Corporation, 1973.

Roberson, William H. *George Washington Cable: An Annotated Bibliography*. Lanham, Md.: Scarecrow Press, 1982.

Schulz, Suzanne. *Horace Greeley: A Bio-Bibliography*. Westport, Conn.: Greenwood Press, 1992.

About the Author

T. Adams Upchurch, Ph.D., is a history professor at East Georgia College in Statesboro, Georgia. He is the author of *Legislating Racism: The Billion Dollar Congress and the Birth of Jim Crow* (2004); *A White Minority in Post-Civil Rights Mississippi* (2005); and *Race Relations in the United States, 1960–1980* (2008). He is associate editor of *The Greenwood Encyclopedia of African American Civil Rights: From Emancipation to the Twenty-First Century* (2003) and the award-winning author of "Why Populism Failed in Mississippi," an article published in the *Journal of Mississippi History*. He has also authored several scholarly history articles and book reviews in peer-reviewed journals.